Safety and Reliability in Pediatrics

Editors

BRIAN R. JACOBS
MAX J. COPPES

PEDIATRIC CLINICS
OF NORTH AMERICA

www.pediatric.theclinics.com

December 2012 • Volume 59 • Number 6

ELSEVIER

1600 John F. Kennedy Boulevard • Suite 1800 • Philadelphia, Pennsylvania 19103-2899

http://www.theclinics.com

THE PEDIATRIC CLINICS OF NORTH AMERICA Volume 59, Number 6
December 2012 ISSN 0031-3955, ISBN-13: 978-1-4557-4919-5

Editor: Kerry Holland
Developmental Editor: Donald Mumford

The Pediatric Clinics of North America (ISSN 0031-3955) is published bimonthly by Elsevier Inc., 360 Park Avenue South, New York, NY 10010-1710. Months of issue are February, April, June, August, October, and December. Periodicals postage paid at New York, NY and additional mailing offices. Subscription prices are $191.00 per year (US individuals), $444.00 per year (US institutions), $259.00 per year (Canadian individuals), $591.00 per year (Canadian institutions), $308.00 per year (international individuals), $591.00 per year (international institutions), $93.00 per year (US students and residents), and $159.00 per year (international and Canadian residents and students). To receive students/resident rare, orders must be accompanied by name of affiliated institution, date of term, and the signature of program/residency coordinator on institution letterhead. Orders will be billed at individual rate until proof of status is received. Foreign air speed delivery is included in all *Clinics* subscription prices. All prices are subject to change without notice. **POSTMASTER:** Send address changes to *The Pediatric Clinics of North America*, Elsevier Health Sciences Division, Subscription Customer Service, 3251 Riverport Lane, Maryland Heights, MO 63043. **Customer Service: 1-800-654-2452 (US and Canada). From outside of the US and Canada: 1-314-447-8871. Fax: 1-314-447-8029. For print support, E-mail: JournalsCustomerService-usa@elsevier.com. For online support, E-mail: JournalsOnlineSupport-usa@elsevier.com.**

Reprints. For copies of 100 or more, of articles in this publication, please contact the Commercial Reprints Department, Elsevier Inc., 360 Park Avenue South, New York, NY 10010-1710. Tel.: 212-633-3812; Fax: 212-462-1935; E-mail: reprints@elsevier.com.

The Pediatric Clinics of North America is also published in Spanish by McGraw-Hill Inter-americana Editores S.A., Mexico City, Mexico; in Portuguese by Riechmann and Affonso Editores, Rua Comandante Coelho 1085, CEP 21250, Rio de Janeiro, Brazil; and in Greek by Althayia SA, Athens, Greece.

The Pediatric Clinics of North America is covered in *MEDLINE/PubMed (Index Medicus), Excerpta Medica, Current Contents, Current Contents/Clinical Medicine, Science Citation Index, ASCA, ISI/BIOMED,* and *BIOSIS.*

Printed and bound by CPI Group (UK) Ltd, Croydon, CR0 4YY

Transferred to digital print 2012

Contributors

GUEST EDITORS

BRIAN R. JACOBS, MD, MS, FAAP
Vice President and Chief Medical Information Officer; Executive Director, Center for Pediatric Informatics, Children's National Medical Center, Washington, DC

MAX J. COPPES, MD, PhD, MBA
President, BC Cancer Agency; Professor of Medicine and Pediatrics, University of British Columbia, Vancouver, British Columbia, Canada

AUTHORS

ERIKA L. ABRAMSON, MD, MS
Assistant Professor, Departments of Pediatrics and Public Health, Weill Cornell Medical College; New York-Presbyterian Hospital; Health Information Technology Evaluation Collaborative; Center for Healthcare Informatics and Policy, New York, New York

MARIE M. BISMARK, MBChB, LLB, MBHL, MPH
The University of Melbourne, Carlton, Victoria, Australia

RICHARD J. BRILLI, MD, FAAP, FCCM
Chief Medical Officer, Nationwide Children's Hospital, The Ohio State University College of Medicine, Columbus, Ohio

KATE CARR, BA
President and CEO, Safe Kids Worldwide, Washington, DC

WALLACE V. CRANDALL, MD
Nationwide Children's Hospital, The Ohio State University College of Medicine, Columbus, Ohio

MOIRA DAVENPORT, MD
Department of Emergency Medicine, Allegheny General Hospital, Pittsburgh, Pennsylvania

J. TERRANCE DAVIS, MD
Nationwide Children's Hospital, The Ohio State University, College of Medicine, Columbus, Ohio

JAYANT K. DESHPANDE, MD, MPH
Professor of Pediatrics and Anesthesiology, Arkansas Children's Hospital, University of Arkansas for Medical Sciences, Little Rock, Arkansas

ELLEN S. DEUTSCH, MD
The Center for Simulation, Advanced Education and Innovation, The Children's Hospital of Philadelphia, Philadelphia, Pennsylvania

MARILYN NEDER FLACK, MA, PMP
Director, Division of Patient Safety Partnerships; Office of Surveillance and Biometrics, Center for Devices and Radiological Health, Food and Drug Administration, Silver Spring, Maryland

JACQUELINE FRANCIS, MD, MPH
Pediatric Champion, Office of the Center Director, Center for Devices and Radiological Health, Food and Drug Administration, Silver Spring, Maryland

SHARON GRISWOLD, MD, MPH
Department of Emergency Medicine, Simulation Center, Drexel University College of Medicine, Philadelphia, Pennsylvania

THOMAS P. GROSS, MD, MPH
Director, Office of Surveillance and Biometrics, Center for Devices and Radiological Health, Food and Drug Administration, Silver Spring, Maryland

RAINU KAUSHAL, MD, MPH
Frances and John L. Loeb Professor of Medical Informatics, Departments of Pediatrics, Public Health, and Medicine, Weill Cornell Medical College; New York-Presbyterian Hospital; Health Information Technology Evaluation Collaborative; Center for Healthcare Informatics and Policy, New York, New York

CHRISTOPHER P. LANDRIGAN, MD, MPH
Associate Professor, Division of General Pediatrics, Department of Medicine, Harvard Medical School, Children's Hospital Boston; Harvard Work Hours, Health, and Safety Group, Division of Sleep Medicine, Department of Medicine, Harvard Medical School, Brigham and Women's Hospital; Division of Sleep Medicine, Harvard Medical School, Boston, Massachusetts

VALERE LEMON, RN, BSN, MBA
Nurse Investigator, Center for Pediatric Informatics, Children's National Medical Center, Washington, DC

CHRISTOPHER A. LONGHURST, MD, MS
Clinical Associate Professor of Pediatrics, Division of Systems Medicine, Department of Pediatrics, Stanford University School of Medicine, Menlo Park, California; Division of General Pediatrics, Department of Pediatrics, Stanford University School of Medicine; Lucile Packard Children's Hospital, Palo Alto, California

RICHARD MCCLEAD, MD
Nationwide Children's Hospital, The Ohio State University, College of Medicine, Columbus, Ohio

DALE ANN MICALIZZI, AAS
Founder/Director of Justin's HOPE project, The Task Force for Global Health, Decatur, Georgia

ANGELA MICKALIDE, PhD, MCHES
Director of Research, Safe Kids Worldwide, Washington, DC

THALIA T. MILLS, PhD
Physicist, Office of In Vitro Diagnostics and Radiological Health, Center for Devices and Radiological Health, Food and Drug Administration, Silver Spring, Maryland

VINAY NADKARNI, MD, MS
The Center for Simulation, Advanced Education and Innovation, The Children's Hospital of Philadelphia; Endowed Chair, Division of Pediatric Critical Care, Department of Anesthesiology, Critical Care, and Pediatrics, The Children's Hospital of Philadelphia, University of Pennsylvania Perelman School of Medicine, Philadelphia, Pennsylvania

DANIEL R. NEUSPIEL, MD, MPH
Clinical Professor of Pediatrics, University of North Carolina School of Medicine; Department of Pediatrics, Levine Children's Hospital, Charlotte, North Carolina

AKIRA NISHISAKI, MD, MSCE
The Center for Simulation, Advanced Education and Innovation, The Children's Hospital of Philadelphia; Division of Pediatric Critical Care, Department of Anesthesiology, Critical Care, and Pediatrics, The Children's Hospital of Philadelphia, University of Pennsylvania Perelman School of Medicine, Philadelphia, Pennsylvania

SRIKALA PONNURU, MD
Department of Emergency Medicine, Simulation Center, Drexel University College of Medicine, Philadelphia, Pennsylvania

JOY SAMUELS REID, MD
Medical Officer, Office of Device Evaluation, Center for Devices and Radiological Health, Food and Drug Administration, Silver Spring, Maryland

GLENN ROSENBLUTH, MD
Associate Clinical Professor, Division of Hospital Medicine, Department of Pediatrics, UCSF Benioff Children's Hospital, University of California San Francisco School of Medicine, San Francisco, California

MATTHEW SCANLON, MD
Associate Professor of Pediatrics, Critical Care, Medical College of Wisconsin; Associate Medical Director of Information Services, Children's Hospital of Wisconsin, Wisconsin

PAUL J. SHAREK, MD, MPH
Clinical Associate Professor, Division of General Pediatrics, Department of Pediatrics, Stanford University School of Medicine; Center for Quality and Clinical Effectiveness, Lucile Packard Children's Hospital, Palo Alto, California

ANDREW Y. SHIN, MD
Clinical Assistant Professor, Division of Cardiology, Department of Pediatrics, Stanford University School of Medicine; Center for Quality and Clinical Effectiveness, Lucile Packard Children's Hospital; Lucile Packard Children's Hospital, Palo Alto, California

JENNIFER M. SLAYTON, RN, MSN
Administrative Director, Performance Management and Improvement, Monroe Carell Jr Children's Hospital at Vanderbilt, Nashville, Tennessee

DAVID C. STOCKWELL, MD, MBA
Executive Director, Improvement Science at Children's National Medical Center; Assistant Professor of Pediatrics, The George Washington University School of Medicine, Washington, DC

ERIN H. STUBBS, MD
Clinical Assistant Professor of Pediatrics, University of North Carolina School of Medicine; Department of Pediatrics, Levine Children's Hospital, Charlotte, North Carolina

DEMIAN SZYLD, MD, EdM
Department of Emergency Medicine and New York Simulation Center for the Health Sciences, New York University School of Medicine, New York, New York

PATRICIA G. THROOP, BSN, CPHQ
Quality Consultant, Performance Management and Improvement, Monroe Carell Jr Children's Hospital at Vanderbilt, Nashville, Tennessee

Contents

array of adverse events has always been in question. The electronic health record (EHR) contains clinical data that can be systematically reviewed to identify adverse events and improve adverse event detection. Active use of an automated trigger tool that is embedded in an EHR can identify systematic issues with delivery of high-risk medications and is cost-effective and efficient. Further development of an automated adverse event detection protocol for pediatrics is needed to apply this approach systematically across pediatric institutions.

Despite increasing attention and discussion, patient harm remains an important issue in health care. Defining and identifying harm remains challenging, and little standardization in approach exists. This summary describes an approach to identifying hospital-wide preventable harm with focused safety efforts using the Preventable Harm Index as a measure of progress and as a metric to motivate improvement. Our hospital's significant decrease in serious safety events, mortality, and preventable harm is outlined.

Since the launch of the 100,000 Lives Campaign by the Institute for Healthcare Improvement (IHI), preventing medical adverse events to reduce avoidable mortality has emerged as a central focus for health care providers, institutions, regulators, insurance companies, and patients. Evidence-based interventions targeting the 6 interventions in the campaign have been associated with a reduction in preventable hospital deaths in the United States. The generalizability of the IHI's campaign to the pediatric population is only partly applicable. Pediatric experiences with rapid response teams and preventing central-line infections parallel the published experience of adults, with promise to significantly reduce preventable pediatric mortality.

The morbidity and mortality conference (M&M) is a long-standing practice in medicine. Originally created to identify errors and improve care, the primary focus of M&M has moved toward an emphasis on education of trainees. A structured format for the M&M conference can help the interdisciplinary team address causes of adverse patient outcomes and identify opportunities for systems improvement.

Sleep deprivation is common among resident physicians and clinical fellows. Current evidence about sleep science, performance, shift work, and medical errors consistently demonstrates positive impact from reduction of excessive duty hours, particularly when shift length is shortened. This article provides an overview of this literature, highlighting research on diminished physician cognitive performance due to sleep deprivation and the increase in the number of medical errors that is seen under these conditions. Accreditation Council on Graduate Medical Education trainee duty hour guidelines are reviewed. Practical approaches to evidence-based scheduling of shift-work are also discussed, with attention to improving patient safety.

Sharon Griswold, Srikala Ponnuru, Akira Nishisaki, Demian Szyld, Moira Davenport, Ellen S. Deutsch, and Vinay Nadkarni

Simulation-based educational processes are emerging as key tools for assessing and improving patient safety. Multidisciplinary or interprofessional simulation training can be used to optimize crew resource management and safe communication principles. There is good evidence that simulation training improves self-confidence, knowledge, and individual and team performance on manikins. Emerging evidence supports that procedural simulation, deliberate practice, and debriefing can also improve operational performance in clinical settings and can result in safer patient and population/system outcomes in selected settings. This article highlights emerging evidence that shows how simulation-based interventions and education contribute to safer, more efficient systems of care that save lives.

Daniel R. Neuspiel and Erin H. Stubbs

Understanding of the types and frequency of errors among children in the outpatient setting is paramount. The most commonly described errors involve medical treatment, communication failures, patient identification, laboratory, and diagnostic errors. Research suggests that adverse events and near misses are frequent occurrences in ambulatory pediatrics, but relatively little is known about the types of errors, risk factors, or effective interventions in this setting. This article will review current information on the descriptive epidemiology of pediatric outpatient medical errors, established risk factors for these errors, effective interventions to enhance reporting and improve safety, and future research needs in this area.

Marilyn Neder Flack, Thomas P. Gross, Joy Samuels Reid, Thalia T. Mills, and Jacqueline Francis

Special initiatives exist in FDA's Center for Devices and Radiological Health (CDRH), the Center for Drug Evaluation and Research, and the Center for Biologics Evaluation and Research to ensure the safety and effectiveness of medical products used in the vulnerable pediatric population. This article focuses on the special programs, projects, and special studies implemented by CDRH to ensure this safety and effectiveness in devices used in pediatric patients throughout the devices' total product life-cycles. Pediatricians play a major role in keeping medical devices safe for use in children by reporting device problems to FDA.

Angela Mickalide and Kate Carr

Unintentional injuries are predictable and preventable. Yet every hour, a child in the United States dies from an unintentional injury. Globally, the number is even more staggering, with nearly 1 million children dying from unintentional injuries each year. Motor vehicle–related injuries, burns, drowning, falls, suffocation or choking, and poisoning are just a few of the unintentional injury risks threatening children. Patient safety requires a three-pronged strategy of behavior change, use of safety devices, and improvement of laws and regulations to ensure that all children lead healthy and productive lives.

PEDIATRIC CLINICS OF NORTH AMERICA

NOW AVAILABLE FOR YOUR iPhone and iPad

Preface

Safe Pediatric Care Delivery

Brian R. Jacobs, MD, MS, FAAP   Max J. Coppes, MD, PhD, MBA
Guest Editors

This is the second publication of *The Pediatric Clinics of North America* dedicated to patient safety. The 2006 safety issue provided some excellent contributions highlighting the importance of actively involving executive hospital leadership in safety, identifying the importance of effective patient care handoffs, minimizing clinician fatigue, and reviewing challenges associated with disclosure of medical errors. That edition also touched on the role of computers and reliability science in health care safety. Patient safety is so important that we felt that it was time to assess our journey over the last 7 years as well as where we believe some of the major opportunities for further advancements may be found.

As alarming as the momentous Institute of Medicine 2000 report *To Err is Human: Building a Safer Healthcare System* may have been, it needed not come as a surprise. As medical caregivers, we need only to listen to our patients and their families to realize that, despite our best intentions, we regularly fall short in meeting their expectations. We therefore elected to kick off this issue of *The Pediatric Clinics of North America* by giving parents a voice on safety. The article by Dale Ann Micalizzi and Marie Bismark is poignant. We encourage our readers to heed the comments and quotes made in this article by patients and family members and "to interpret such comments within the context they were made." While certainly true, the issue is not to find excuses or extenuating circumstances for why we failed patients and parents; rather, the point is that we did fail them and in doing so also lost their trust. We contend that none of us get up in the morning with the intention of failing or making a mistake, quite the contrary. But it is essential for us all to start accepting that, despite our training, expertise, team work, experience, and commitment to providing the very best care possible to each and every patient with high reliability performance, we remain human and therefore prone to making errors both at work and at home. Embracing this reality seems essential to developing systems that minimize the number of errors we providers make as well as the number of errors that reach our patients. If one thing is clear from Micalizzi and Bismark, parents do not expect infallibility or perfection, but they do expect us to

Pediatr Clin N Am 59 (2012) xv–xvii
http://dx.doi.org/10.1016/j.pcl.2012.10.006
0031-3955/12/$ – see front matter © 2012 Published by Elsevier Inc.

recognize and acknowledge our own failures immediately and respond empathetically to those we affect by our failing. Parenthetically, this likely includes coworkers and colleagues, although little research has been performed to document this. Similarly, we suggest that failure also affects one's trust. In short, performance failure in health care has many serious consequences beyond patient morbidity or even mortality. Therefore high reliability performance and patient safety have increasingly become an important focus in health care.

This issue spends a considerable amount of time examining what we know today regarding the role of technology in ensuring patient safety. In the last decade, health information technology has taken on an important worldwide role and is often discussed as a centerpiece of health care reform. Erika Abramson and Rainu Kaushal kick off the technology discussion examining the growing body of information on the role of computerized provider order entry in patient safety. The authors review how computerization has affected the safety of the front end of the medication management cycle—prescribing and transcribing. Continuing in the technology theme, Matthew Scanlon reviews the positive and negative aspects of smart infusion pumps on the sharp end of medication safety—drug administration. Dr Scanlon's article presents compelling information on these devices, which should leave the reader well informed on their role in preventing administration errors. Next up, Valere Lemon and David Stockwell from Children's National Medical Center describe their innovative journey automating the detection of potential adverse events and errors using data derived from the electronic health record. Their work in building a national collaborative around this methodology is both novel and exciting.

Wallace Crandall and his colleagues at Nationwide Children's Hospital then take the reader on a deep dive into the study of preventable harm. They elaborate on a new approach utilizing aggregated safety metrics. Andrew Shin and associates at Lucille Packard Children's Hospital then launch a wonderfully insightful discussion on their work around mortality associated with adverse events. We next turn to Jay Deshpande from Arkansas Children's Hospital for information on the methods used in his organization to standardize the way morbidity and mortality reviews are conducted and the lessons learned from their approach at that organization.

Fatigue clearly plays a role in the safety cultures of many industries across the world. Health care is perhaps the last industry to recognize the importance of adequate rest on good outcome for both patients and providers. Glenn Rosenbluth and Chris Landrigan elaborate on the role of sleep and work fatigue in both patient and provider safety in the health care setting. These authors leave us all with a comprehensive background in the necessary balance between work and rest. Sharon Griswold and colleagues then move us into the area of simulation training, reviewing the role and great importance of simulation in the promotion of patient safety in a variety of medical disciplines.

Much of the work in this issue is devoted to safety-related issues in the acute and critical care environment. Not to be ignored, the ambulatory environment has its own set of safety concerns in pediatric health care. Daniel Neuspiel's article focuses on what we know and what we can do in this important care delivery setting. Although much of the weight of safety prevention in children lies on the shoulders of the health care provider and the family, there remains a clear and important role of the regulatory agency in device, medication, and biologic product safety. Marilyn Flack and colleagues from the Food and Drug Administration (FDA) review the important role that the FDA plays in ensuring safety for our patients in the provision of health care.

Finally, in rounding out this issue, Kate Carr and Angela Mickalide provide the readers a glimpse of the Safe Kids Worldwide program and the impact that this program has had on patient safety around the globe in recent years.

Patient safety is paramount to our mission of providing the optimal health care delivery environment for children and their families. Patients and families expect their health care providers to be expert in this area. This issue of *Pediatric Clinics of North America* clearly sets the stage in moving forward into the next decade of safe pediatric care delivery.

Sincerely,

Brian R. Jacobs, MD, MS, FAAP
Center for Pediatric Informatics
Children's National Medical Center
Washington, DC, USA

Max J. Coppes, MD, PhD, MBA
BC Cancer Agency
Department of Medicine and Pediatrics
University of British Columbia
Vancouver, British Columbia, Canada

E-mail addresses:
bjacobs@cnmc.org (B.R. Jacobs)
mcoppes@bccancer.bc.ca (M.J. Coppes)

The Heart of Health Care
Parents' Perspectives on Patient Safety

Dale Ann Micalizzi, AAS[a],*,
Marie M. Bismark, MBChB, LLB, MBHL, MPH[b]

KEYWORDS

- Patient safety • HEART model • Service recovery • Medical error • Patient harm
- Healthcare quality

KEY POINTS

- Today there is no lack of discussion about health care delivery and quality.
- Quality from the parent's perspective includes access to care, responsiveness and empathy, good communication and clear information, appropriate treatment, relief of symptoms, improvement in health status, and safety and freedom from medical injury.
- If a medical injury occurs it is important to listen to the parent, acknowledge the damage, give an honest and open explanation and an apology, acknowledge anxieties about future treatment, and provide practical and financial help quickly.
- Nursing shortages, overtime, financial obligations, and insurance company guidelines interfere with the quality of care.
- Work as a team, review all the information, establish a plan, communicate between specialists, remove arrogance and intimidation, and have a common goal to heal.

AUTHORS' BACKGROUND

Dale, a childhood educator in New York, is mother of Dan, Andrea, and Justin and grandmother to Isabella. When Justin was 11 years old he underwent minor surgery on his ankle. During the procedure, something went terribly wrong and Justin's heart arrested. Justin was urgently transported from the surgical hospital to a pediatric intensive care unit where Dale and her husband experienced every parent's worst nightmare: the preventable loss of their loving, healthy child. Error on error killed Dale's son and her faith in a medical system that was meant to comfort and heal. Determined not to let this unbearable pain happen to another family, Dale has spent more than 10 years working with the health care sector, trying to reduce the fear and secrecy that surrounds adverse events. As part of this endeavor, Dale founded the Justin's HOPE Project at the Task Force for Global Health.[1] Justin's HOPE, in partnership

[a] The Task Force for Global Health, 325 Swanton Way, Decatur, GA 30030, USA; [b] The University of Melbourne, 207 Bouverie Street, Carlton, Victoria 3010, Australia
* Corresponding author.
E-mail address: micalizzidag@aol.com

Pediatr Clin N Am 59 (2012) 1233–1246
http://dx.doi.org/10.1016/j.pcl.2012.08.004
0031-3955/12/$ – see front matter © 2012 Elsevier Inc. All rights reserved.

with the Institute for Healthcare Improvement, provides yearly scholarships to health caregivers who are committed to patient safety and providing a safe health care environment for patients and their families.[2]

Marie has three children (Finn, 12; Stella, 10; and Zoe, 8) who have experienced the usual spectrum of childhood bumps and illnesses while living in New Zealand, Australia, and the United States. For the last 10 years Marie has worked in the field of patients' rights and complaints resolution, including 4 years as an advisor to the New Zealand Health and Disability Commissioner and a year as a Harkness Fellow at the Harvard School of Public Health. Marie currently works as a Senior Research Fellow at the University of Melbourne researching the influence of patients' complaints on quality and safety of health care.

INTRODUCTION

Health care providers that encourage patients and parents to be "the eyes and ears" of patient safety gain many insights into opportunities for improvement and risk prevention.[3] Yet, in the world of quality improvement the voices of patients and their families often go unheard. As mothers of children who have benefited from and been harmed by pediatric care we are grateful for this opportunity to share our perspectives on patient safety.

Our views are informed by our personal experiences, and enriched by conversations and written communications with hundreds of families. Many of the parents we have spoken with lost not only a child, but also their trust in medicine as a result of a senseless and preventable medical error.

> As they were administering the anesthetic to James he looked at the anaesthetist and said "don't hurt me." Those were James' last words.

Others recall extraordinary care and moments of compassion as doctors partnered with them to provide their child with the best possible care.

> It is the memory of one act that still brings tears to my eyes. In the junction between hospital buildings there is a join in the floor. This caring nurse stopped Chloe's trolley and individually lifted each wheel over the join to prevent her broken neck from being jolted. Compassion is revealed in the smallest acts.[4]

There is no substitute for being present with these families as they recall their experiences of pediatric health care: the good and the bad. To communicate some of their sentiments and suggestions with the reader, we have woven their words within this article wherever possible. Through different yet connecting eyes we offer the parents' view of patient safety and share our hopes for the future.

This article is arranged in five sections, which correspond to the five parts of the HEART model for service recovery: Hear, Empathize, Apologize, Resolve, and Thank. Variations of this model are used within[5,6] and outside[7] health care by front-line staff who seek to resolve problems by putting the needs of the affected person first.

SERVICE RECOVERY AND THE HEART MODEL

As parents, we do not expect perfection. We understand that people make mistakes and we understand that no part of life is entirely free from error or harm. However, we do expect that systems are designed with safety in mind and that when things go wrong someone steps in quickly to fix the problem. Unfortunately, health care performs poorly on both counts compared with other industries with stronger cultures of safety, service, and learning. Day after day, children are harmed by care that was intended to heal.[8,9] Frequently, parents seeking to understand what happened and why are faced with a wall of silence.[11,12] Too often, injured families are treated as adversaries rather than allies in the search for safer care.

Much has been written about the negative impact of medical malpractice litigation on doctors' reluctance to speak openly and honestly with families in the aftermath of adverse events. Certainly, the punitive, individualistic, adversarial approach of tort law runs counter to the nonpunitive, systems-oriented, cooperative strategies promoted by leaders of the patient-safety movement.[12] Yet it is too simplistic to suggest that the fear of legal action is the only obstacle standing in the way of true partnership with patients and families who have been injured by the very care that was intended to heal. Medicine has a long tradition of exercising paternalistic sovereignty over patients' information[13] and "circling the wagons" in defense against accusations of patient harm. Even within such countries as New Zealand, where malpractice litigation is effectively barred and compensation is provided on a no-fault basis,[14] fears of reputational damage, professional discomfort with uncertainty and failure, medicolegal myths regarding the risks of disclosure, and an entrenched culture of self-protection still impede the willingness of some doctors to talk openly about and learn from adverse events.[15]

However, the news is not all bad. Many industries outside of health care have effectively designed safety features into the workflow (ie, limited hours for taxi drivers, checklists for pilots).[16] In hospitals and clinics around the world, an increasing number of providers are finding the courage to "do the right thing" with or without the support of legislative or policy reform. Examples include the "3R's program" implemented by COPIC in Colorado[17] and the "seven pillars" process developed by the University of Illinois Medical Center at Chicago.[18]

One simple, yet effective, model of service recovery that goes a long way toward meeting the needs of injured patients and their families is the HEART framework. Variations of the HEART model, including the Cleveland Clinic "Respond with HEART" program,[6] are used by several health care providers in the United States and elsewhere.[5] As explained by Brenda Radford, from Duke University Hospital,[19] HEART has two aims: "The first goal is to prevent patient concerns from occurring … If that fails, service recovery is simply making right what went wrong."

By using the HEART model, providers can respond with compassion and learn from every mistake. The following sections break down each of the five steps and provide context for providers interested in applying the model to their own practices.

Hear

Parents have a critical role to play in the delivery of safe, high-quality pediatric care. We can assist with diagnosis, management, and administration of treatment. We can provide an extra set of "eyes and ears," noticing subtle changes in our child's condition and alerting providers to possible risks and errors in the delivery of care. However, we can only fulfill that role if our voices are heard and respected.

> *It had been extremely distressing that no one would believe Simone was seriously ill, when I – as her mother – was all too aware of her precarious state. Then, when it was almost too late, I was being treated as if I had not acted soon enough.*

Honest information, clear communication, and a participative approach should be the watchwords in promoting safety at all levels of pediatric health care. Some hospitals do this well.

Upon arrival we were shown around, introduced to the nurses, told all about the monitors, and everything was fully explained to us ... Nothing was ever too much bother, every question we asked was answered no matter how silly it sounded ... Whenever a doctor or nurse did anything to Oliver it was explained fully, what and why they were doing it ... Everything was parent and child oriented.

Yet many parents feel unsafe to speak up, worry about being labeled a "difficult parent" if they ask too many questions, or face exclusion from conversations about their child.

When I saw [the doctor] he was always accompanied by other people and seemed to be talking to them and at me as opposed to including me in the conversation and making sure I understood exactly what was going on.

Likewise, many children who are old enough to have a voice in their own care are treated with little respect for their dignity or independence.

No one even told me their name. They just started poking at me and talking amongst themselves like I wasn't even in the room.

For health care providers the hospital environment is a second home: routines are familiar, everyone's role is known and understood, and medical jargon is readily interpretable. However, for parents the hospital environment is a frighteningly unfamiliar place and explanations are often inadequate.

No one gave us any ideas on what to look for, to check if there was a change in her condition.

From clothing to meals, from visiting hours to pain relief, choices are repetitively taken away from parents. Little is posted, little is clear.

The worst aspect of her second operation was the "losing control." There was nothing we could do. We had to rely entirely upon the "experts."

Even the process of informed consent, which is intended to support choice and understanding, is frequently derailed through the use of vague and legalistic documents and forms. For a patient or family member who is already feeling frightened and vulnerable, quickly signing and pushing the form away may feel safer than struggling to work through language and concepts they are ill-equipped to understand.

From a parents' perspective, three key elements in being heard are (1) trust, (2) openness, and (3) respect. Trust is present when we feel confident that a provider has our child's best interests at heart, that he or she has the time to listen, and that he or she will take our concerns seriously. If we feel unable to trust our child's doctor, we may turn to another member of the team (a nurse, a social worker, a health care assistant, or patient advocate) or we may simply remain silent and uneasy.

My concern at the time was that she was on a general nursing ward with a severe condition and no attempt of barrier nursing to help prevent her contracting further infections. I did not voice my concern at the time. It was difficult to criticize professionals.

Openness requires providers to share the information we need to participate in meaningful dialogue about our child's care. How can we understand our child's illness and medical needs when we do not have easy access to his or her test results and medical record? How can we explore our options when medical journals keep important research findings locked behind expensive pay walls? How can we choose the safest care for our child when we do not know how many times the surgeon has performed this procedure or how the local hospital's infection rate compares with the facility down the road? The health care system's ongoing failure to provide parents' with ready and timely access to information relevant to their children's care is inexcusable.

We were not offered any part in the decision making. We were just told what would happen. The alternatives were not discussed with us ... With hindsight we feel that it would have been helpful to have been confronted with the full facts, and to have been given an indication of the implications and the options open to us.

Finally, respect involves recognizing and valuing parents' knowledge and perspectives. Many parents experience a powerful sense of intuition that something is wrong long before a doctor is able to put a name to the problem[20]: a voice inside our heads warning us to be watchful and wary. Doctors disregard a parent's inner voice at their peril.

My wife had always felt sure that there was something else wrong with Oliver. But the doctors brushed it aside. It would be another two years before anyone else would take my wife's fears seriously.

Moms and dads should be reassured that their gut feelings matter and encouraged to speak up if they feel worried about their child's care or clinical condition. A good clinician will ask: "Do you have anything inside that is bothering you because we would really like to hear it? Your thoughts can change the plan for the better." For some children, having their parents' voices heard in time can mean the difference between life and death.

Empathy

When an adverse event does occur, parents have different needs depending on the nature of the injury, relationship with the providers involved, previous health care experience, and cultural values and norms. Regardless of background, parents of an injured child always remember a compassionate moment from a child's caregiver; a gentle touch or a shoulder to cry on:

Two nurses impressed us with their care in particular. They communicated empathy to us in our distress and demonstrated concern for our child.

Facing the raw emotions of a parent whose child has been injured is not easy. The providers involved often are dealing with their own shame and fear, and they may be ill-prepared and poorly supported in responding to the consequences of an adverse event. Yet, it is at that very moment when the injured patient and family need their care the most.

She seemed uneasy with us and the situation we were in. It was as if she was not sure what to say or was unsure how we would react. She remained detached from us. [It] was a deeply lonely experience.

The death of a child is a time of unparalleled grief and vulnerability. **Table 1** illustrates the scope and severity of symptoms reported by a group of 75 parents after the loss of a child. Many of these parents recall that being left alone at their lowest moment of despair was the most painful part of an already devastating experience. Parents need comfort when there is nothing else left to give.

Many health care providers could learn a lot about empathy and compassion from the end of life care provided in pediatric intensive care units and hospices. The doctors

Table 1
Symptoms reported by 75 parents after the loss of a child

Emotional and Psychological Symptoms	Percentage (n = 75)
Sleeplessness	82%
Depression	82%
Anxiety	73%
Lack of joy	68%
Fatigue	65%
Lack of concentration	60%
Alcohol or drug abuse	59%
Mood changes	58%
Lack of motivation	55%
Posttraumatic stress	53%
Uncontrollable crying	50%
Suicidal thoughts	45%
Irritability	40%
Morbid thoughts	33%
Lack of emotions	28%
Obsessive-compulsive tendencies	23%
Unable to return to work	22%
Unable to leave home	18%
Anger management concerns	18%
Uncontrollable laughing	3%
Bipolar diagnosis	2%
Delirium	2%

and nurses in these units know all too well the devastation that follows the death of a child, they have heard the animal-like cries of loss from bereaved parents, and they have shared tears of sadness with the families they serve. They understand the importance of listening, rituals of care, support, and comfort while facing the reality that sometimes your best is not good enough.

Keeping promises is essential. A provider who promises to stop by, bring a cup of coffee, or plan a family meeting must follow through. Broken promises are always remembered; forgiven usually but not forgotten.

After returning home I telephoned the hospital several times. On each occasion I was told that no one was available to speak to me, or alternatively, I was just put on hold and ignored.

Acknowledging the individuality of the child and the family is important too. Our children are important to us and should be important to providers, too. After an adverse event, providers should sit down, make eye contact with family members, and listen with an open mind and heart.

Hospital staff deal with countless patients and the individuality of the person may be lost amongst all the flesh and tissue.

When a child has been injured by medical care, the need for empathy and care extends long beyond the initial period of grief and well beyond the immediate family.

I remember walking up the steps out of the hospital feeling empty, leaving Daniel there and going home. The whole way home I was sobbing and then I had to tell people that he had died after an operation which was to give him life. There was no offer of counseling, though we were given a blue leaflet on how to cope with death.

Health professionals cannot always be there, but they can put parents in touch with groups and individuals who can help. Some support groups take advantage of the social media transformation that brings together parents from around the world to share support and guidance. Such Web sites as Caring Bridge,[21] Patients Like Me,[22] and many disease-specific sites are full of parents who want to offer a supportive shoulder to other families experiencing similar questions and concerns.

Others, such as those run by Family Voices[23] and The Compassionate Friends International,[24] meet in person. To witness a group of bereaved parents gathering in a support group is an extraordinary experience. Newly grieving parents arrive at their first meeting bent over with despair, and receive strength from other parents quietly listening, advising, holding, supporting, and knowing. At the next meeting they are there again, offering care and compassion to newer parents through their own grief. It is a circle of love and a true testimony of humanity.

I felt very alone so it felt good to be able to communicate with other parents, and share our concerns.

The impact of an adverse event on friends and the wider community should not be forgotten. When Dale returned to Justin's school to clean out his locker, she witnessed one of his friends being scolded and punished for his bad behavior that day. The teacher said "I don't know what's wrong with you!" More than 10 years later Justin's friends still visit his grave each year on his birthday.

Medical schools and postgraduate training programs play a critical role in equipping students with the self-awareness and skills they require to respond to adverse events in an open and empathetic manner. Some, such as the University of Illinois at Chicago Institute for Patient Safety Excellence, already emphasize the importance of sharing information with families and integrate disclosure practices into the course of their practice.[25] Others continue to expose students and trainees to a culture of detachment and denial.

The trauma that parents experience as the result of an adverse event is bad enough. The trauma inflicted when the incident is managed poorly can be even worse. When things go wrong, more than ever before, parents need their child's caregivers to be kind, dependable, and above all to be there.

They may not remember what you said or what you did but they will remember how you made them feel.

~*Maya Angelou*

Apologize

In addition to empathy and compassion, parents dealing with the aftermath of an adverse event need to know that their child mattered to caregivers and that lessons will be learned to prevent another family suffering similar harm. Rapid open disclosure, a thorough investigation, appropriate accountability, and a sincere apology can save relationships and save lives.

All I kept thinking was ... why had this happened? The following day we asked to see [the doctor] for an explanation. I can remember him saying words to the effect "It's one of those things that happens." I did not feel at all happy with the explanations – or rather, lack of explanations. We were receiving no straight answers ...

When we suspect that information is being withheld or altered, when we face barriers to accessing our child's medical record, when we wait and wait for telephone calls to be returned, when we hear whispers in the hallways—we become suspicious. Secrecy is damaging. Being open brings comfort and respect.

We wanted to know why our daughter had died. We did not understand why the report should have been hidden from us.

Many patients and families (particularly the parents of children who have died or suffered permanent disability) wonder whether they are in some way to blame for the harm that occurred. The thought that this catastrophe could have been prevented if we, the family, had done something differently may nag parents and siblings for years.

It was our job to keep our child safe. If we don't know what happened, we inevitably blame ourselves for having failed in our duty as parents.

An apology from the doctors may provide important confirmation to the family that the health system had more responsibility for the injury than did the patient or the family. By truthfully acknowledging the extent to which the outcome was a result of their actions or of broader aspects of the health care system, health practitioners can lift the burden of uncertainly and guilt from the shoulders of the family and provide an understanding of how and why things went wrong.[26]

At one point we noticed Laura had a burn on her leg caused by drugs which were leaking from her drip. When we brought this burn to the doctor's attention, he said it was not a problem since "we can always do a skin graft." He did not say "I'm sorry."

Kathryn Schulz notes in her book *Being Wrong*: "As a culture, we haven't... mastered the basic skill of saying 'I was wrong.' This is a startling deficiency, given the simplicity of the phrase, the ubiquity of error, and the tremendous public service that acknowledging it could provide."[27]

There was complete silence from the hospital. It made us feel that something had gone wrong and that the hospital staff were too embarrassed to face us.

Resolve

What differentiates health care organizations—positively or negatively—is the way they respond in a crisis. Are they willing to work with patients and their families to resolve a problem in a positive and proactive manner, or do they run and hide?

Resolving the harm caused by an adverse event usually takes two forms: remedying the harm to the individual patient and family wherever possible (by way of treatment, rehabilitation, and compensation where appropriate[28]); and addressing the underlying problem to provide safer care in the future. Such restorative measures—combined with timely and compassionate communication—benefit patients and their families, may avert potential medicolegal action,[17] support safer care, and strengthen trust in health care systems. Given the opportunity, the families of children injured by health care will give the best that they have to give to protect another child from suffering similar harm.

I could not bear the thought of another parent going through what we went through.

Parents' efforts to develop and promote safer care have been arduous and the results slow at times. Yet, great strides have been made toward improving pediatric health care for the better. Some of the many contributions offered by families of children harmed by health care are shown in **Table 2**.

During the course of a typical hospital admission, parents learn quickly about systems that work and those that do not. Look-alike medication bottles, miscommunication, poor hand hygiene, missing test results, short staffing, inconsistent advice from different doctors, no clear processes for reporting or learning from errors—the opportunities for improvement seem so clear to parents sitting for hours on hours watching the daily activities of care.

We see the difference between well-trained and rested staff and those who are exhausted or out of their depth.

At the shift changeover I remember than an agency nurse took over. He said he did not work on the unit very often and it was apparent that he was not at all used to the equipment ... I was a little worried at his lack of knowledge and experience.

We see what happens when a member of senior hospital leadership does a safety walk and what happens when his or her back is turned. We see which protocols are followed and which are ignored when the ward becomes busy.

We noticed that some staff were more stringent in matters of hygiene than others. Some members of staff neglected to wear plastic gloves and masks [when undertaking procedures in the intensive care unit]. We found this worrying at the time and wonder, in retrospect whether such lapses in hygiene might have been responsible for Laura's primary infection which led to her septicaemia.

We see which doctors roll their eyes when required to complete a checklist and which ones understand their importance for safe, reliable care. We see the way that alarms are ignored like the boy who cried wolf, until one day there really is a wolf.

We observed that one of Michael's monitors went haywire for a few seconds and we pointed this out to a nurse who dismissed this as a problem that happened quite frequently with that piece of equipment. We found that quite strange: how would they then know when there really was a problem?

We see the value of premixed medications and dedicated ward pharmacists. We see the opportunities to save money while still providing great care through the avoidance of duplicate tests and unnecessary delays.

Staff were unable to find her previous X-rays for comparison ... I was appalled at the lack of information technology systems available to the staff.

We see the care provided to our children across different shifts, different professions, different locations, and different times.

For those providers interested in improving patient safety, parents can provide an extraordinary resource. No one else has a greater insight into the day-to-day workings of the hospital, from the patient and family perspective, and no one else has a stronger incentive to ensure that the care provided is safe and effective.

As parents, we want to know that our child will be safe at any hospital and we are willing to help resolve any problems that might stand in the way of that goal. We are not looking for a tokenistic patient safety office but rather an embedded culture in which the safety of our child matters to each and every person caring for them. This is what we mean when we say "take care of my baby." Is that naive? Or is it what our children deserve?

Table 2
Ways in which parents contribute to patient safety

	Examples	Case Study
Education and information	Grand rounds Medical student teaching Curriculum design	Dale Ann Micalizzi has presented her son Justin's story to many medical students including students at Yale Medical School
Advice and support	Face-to-face support groups Online support groups Web sites	Through a network of more than 600 chapters, The Compassionate Friends supports bereaved families after the death of a child[24]
Empowerment	Workshops Family rounds Advocacy	Cincinnati Children's Hospital has developed and implemented a process that allows families to decide if they want to be part of attending-physician rounds[31]
Medicolegal action	Complaints Lawsuits Inquiries	Many parents gave evidence at the Inquiry into the management of care of children receiving complex heart surgery at the Bristol Royal Infirmary[32]
Research and analysis	Root cause analyses Surveys Research collaborations	The Young and Well CRC undertakes research in collaboration with young people and their families to reduce disengagement from health services[33]
Writing and presenting	Editorials Conference presentations Articles and books	*Time to Care* was authored by Robin Youngson after his daughter's spinal injury[4]
Technology and design	Smart phone applications Patient education tools	A charity founded by Parool Shah, the mother of a premature baby, has developed a smart phone application to help parents understand the medical speak they face in neonatal intensive care units[34]
Funding	Fundraising Scholarships Foundations	The Justin's HOPE project awards scholarships to health care givers who are committed to improving patient safety for patients and families[35]
Policies and standards	White papers Accreditation standards	The IHI White Paper "When things go wrong: Responding to adverse events" represents the collaborative effort of a group of clinicians, risk managers, and patients[36]

(continued on next page)

Table 2 (continued)		
	Examples	**Case Study**
Governance	Advisory councils Directorships	All hospitals in Massachusetts are required to have a Patient and Family Advisory Council to advise the hospital on patient and provider relationships, quality improvement initiatives, and patient education[37]
Legislation and regulation	Lobbying Drafting bills	The Michael Skolnik Medical Transparency Act 2007 requires physicians in Colorado to disclose specific information that can be accessed by the public[38]
Art and culture	Music Gardens Art	Regina Holliday paints the stories of dozens of patients (including children and their families) on the backs of jackets to form a "Walking Gallery"[39]

Thank

As Sheridan and Hatlie[29] point out, when it comes to improving patient safety, parents "are not the enemy." The focus of providers and parents should be on learning from adverse events to improve the quality of care and thus decrease the risk of similar events in future. Although parents do not expect to be thanked for raising concerns we do expect to be treated as partners in care. In the long run partnering with parents to redesign health care saves time, money, and lives.

There is no doubt that experienced pediatric patients and their families can teach health care a thing or two.

To get their attention, providers need to know "Why is this important to me?" Having heard Dale Ann Micalizzi quietly but forcefully speak of her experience, a provider recounted to me that "everyone in the room was in tears." After that kind of experience, each time a provider undertakes their daily duties, that family and their adversity and tragedy will be in the back of the provider's mind. Identifying with the patient's experience can change behaviors for the better.[30]

Yet, many hospitals continue to exclude families from care improvement processes, and treat parents' suggestions for improvement as a threat or a distraction from their "real" work. The risks of this adversarial approach are significant, and include losing trust, impairing healing, preventing learning, increasing regulatory action and lawsuits, attracting adverse media comment, and contributing to staff burnout.

For hospitals who chose to see every error as an opportunity to learn and improve, and who want to acknowledge the valuable contribution of parents to improving pediatric care there are many ways to do so. The most effective way of thanking parents for their contribution to patient safety is by implementing meaningful changes in response to their suggestions.

The father of a child receiving radiation treatment emphasized that his child was at increased risk of infection because of the cancer treatments and should not be exposed to many people for no reason. This led to streamlining and improvements in the process of patient admission and discharge for radiation treatment.

What steps are being taken in your hospital to recognize and respect the role of parents in improving patient safety? Are expressions of concern and suggestions for change viewed as a burden or as a gift?

SUMMARY

Today there is no lack of discussion about health care delivery and quality. We hear leaders in the field professing that improving quality is the industry's first priority. Quality from the parent's perspective includes access to care, responsiveness and empathy, good communication and clear information, appropriate treatment, relief of symptoms, improvement in health status, and safety and freedom from medical injury. When we who have experienced the trauma of errors see more providers engaging parents and patients, we believe we will see true quality improvement.

If a medical injury occurs it is important to listen to the parent, acknowledge the damage, give an honest and open explanation and an apology, acknowledge anxieties about future treatment, and provide practical and financial help quickly. By following the HEART model (or another patient-centered framework of service recovery), providers and parents can become allies rather than adversaries in the quest for safer care.

We know about the nursing shortages, the overtime, the financial obligations, and the insurance company guidelines that interfere with the quality of care. We also know, when it comes time for a child's care, providers must find a way to remove the chaos. Work as a team, review all the information, establish a plan, communicate between specialists, remove arrogance and intimidation, and have a common goal to heal. Complete checklists, double check medications and dosages, and treat every case as a possible emergency with our child as your only focus for as long as it takes. Because if the child in that hospital bed was your child, that is what you would want too.

The highest courage is to dare to be yourself in the face of adversity. Choosing right over wrong, ethics over convenience, and truth over popularity...these are the choices that measure your life. Travel the path of integrity without looking back, for there is never a wrong time to do the right thing.

~unknown

ACKNOWLEDGMENTS

Special thanks to Jean DerGurahian, health care safety and information technology journalist, for her thoughtful suggestions and editorial assistance on this project. The quotes in this paper are drawn from more than 10 years of personal conversations and written communications between the authors and families of children who were injured during medical care, along with publicly available documents, such as media reports and statements to public inquiries. Where appropriate, minor details have been changed to protect the anonymity of the family concerned.

REFERENCES

1. Available at: http://www.taskforce.org/our-work/projects/justins-hope.
2. Available at: http://app.ihi.org/marketing/program_documents/2012_NatnForum/Justin_Micalizzi_Memorial_IHI_Forum_Scholarship_2012.pdf.
3. Hayden AC, Pichert JW, Fawcett J, et al. Best practices for basic and advanced skills in healthcare service recovery: a case study of a re-admitted patient. Jt Comm J Qual Patient Saf 2010;36(7):310–8.

4. Youngson R. Time to care. Auckland (New Zealand): Rebelheart Publishers; 2012.
5. Govern P. Plan turns complaints into opportunities. Reporter Vanderbilt University Medical Center's Weekly Newspaper; 2005. Available at: http://www.mc.vanderbilt.edu/reporter/index.html?ID=4220.
6. Merlino J, Sinclair S. Respond with H.E.A.R.T. Cleveland Clinic Focus on the Patient Experience. 2010:6.Available at: http://my.clevelandclinic.org/Documents/Patient-Experience/OPE-Newsletter-5-26-10.pdf.
7. Available at: http://www.quibblo.com/quiz/bHeQPEv/Front-Desk-Service-Recovery-The-HEART-Model.
8. Kaushal R, Bates DW, Landrigan C, et al. Medication errors and adverse drug events in pediatric inpatients. JAMA 2001;285(16):2114–20.
9. Woods D, Thomas E, Holl J, et al. Adverse events and preventable adverse events in children. Pediatrics 2005;115(1):155–60.
10. Gibson R, Singh JP. The wall of silence. Washington: Lifeline Press; 2003.
11. Garbutt J, Brownstein DR, Klein EJ, et al. Reporting and disclosing medical errors: pediatricians' attitudes and behaviors. Arch Pediatr Adolesc Med 2007; 161(2):179–85.
12. Studdert DM, Mello MM, Brennan TA. Medical malpractice. N Engl J Med 2004; 350(3):283–92.
13. Katz J. The silent world of doctor and patient. Baltimore (MD): John Hopkins University Press; 2002.
14. Bismark M, Paterson R. No-fault compensation in New Zealand: harmonzing injury compensation, provider accountability and patient safety. Health Aff 2006;25(1):278–83.
15. Lamb R. Open disclosure: the only approach to medical error. Qual Saf Health Care 2004;13(1):3–5.
16. Gawande A. The checklist manifesto: how to get things right. New York: Picador; 2011.
17. Quinn RE, Eichler MC. The 3Rs program: the Colorado experience. Clin Obstet Gynecol 2008;51(4):709–18.
18. McDonald TB, Helmchen LA, Smith KM, et al. Responding to patient safety incidents: the "seven pillars." Qual Saf Health Care 2010;19(6):e11.
19. Williamson S. Tools for building satisfied patients. Inside 2004;13(7).
20. Graedon J, Graedon T. Enlisting families as patient safety allies. Clin Pediatr Emerg Med 2006;7(4):265–7.
21. Available at: http://www.caringbridge.org/.
22. Available at: http://www.patientslikeme.com/.
23. Available at: http://www.familyvoices.org/.
24. Burnell G, Burnell AL. The compassionate friends: a support group for bereaved parents. J Fam Pract 1986;22(3):295–6.
25. Mayar D, Klamen DL, Gunderson A, et al. Designing a patient safety undergraduate medical curriculum. Teach Learn Med 2009;21(1):52–8. Available at: http://www.yuhuihuang.com/IPSE/index.php.
26. Bismark M. The power of apology. N Z Med J 2009;122:96–106.
27. Shulz K. Being wrong: adventures in the margin of error. New York: Ecco / Harper Collins; 2010.
28. Bismark M, Dauer E, Paterson R, et al. Accountability sought by patients following adverse events from medical care. CMAJ 2006;175(8):889–94.
29. Sheridan SS, Hatlie MJ. We're not your enemy: an appeal from a consumer to re-imagine tort reform. Patient Safety and Quality Healthcare 2007; July/August. Available at: www.psqh.com/julaug07/tortreform.html.

30. MBW Health Communications Specialist. 2012.
31. Muething SE, Kotagal UR, Schoettker PJ, et al. Family-centered bedside rounds: a new approach to patient care and teaching. Pediatrics 2007;119(4):829–32.
32. Bristol Royal Infirmary Inquiry. The inquiry into the management of care of children receiving complex heart surgery at the Bristol Royal Infirmary 1984-1995. London: Stationery Office; 2001.
33. Young and Well Cooperative Research Centre. Available at: http://www.yawcrc.org.au/.
34. Smith S. App helps new parents crack intensive care medical jargon. Life's Little Treasures Foundation. 2012. Available at: http://ahha.asn.au/news/app-helps-new-parents-crack-intensive-care-medical-jargon.
35. Justin Micalizzi Memorial IHI Forum Scholarship. Available at: http://app.ihi.org/marketing/program_documents/2012_NatnForum/Justin_Micalizzi_Memorial_IHI_Forum_Scholarship_2012.pdf.
36. When things go wrong: responding to adverse events. A consensus statement of the Harvard Hospitals. Burlington (MA): Massachusetts Coalition for the Prevention of Medical Errors; 2006.
37. Patient and Family Advisory Councils. Commonwealth of Massachusetts Circular Letter: DHCQ 09-07-514. Available at: http://www.mass.gov/eohhs/docs/dph/quality/hcq-circular-letters/dhcq-0907514.pdf.
38. Available at: http://citizensforpatientsafety.org/history.html.
39. Small V. Walking gallery tells medical stories. The Washington Post; 2012. Available at: http://www.washingtonpost.com/business/capitalbusiness/2012/06/08/gJQAs5NNTV_story.html.

Computerized Provider Order Entry and Patient Safety

Erika L. Abramson, MD, MS[a,b,c,d,e,*],
Rainu Kaushal, MD, MPH[a,b,c,d,e,f]

KEYWORDS

- CPOE - Pediatrics - Medication safety

KEY POINTS

- Pediatric patients are particularly vulnerable to prescribing errors.
- Research on the impact of CPOE systems for pediatric patients is growing.
- CPOE has tremendous potential for improving patient safety but can also have unintended consequences.
- Much of the research on the effectiveness of CPOE among pediatric patients has been on reduction in prescribing errors.
- Future research should focus on the effectiveness of CPOE with CDS on actual outcomes for pediatric patients, and other workflow and implementation factors.

INTRODUCTION

Medical errors are a leading cause of morbidity and mortality in the United States and result in tremendous health care cost.[1] Medication errors are the most common type of medical error, and most medication errors occur at the prescribing stage.[1] Although medication errors affect adult and pediatric patients, children are particularly vulnerable, and thus the need to improve prescribing safety for this population is critical.[1–3]

Health information technology (HIT), including computerized provider order entry (CPOE), is believed to hold tremendous promise for improving medication safety and unprecedented federal initiatives are currently promoting its adoption and use.[4] Leading pediatric organizations, such as the American Academy of Pediatrics, are also endorsing the use of CPOE for the prevention of medication errors.[5] Although

[a] Department of Pediatrics, Weill Cornell Medical College, 525 East 68th Street, New York, NY, USA; [b] Department of Public Health, Weill Cornell Medical College, 525 East 68th Street, New York, NY, USA; [c] New York-Presbyterian Hospital, 525 East 68th Street, New York, NY, USA; [d] Health Information Technology Evaluation Collaborative, New York, NY, USA; [e] Center for Healthcare Informatics and Policy, New York, NY, USA; [f] Department of Medicine, Weill Cornell Medical College, 525 East 68th Street, New York, NY, USA
* Corresponding author. Departments of Pediatrics and Public Health, Weill Medical College of Cornell University, 530 East 70th Street, Room M-610A, New York, NY 10065.
E-mail address: err9009@med.cornell.edu

Pediatr Clin N Am 59 (2012) 1247–1255
http://dx.doi.org/10.1016/j.pcl.2012.08.001
0031-3955/12/$ – see front matter © 2012 Elsevier Inc. All rights reserved.

pediatric.theclinics.com

much research on the impact of CPOE has been conducted among adult patients, research has increasingly begun to focus on the impact of CPOE on pediatric patients.

Understanding the effects of CPOE in actual use is critical to inform health care policy. This article (1) reviews the epidemiology of medication errors in children, (2) examines the literature on the impact of CPOE on pediatric patient safety in the hospital and outpatient setting, and (3) discusses policy implications and future directions for research.

DEFINITIONS

CPOE refers to a provider's use of computer assistance to directly enter medical orders, such as medications, consultations with other providers, laboratory services, imaging studies, and other auxiliary services. CPOE is often used to describe this process in the inpatient setting. Electronic transmission of prescriptions directly to pharmacies (ePrescribing) is commonly an associated functionality.

Much of the value of CPOE is believed to come from clinical decision support (CDS). CDS refers to electronic suggestions or reminders, delivered at the point of care, to aid in the prescribing process. CPOE systems are often categorized as basic or advanced, depending on the amount of available CDS. Examples of CDS include drug-allergy checking, basic dosing guidance, formulary decision support, duplicate therapy checking, dosing support for renal insufficiency, and guidance for medication-related laboratory testing. CPOE systems might also have order sets (bundled groups of orders to standardize ordering around a specific disease or condition) or provide reminders or guidelines to promote best practices by prescribing physicians.

MEDICATION ERRORS

Medication errors can occur at any step in the medication process (defined by the Institute of Medicine as prescribing, transcribing, dispensing, administering, and monitoring a medication).[1] CPOE largely targets prescribing errors. Common types of prescribing errors include incorrect dosing (overdosing and underdosing); incorrect drug selection; incorrect frequency; wrong patient; incorrect route of administration; and illegibility (for handwritten orders). Near misses are a type of error with high potential for serious patient harm that do not harm the patient either fortuitously or because the error was intercepted. Adverse drug events (ADEs) are harm from a medication. Some ADEs are associated with errors and therefore preventable, whereas others are not associated with an error and are considered nonpreventable. Lastly, ameliorable ADEs are nonpreventable ADEs whose severity could have been substantially reduced if there had been an appropriate and timely response by the provider.[6] **Table 1** provides examples of various types of prescribing errors.

THE EPIDEMIOLOGY OF PEDIATRIC MEDICATION ERRORS

Research on the epidemiology of pediatric medication errors suggests these errors occur with great frequency. In the inpatient setting, a study conducted by Kaushal and colleagues[3] found that 5.7% of handwritten inpatient orders contained prescribing errors with low potential for harm; 1.1% contained near misses; and 0.24% resulted in ADEs, of which 19% were preventable. Importantly, the rate of near misses was triple that compared with adults.[7] Most errors occurred at the prescribing stage and most prescribing errors were related to incorrect dosing. Subsequent studies have similarly found high error rates, with most errors occurring at the prescribing stage for pediatric patients.[8,9] For example, a study by Otero and colleagues[8] found prescribing errors in

Table 1
Examples of prescribing errors

Type of Error	Example
Prescribing error with low potential for harm	Failure to specify frequency for a topical cream, such as 1% hydrocortisone
Near miss	Prescribing amoxicillin for a patient with a penicillin allergy that is not administered because the pharmacist intercepts the error
Preventable adverse drug event	Prescribing amoxicillin for a patient with a penicillin allergy who then experiences anaphylaxis
Ameliorable adverse drug event	Patient experiences severe diarrhea from an antibiotic but does not report this to the provider for several days

every five or six orders among all hospitalized children in their institution. Also importantly, of all pediatric inpatients, neonates and critically ill children seem to be particularly vulnerable to errors.[3,10–12]

As in the inpatient setting, prescribing errors are extremely common in the outpatient setting, although research in this setting is much more limited. A study of six outpatient offices in Massachusetts found prescribing errors in 53% of prescriptions and near misses in 20% of prescriptions.[13] As in the inpatient setting, most errors occurred at the prescribing stage. Inappropriate abbreviation errors and dosing errors were most common, and the most frequent cause of errors was illegibility. A more recent study of handwritten prescriptions for pediatric patients in a renal outpatient clinic found an even higher rate of errors at 77.4%.[14]

THE UNIQUE VULNERABILITY OF CHILDREN TO MEDICATION ERRORS

Children seem to be particularly vulnerable to medication errors and ADEs for a variety of reasons (**Box 1**).[1–3] Some factors are intrinsic to the nature of being a child, whereas others are related to how medications are ordered and used among pediatric patients.

PROPOSED BENEFITS OF CPOE

Given the scope of the problem facing pediatric patients, HIT is increasingly being promoted and used as a way to improve patient safety. Indeed, use of CPOE is one

Box 1
Factors associated with the increased risk of children to medication errors and preventable ADEs

- Immature renal and hepatic systems affecting drug metabolism
- Limited reserve to withstand errors
- Limited ability to communicate to prevent an error or signal that an error has occurred
- Neonatal drugs often dosed based on chronologic and postconceptual age
- Weight-based dosing (requires calculations by prescribers and knowledge of dosing maximums)
- Wide range of correct drug doses depending on indication
- Unique risk for 10-fold medication errors
- More frequent off-label use of medications in pediatrics

of the core requirements providers must demonstrate to be eligible for financial incentives through the electronic health record (EHR) incentive program, an unprecedented federal initiative promoting adoption and meaningful use of EHRs.[4] The emphasis being placed on use of CPOE stems from the many potential benefits of CPOE use. **Box 2** summarizes those benefits, a few of which are highlighted later.

One of the primary benefits of CPOE use is eliminating illegibility, a significant problem among handwritten prescriptions. In a study conducted at an acute care children's hospital that reviewed records for 132 patients, medication order legibility rates were 13% in the neonatal intensive care unit, 53% in the pediatric intensive care unit (PICU), and 50% to 80% in the medical-surgical units.[15] In the outpatient setting, a recent study reviewing handwritten prescriptions by 78 community-based adult ambulatory care providers across two states found that illegibility errors occurred on average more than once per prescription.[16] Although there are no comparable large-scale pediatric studies that the authors are aware of, a study of prescriptions in a pediatric renal outpatient clinic found that 12.3% of items were judged to be illegible.[14]

In addition to eliminating illegibility, CPOE can also help ensure completeness in prescribing fields. In the same study of pediatric patients at an outpatient clinic, 73% of handwritten items were found to be missing essential information.[14] In the inpatient setting, a PICU study estimated the error rate related to incomplete information was 18.7%.[17]

Another proposed benefit of CPOE is improved prescribing practices through addition of CDS. CDS provides timely, point-of-care information that can guide the provider in prescribing choices, avert potential errors, and improve adherence to guidelines. For CDS to be useful, however, it must be integrated within clinical workflow and provide information perceived as useful. Multiple studies have highlighted the problem of alert fatigue, resulting in routine overriding of alerts by providers.[18–21] A study of more than 54,000 orders entered into a CPOE system for pediatric inpatients at a large, urban academic medical center found that of the 27,000 alerts generated, providers did not accept alerts nearly two-thirds of the time, and most overridden orders differed by more than 50% from the suggested computer dosing.[22]

CPOE, when integrated with pharmacy systems and with electronic medication administration records, can also help improve the tracking of orders and eliminate the need for transcription of information, reducing the potential for error. Each time transcription is performed, potential for error is introduced. A recent study looking at transcription errors associated with intravenous medications in a regional pediatric hospital found that 6% of transcriptions had at least one error.[23]

IMPACT OF CPOE SYSTEMS ON PATIENT SAFETY

In the inpatient and outpatient setting, multiple studies have shown that CPOE can reduce the frequency of medication errors for adult patients.[24–28] For example, a study

---

Box 2
Potential benefits of CPOE
Eliminate illegibility of prescribing fields
Ensure completeness of prescribing fields
Reduce transcription errors
Provide CDS to aid in the prescribing process (this includes order sets, alerts, reminders, and screening guidelines)
Improve tracking of orders

conducted by Bates and colleagues[25] evaluating medication errors among adult inpatients found that CPOE eliminated more than 80% of nonmissed drug medication errors. In the outpatient setting, a recent study of community-based ambulatory care adult providers found that introduction of electronic order entry integrated within an EHR decreased prescribing errors nearly 1.5-fold, and introduction of a stand-alone prescribing system reduced errors nearly sevenfold.[27,28]

In pediatric inpatients, several studies have similarly demonstrated decreases in medication errors after implementation of a CPOE system. For example, a systematic review by van Rosse and colleagues[29] reviewed a total of 12 observational studies conducted in a mixture of pediatric general inpatient units, neonatal intensive care units, and PICUs. The authors found that prescribing errors were reduced in all studies.

In the pediatric outpatient setting, few studies have been conducted examining the impact of CPOE on prescribing errors and results are more mixed. One study examining the prevalence of dosing errors among 22 commonly used medications for children found no difference in prescribing error rates in sites with and without electronic order entry.[30] Notably, however, this study did not evaluate handwritten prescriptions but instead evaluated automated pharmacy data. Thus, the study could not assess the impact that CPOE would have on prescribing illegibility errors.

A more recent study of prescribing errors in a pediatric outpatient renal clinic found that electronic prescribing completely eliminated illegibility errors, which occurred at a high rate at baseline, and significantly reduced errors related to completeness of prescriptions.[14] Another study assessed the effectiveness of an automated weight-based dosing calculator integrated into an EHR for reducing antipyretic prescribing errors in an outpatient pediatric clinic and found a significant reduction in prescribing errors, particularly overdosing errors.[31]

Studying the effect of CPOE systems on prescribing errors is important for several reasons. First, these types of errors often lead to tremendous rework for pharmacists, patients, and physicians. Second, these types of errors also lead to clinically significant delays in patients receiving medications. For example, one study of pharmacies showed that callbacks to clarify prescriptions led to delays in the dispensing of acute medications (eg, antibiotics or pain medications) such that the problem could not be resolved on the same day 34% of the time.[32]

Notably, few pediatric studies have been able to demonstrate the effectiveness of CPOE systems on actual patient outcomes, such as ADEs, morbidity, or mortality.[29] A prospective study on the impact of CPOE with CDS on the incidence of ADEs in pediatric inpatients demonstrated that CPOE led to a reduction in potential and actual ADEs. The authors determined that CPOE was associated with the avoidance of 1 preventable ADE every 59 admissions.[33] Another recent study evaluating the effect of an electronic order entry tool for pediatric oncology patients found that reported medication error events decreased by 39% and that of these, the number of events that reached the patient decreased by 40%.[34] In addition, a study of reported adverse events among patients in pediatric hospitals found that patients in hospitals without CPOE were 42% more likely to experience reportable ADEs than patients in hospitals with CPOE.[35]

Perhaps most notably, a 2010 study by Longhurst and colleagues[36] evaluating the effect of CPOE implementation on the hospital-wide mortality rate in a freestanding, quaternary care academic children's hospital in California found a 20% decrease in the mean monthly adjusted mortality rate after CPOE implementation. This is one of only a few published studies to the authors' knowledge demonstrating a decrease in hospital-wide mortality rates after CPOE implementation. In 2006, Cincinnati Children's Hospital also published their experience after CPOE implementation, which showed a decrease in the raw mortality rates and no change in the severity-adjusted mortality rate.[37]

UNINTENDED CONSEQUENCES OF CPOE

Although CPOE has tremendous promise, there are also important pitfalls. Several studies have evaluated unintended consequences after CPOE implementation. Unintended consequence is the term often used to describe a consequence that is unanticipated and undesirable.

One important type of unintended consequence of CPOE implementation is the fostering of new types of errors.[38–42] One such error is a juxtaposition error, in which the clinician inadvertently chooses the incorrect patient or medication name from a drop-down list. Systems with long, dense pick lists predispose to this particular error type.

A study conducted among adult inpatients evaluating the effectiveness of a nearly "hard stop" alert to reduce concomitant orders for warfarin and trimethoprim-sulfamethoxazole highlights another type of dangerous unintended consequence from CDS implemented within a CPOE system, specifically, failure to administer appropriate therapy in response to computer alerts.[43] In this study, the electronic hard stop alert was extremely effective in stopping co-ordering of the two medications. However, the study had to be terminated early because of four instances in which patients experienced a delay in appropriate therapy being administered.

In addition, CPOE implementation can significantly alter workflow, creating more work for providers, and changes in communication patterns. Specifically, direct communication between different providers on a care team is often reduced because of the "illusion of communication" created by electronic systems.[42] This unintended consequence can in turn lead to errors.

One study that has generated much discussion about the unintended consequences of CPOE implementation is a study by Han and colleagues[44] describing an unexpected increase in mortality after rapid implementation of a minimally modified CPOE system in a PICU at Children's Hospital of Pittsburgh. Although several studies have since demonstrated no increase in mortality after CPOE implementation, and in the recent Longhurst[36] study discussed previously an actual decrease in mortality after CPOE implementation, Han's study highlights the importance of proper implementation, training for providers, and attention to workflow when implementing a CPOE system.[45,46]

POLICY IMPLICATIONS AND FUTURE DIRECTIONS

For many years, rates of CPOE adoption and use by hospitals and ambulatory providers were extremely low. However, these rates have been steadily increasing, and are expected to continue to increase dramatically in light of the federal incentives provided through the EHR incentive program. As of 2010, an estimated 21.7% of US hospitals had CPOE, compared with only 15.7% in 2009.[47] Among eligible ambulatory providers, 390,000 prescribed electronically (58% of all office-based prescribers). This is up from 234,000 providers in 2010.[48] Although no study that the authors are aware of has specifically compared use of CPOE among pediatricians with nonpediatricians, there is evidence to suggest that primary care physicians, including pediatricians, are more likely to use CPOE than subspecialists.[49]

To understand whether or not CPOE is effective in improving patient safety for pediatric patients, more research is needed in this population in the inpatient and outpatient setting. In particular, studies evaluating the impact of CPOE on actual patient outcomes rather than proxy outcomes (eg, prescribing errors) are urgently needed to determine whether the billions of dollars invested in HIT as a nation is achieving the desired results. In addition, research comparing how different CPOE systems perform in actual use is essential to understand what features of these systems are critical for success and how such factors as implementation, training, and integration into workflow impact system effectiveness. For example, a recent study comparing the effect of two types of e-prescribing systems (a stand-alone system and a system integrated within an EHR) on prescribing errors for adult outpatients found that providers using the stand-alone system had fourfold lower rate of errors.[50] These study results question beliefs that integrated systems represent the best model of care. Variations in provider training and level of enabled CDS likely contributed to some of these differences, but underscore the importance of comparative effectiveness research for HIT applications.

Critical to the success of CPOE in improving pediatric patient safety is the development of pediatric-specific CDS and CPOE systems tailored to meet the unique needs of pediatric providers. There is great variability in the amount of pediatric-specific CDS currently built into CPOE systems. Given the differences between prescribing medications for adult and pediatric patients, most notably the use of weight-based dosing in pediatrics, developing these functionalities is essential. Also important is making such functionalities widely available in commercial systems such that most providers have access.

REFERENCES

1. Kohn LT, Corrigan J, Donaldson MS. To err is human: building a safer health system. Washington: National Academy Press; 2000.
2. Wong IC, Ghaleb MA, Franklin BD, et al. Incidence and nature of dosing errors in paediatric medications: a systematic review. Drug Saf 2004;27:661–70.
3. Kaushal R, Bates DW, Landrigan C, et al. Medication errors and adverse drug events in pediatric inpatients. JAMA 2001;285:2114–20.
4. Department of Health and Human Services. Health information technology: initial set of standards, implementation specifications, and certification criteria for electronic health record technology; final rule. Fed Regist 2010;75(144):44589–654.
5. Stucky ER. Prevention of medication errors in the pediatric inpatient setting. Pediatrics 2003;112:431–6.
6. Glossary: adverse drug event. Available at: http://psnet.ahrq.gov/popup_glossary. aspx?name=adversedrugevent. Accessed August 2, 2012.
7. Bates DW, Cullen DJ, Laird N, et al. Incidence of adverse drug events and potential adverse drug events. Implications for prevention. ADE Prevention Study Group. JAMA 1995;274:29–34.
8. Otero P, Leyton A, Mariani G, et al. Medication errors in pediatric inpatients: prevalence and results of a prevention program. Pediatrics 2008;122:e737–43.
9. Marino BL, Reinhardt K, Eichelberger WJ, et al. Prevalence of errors in a pediatric hospital medication system: implications for error proofing. Outcomes Manag Nurs Pract 2000;4:129–35.
10. Kadmon G, Bron-Harlev E, Nahum E, et al. Computerized order entry with limited decision support to prevent prescription errors in a PICU. Pediatrics 2009;124: 935–40.
11. Rothschild JM, Landrigan CP, Cronin JW, et al. The Critical Care Safety Study: the incidence and nature of adverse events and serious medical errors in intensive care. Crit Care Med 2005;33:1694–700.

12. Kopp BJ, Erstad BL, Allen ME, et al. Medication errors and adverse drug events in an intensive care unit: direct observation approach for detection. Crit Care Med 2006;34:415–25.
13. Kaushal R, Goldmann DA, Keohane CA, et al. Medication errors in paediatric outpatients. Qual Saf Health Care 2010;19:e30.
14. Jani YH, Ghaleb MA, Marks SD, et al. Electronic prescribing reduced prescribing errors in a pediatric renal outpatient clinic. J Pediatr 2008;152:214–8.
15. Ettel DL, Wilson CM. Medication errors: focus on legibility. Patient Safety and Quality Healthcare 2006. Available at: http://www.psqh.com/janfeb06/mederrors.html. Accessed October 2, 2012.
16. Abramson EL, Bates DW, Jenter C, et al. Ambulatory prescribing errors among community-based providers in two states. J Am Med Inform Assoc 2012;19(4): 644–8.
17. Cimino MA, Kirschbaum MS, Brodsky L, et al. Assessing medication prescribing errors in pediatric intensive care units. Pediatr Crit Care Med 2004;5:124–32.
18. Taylor LK, Kawasumi Y, Bartlett G, et al. Inappropriate prescribing practices: the challenge and opportunity for patient safety. Health Care Q 2005;8(Spec No):81–5.
19. Shah NR, Seger AC, Seger DL, et al. Improving acceptance of computerized prescribing alerts in ambulatory care. J Am Med Inform Assoc 2006;13:5–11.
20. van der Sijs H, Aarts J, Vulto A, et al. Overriding of drug safety alerts in computerized physician order entry. J Am Med Inform Assoc 2006;13:138–47.
21. Weingart SN, Massagli M, Cyrulik A, et al. Assessing the value of electronic prescribing in ambulatory care: a focus group study. Int J Med Inform 2009;78:571–8.
22. Killelea BK, Kaushal R, Cooper M, et al. To what extent do pediatricians accept computer-based dosing suggestions? Pediatrics 2007;119:e69–75.
23. Rivas E, Rivas A, Bustos L. Frequency of prescription and transcription errors for intravenous medications in four pediatric services. Rev Med Chil 2010;138:1524–9.
24. Ammenwerth E, Schnell-Inderst P, Machan C, et al. The effect of electronic prescribing on medication errors and adverse drug events: a systematic review. J Am Med Inform Assoc 2008;15:585–600.
25. Bates DW, Teich JM, Lee J, et al. The impact of computerized physician order entry on medication error prevention. J Am Med Inform Assoc 1999;6:313–21.
26. Bates DW, Leape LL, Cullen DJ, et al. Effect of computerized physician order entry and a team intervention on prevention of serious medication errors. JAMA 1998;280:1311–6.
27. Abramson E, Barron Y, Quaresimo J, et al. Electronic prescribing within an electronic health record reduces ambulatory prescribing errors. Jt Comm J Qual Patient Saf 2011;37:470–8.
28. Kaushal R, Kern LM, Barron Y, et al. Electronic prescribing improves medication safety in community-based office practices. J Gen Intern Med 2010;25(6):530–6.
29. van Rosse F, Maat B, Rademaker CM, et al. The effect of computerized physician order entry on medication prescription errors and clinical outcome in pediatric and intensive care: a systematic review. Pediatrics 2009;123:1184–90.
30. McPhillips HA, Stille CJ, Smith D, et al. Potential medication dosing errors in outpatient pediatrics. J Pediatr 2005;147:761–7.
31. Ginzburg R, Barr WB, Harris M, et al. Effect of a weight-based prescribing method within an electronic health record on prescribing errors. Am J Health Syst Pharm 2009;66:2037–41.
32. Hansen LB, Fernald D, Araya-Guerra R, et al. Pharmacy clarification of prescriptions ordered in primary care: a report from the Applied Strategies for Improving Patient Safety (ASIPS) collaborative. J Am Board Fam Med 2006;19:24–30.

33. Holdsworth MT, Fichtl RE, Raisch DW, et al. Impact of computerized prescriber order entry on the incidence of adverse drug events in pediatric inpatients. Pediatrics 2007;120:1058–66.
34. Chen AR, Lehmann CU. Computerized provider order entry in pediatric oncology: design, implementation, and outcomes. J Oncol Pract 2011;7:218–22.
35. Yu F, Salas M, Kim YI, et al. The relationship between computerized physician order entry and pediatric adverse drug events: a nested matched case-control study. Pharmacoepidemiol Drug Saf 2009;18:751–5.
36. Longhurst CA, Parast L, Sandborg CI, et al. Decrease in hospital-wide mortality rate after implementation of a commercially sold computerized physician order entry system. Pediatrics 2010;126:14–21.
37. Jacobs BR, Brilli RJ, Hart KW. Perceived increase in mortality after process and policy changes implemented with computerized physician order entry. Pediatrics 2006;117:1451–2 [author reply: 5–6].
38. Koppel R, Metlay JP, Cohen A, et al. Role of computerized physician order entry systems in facilitating medication errors. JAMA 2005;293:1197–203.
39. Ash JS, Berg M, Coiera E. Some unintended consequences of information technology in health care: the nature of patient care information system-related errors. J Am Med Inform Assoc 2004;11:104–12.
40. Ash JS, Sittig DF, Dykstra RH, et al. Categorizing the unintended sociotechnical consequences of computerized provider order entry. Int J Med Inform 2007; 76(Suppl 1):S21–7.
41. Ash JS, Sittig DF, Dykstra R, et al. Exploring the unintended consequences of computerized physician order entry. Stud Health Technol Inform 2007;129: 198–202.
42. Ash JS, Sittig DF, Poon EG, et al. The extent and importance of unintended consequences related to computerized provider order entry. J Am Med Inform Assoc 2007;14:415–23.
43. Strom BL, Schinnar R, Aberra F, et al. Unintended effects of a computerized physician order entry nearly hard-stop alert to prevent a drug interaction: a randomized controlled trial. Arch Intern Med 2010;170:1578–83.
44. Han YY, Carcillo JA, Venkataraman ST, et al. Unexpected increased mortality after implementation of a commercially sold computerized physician order entry system. Pediatrics 2005;116:1506–12.
45. Del Beccaro MA, Jeffries HE, Eisenberg MA, et al. Computerized provider order entry implementation: no association with increased mortality rates in an intensive care unit. Pediatrics 2006;118:290–5.
46. Keene A, Ashton L, Shure D, et al. Mortality before and after initiation of a computerized physician order entry system in a critically ill pediatric population. Pediatr Crit Care Med 2007;8:268–71.
47. Hess J. CPOE: the ARRA effect. 2011.
48. The National Progress Report on E-prescribing and Interoperable Health Care. In: Surescripts; 2011.
49. Menachemi N, Ford EW, Chukmaitov A, et al. Managed care penetration and other factors affecting computerized physician order entry in the ambulatory setting. Am J Manag Care 2006;12:738–44.
50. Kaushal R, Barron Y, Abramson EL. The comparative effectiveness of 2 electronic prescribing systems. Am J Manag Care 2011;17:SP88–94.

The Role of "Smart" Infusion Pumps in Patient Safety

Matthew Scanlon, MD[a,b,*]

KEYWORDS

- Smart infusion pumps • Medication safety • Errors • Usability

KEY POINTS

- There are limited data on the value of smart pump technology in preventing errors and even less data measuring prevention of harm.
- Smart pumps work by mitigating the extent of potential errors through medication dosing limits.
- Outstanding issues with smart pump technology include usability issues with design, issues with user acceptance, and their benefit being contingent on no errors occurring earlier in the medication management process.

INTRODUCTION

"Smart" infusion pumps, computerized provider order entry (CPOE), and bar coding of medication administration (BCMA) constitute the troika of medication safety-related health care information technology. Although CPOE is intended to optimize safe medication ordering and BCMA is intended to ensure that the drug and dose of medication match the intended patient, smart infusion pumps are intended to ensure that infused medications are delivered within a safe range of doses (if not the exact prescribed dose). Unfortunately, all three of these safety technologies merit the same criticism of that given an underachieving student: "They are definitely smart but not living up to their potential." This article helps readers understand the realized and unrealized potential of smart infusion pumps, while exploring limitations and barriers of this technology in the larger scope of medication delivery systems.

WHAT MAKES SMART PUMPS SO SMART?

A skeptical reader might instead ask why these infusion pumps are even considered smart. In contrast to traditional infusion pumps, smart pumps are infusion devices that

[a] Department of Pediatrics, Critical Care, Medical College of Wisconsin, 9000 West Wisconsin Avenue, PO Box 1997, Milwaukee, WI 53226, USA; [b] Children's Hospital of Wisconsin, WI, USA
* Corresponding author. Department of Pediatrics, Critical Care, Medical College of Wisconsin, 9000 West Wisconsin Avenue, PO Box 1997, Milwaukee, WI 53226.
E-mail address: mscanlon@mcw.edu

Pediatr Clin N Am 59 (2012) 1257–1267
http://dx.doi.org/10.1016/j.pcl.2012.08.005
0031-3955/12/$ – see front matter © 2012 Published by Elsevier Inc.
pediatric.theclinics.com

have a computer embedded within the device.[1] These computers run vendor-specific software that is intended to reduce dosing errors through the use of drug-specific limits to allowable doses. Particularly in the context of pediatrics, these software libraries of medications and their specific doses are not provided as "ready to implement." Instead, a hospital must create organization-specific (and often unit-specific) libraries, which list the different medications that might be infused, and the associated dosing limits. Additionally, organizations must decide if crossing a limit results in a warning or alert that can be overridden by the programmer (a "soft limit") or absolutely prevents the programmer from entering the dose outside the predetermined limit (a "hard limit").

UNDERSTANDING SMART PUMPS IN THE CONTEXT OF SYSTEMS

Safe patient care increasingly is known to be an emergent property of systems. Whether patient care is safe or not results from the interactions and properties of individual systems elements and not simply the elements themselves. One model for thinking about patient safety is the Systems Engineering Initiative for Patient Safety model.[2]

This model consists of five interacting components (**Fig. 1**). The first component is people: this component includes patients, their families, clinicians, and other support staff working in the environment of interest. Importantly, each person brings to the system his or her own culture including culture of safety. The people use the second component, tools and technologies. These tools and technologies can range from pens and paper documents to CPOE and smart pumps. The people use the tools and technology to perform tasks, the third component of a system. The tasks include gathering data, assessing patients, prescribing medications, dispensing medications, and programming of an infusion pump. These three components occur and interact within an environment, the fourth component, which has its own impact in the form of noise, temperature, lighting, and physical layout. Finally, all of the previously components interact within the larger context of an organization. The component of an organization includes leadership behaviors, policies and procedures, purchasing decisions, and the organization's culture of safety. The presence or absence of safety is an emergent property of the system: it is more than the sum of the individual components. As a result, any change to a system, such as the introduction of new infusion pump technology, inevitably impacts every other component and the resultant safety of the system.

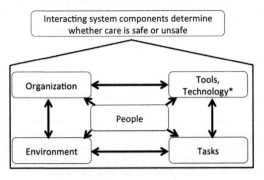

*Technology would include "smart" or tradition pumps

Fig. 1. Adaptation of Systems Engineering Initiative for Patient Safety model to smart pump technology illustrating the systems nature of medication delivery with pumps and the implications for patient safety.

When smart pumps are framed using this model, their strengths and limitations become more transparent. Although the pumps have the potential to limit programming errors, they depend on how people interact with them. However, how people interact with the pumps is subject to other system components. These include other technologies used for patient care; other people involved in the care of patients (directly or indirectly); the culture of the individuals and the organization in which they work; environmental factors (eg, noise and lighting); and organizational decisions, such as how the pumps are implemented, training, and decisions on the drug libraries.

JUST HOW SMART ARE THESE PUMPS?

The principle goal of smart pumps is to prevent dosing errors when administering medications. Fanikos and colleagues[3] analyzed alerts from smart pumps used for delivering anticoagulants to adult patients and found an association between the use of smart pumps and fewer infusion rate errors. Although the authors perhaps overstated the association as being a causative relationship, particularly because not all anticoagulant infusions necessarily used the libraries and thus may have missed inclusion, this study is notable for showing a potential reduction in errors as a result of this technology.

Another study of 3 days of smart pump data from a Canadian adult heart hospital revealed that the pumps intercepted 14 infusion errors.[4] An additional 67 overridden alerts were captured in the same time period. Perhaps most intriguing was the observation that of 1306 infusions started during this time period, 973 (74.5%) of the medications were infused in a mode that bypassed the smart functionality. This is consistent with findings by Malashock and colleagues,[5] who studied alerts in smart pumps from three subspecialty units and found evidence of 157 alerts that led to reprogramming of the pumps. The authors provided no denominator of number of unique infusions. An additional 696 alerts were reported as overridden and, without clear evidence for the conclusion, attributed this to medication boluses or loads.

Two other publications draw unsubstantiated conclusions about the impact of smart pumps. In a 2003 newsletter of the Anesthesia Patient Safety Foundation, Reves[6] cites unpublished data to state "smart pump" technology reduces errors. One source of Reves' data was an award winning presentation by Kinneally.[7] The Kinneally data reflected a drop in the number of voluntarily reported administration errors from the pre–smart pump to post–smart pump time period. Unfortunately, Reves[6] later observes, "While the full impact of the new "smart pumps" on the reduction of intravenous medication errors has yet to be measured, the preliminary data are very encouraging."

Similarly, Rosenkoetter and colleagues[8] reach several disturbingly unsupported conclusions about smart pump use. Drawing from surveys of nurses and pharmacists, the authors state in their abstract that "the pump offers an effective approach to the reduction of intravenous medication errors," and that "use of smart pumps had no effect on use of pharmacy staff and did not negatively affect staff nursing work load." The authors, however, neither measured intravenous medication errors nor pharmacy or staff workload. Instead, they cited survey data about perceptions. The sole evidence supportive of error reduction was a reference to work by Wilson and Sullivan[9] that measured 1 prevented error among 80 analyzed infusions.

Finally, Larsen and coworkers[10] reported a drop in "reported errors" after three interventions: (1) the implementation of standard drug concentrations, (2) smart pump technology, and (3) user-friendly medication labels. This was despite the absence of any direct error measurement and the fact that the reduction in reported errors might be explained by the possibility that nurses were too busy responding to these three system changes to report errors that occurred.

In summary, the available evidence shows minimal to moderate error reduction as a result of smart pump technology and no measured evidence of a reduction in patient harm.

ARE SMART PUMPS LIVING UP TO THEIR POTENTIAL?

The literature on smart infusion pumps is particularly enlightening on the aforementioned charge of "not living up to their potential." A 2006 study observed the infusions of 426 medications and identified 389 different errors. Of these, only one error would have been prevented by smart pump technology without the use of additional interface technology that was not available at that time.[11] This finding is consistent with that of Nuckols and colleagues,[12] who found that of 100 identified intravenous adverse drug events that caused harm, only 4% were potentially addressed by available smart pump technology.

Using high-fidelity simulation, Trbovich and colleagues[13] observed that the use of soft limits with smart pumps "had no significant effect in preventing dosing errors." This simulated study reached similar conclusions to a controlled trial of smart pumps used with adult cardiac patients, which found that although errors occurred frequently, the smart pumps had no measurable effect on the rate of serious medication errors.[14]

Finally, Schroeder and colleagues[15] published a chilling case report of a tubing misload resulting in free-flow administration of nitroglycerin administered with a smart pump. Ironically, the same technology had undergone proactive risk assessment using a failure modes and effects analysis. Although the manufacture has addressed the design defect that resulted in the event, the documentation of preventable harm (by a pump manufacturer) in the absence of error prevention or harm reduction data is concerning.

WHAT IS THE COST OF THESE PUMPS?

In 2005, smart pumps were described as attractive because of the cost and speed of installation in a facility.[16] At that time, implementation was reported to be as quick as 90 days for a facility with a cost from $2 to $3.5 million for 1000 pumps. These cited costs are strictly that for hardware and software. There are additional hidden costs related to training staff, server and networking, maintenance, and support. Pediatric facilities are faced with even greater hidden costs associated with the time required to develop context-appropriate drug libraries for installation. Whether or not the technology is viewed as attractive depends on the actual cost of all implementation and ongoing maintenance.

Even then, a published analysis of alerts during the first 4 months of smart pump implementation in a pediatric intensive care unit identified numerous problems that necessitated retraining of nursing staff, and changes to previously selected limits because of clinical alert irrelevance and errors in library programming.[17] Readers should not underestimate the cost associated with changes to a smart pump library. In the absence of additional network technology, which is not standard on smart pumps, changing the library (be it additions, corrections, or deletions) requires manual interaction with every pump in an organization. This is no small task. In one freestanding children's hospital, each manual upgrade was associated with an operational cost estimated at $25,000 and requiring 3 days (Brian Jacobs, personal communication, 2012). Additionally, infusion pumps that are used to provide life-sustaining vasopressors and inotropes cannot be updated until the pump is no longer in active use with a patient. After a center implements pump networking, the pumps can be upgraded as soon as the pumps are powered on, as long as the end-user accepts the update and the pump is not in active use.

Thus, the true cost of ownership (implementation and maintenance) is difficult to quantify and arguably greater at a per-pump level for pediatric centers than adult centers, which can standardize libraries and have fewer weight-based infusion types.

CONTEXT IS EVERYTHING

Patient safety is a property of systems. Although this requires pediatric providers and safety professionals to consider all the identified system components and their interactions before making changes to a system, it is worth noting the complexity of just the steps in medication delivery (**Fig. 2**).

The first steps of ordering and taking delivery of a medication from a vendor have taken on added risk and complexity in light of ongoing medication shortages. As a result, pharmacists are forced to identify potential substitute medications for providers to order. This presumes that the medications selected for infusion exist in the preconfigured smart pump library. Otherwise, every pump (or at least a dedicated subset of all infusion pumps) requires reprogramming, another potential source of delay, expense, and error.

Pediatric pharmacists frequently are left to repackage medications for infusion from adult formulations, particularly when dealing with small children, infants, and neonates. These steps introduce errors when the medications are prepared in accordance with the hospital's standardized formulary and then relabeled including with a bar code, when applicable. This step is critical because after a labeled syringe leaves the pharmacy destined for infusion, the bedside nurses and physicians are acting entirely on faith that the medication in the syringe is the correct medication and concentration. No components of smart pumps guard against this hazard.

Finally, the nurse or physician who is programming the smart pump must correctly follow a sequence of steps. Error at any of these steps may undermine any potential benefit of the dosing limits. These steps include selecting the appropriate library; selecting the correct medication and concentration (when more than one exists); and entering the patient's weight correctly, the desired drug to be administered, and the rate at which the administration should occur. If the combination of these inputs results in a drug delivery that is outside the preset limits, then a soft stop or hard stop alert may occur. At this point a provider may or may not recognize their error and back up in the process. However, as identified by Rothschild and coworkers,[14] soft stop overrides can result in realized and potential adverse drug events.

Importantly, most if not all smart pumps have two related additional features, which are notable and potential sources of risk to patient harm. First, as also noted by Rothschild and coworkers,[14] smart pumps feature the ability to bypass the library entering a traditional pump mode that eliminates the potential benefit of the additional hardware and software. In the same vein, even within libraries, there may be "wildcard" entries that allow providers to infuse medications that do not exist in the library. This functionality is critical for administering medications that may not have been in the formulary at the time of the last smart pump library edit. As illustrated in **Box 1**, these "wildcard" modes offer several rates. If the patient's weight is entered, the math calculations are performed, offering some safety compared with traditional pumps. However, these modes gain no benefit from the dosing range limits that are otherwise available in these pumps.

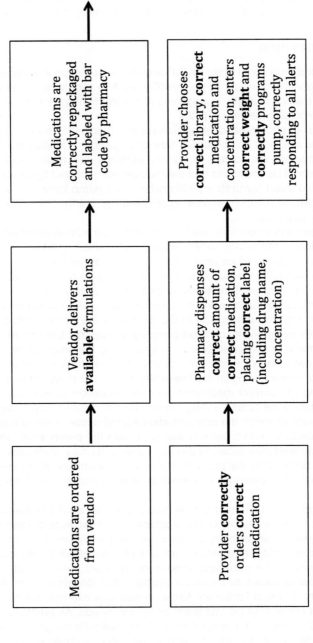

Fig. 2. Steps in medication management process include elements that must occur correctly for smart pumps to be beneficial.

Box 1
Example of "wildcard" settings in "smart" pump library
• units/kg/h
• mg/kg/h
• μg/kg/h
• μg/kg/min
• ng/kg/min

A final context-related consideration is the presumed linearity of infusion pump management. This consideration, which admittedly applies to smart and traditional pumps, centers on the fact that manufacturers of infusion pumps (and other technologies including CPOE) presume a very linear workflow. Specifically, a physician enters an order, informs a nurse, the nurse programs a pump, and thus the infusion and orders match. However, a recent study in a pediatric intensive care unit with smart pumps in use revealed that 24% of medication infusions and 42% of fluids were infusing at rates that did not agree with the order.[18] The authors hypothesized the large number of discrepancies between orders and infusion pump settings can be explained by the nonlinear nature of infusion pump management (eg, clinician changes pump settings and fails to notify nurse or update orders). These findings are relevant to this discussion of smart pumps because the dose-limiting functionality may be irrelevant if the patient is simply receiving the wrong dose within the acceptable dosing limits.

THINGS THAT ARE DECIDEDLY NOT SMART ABOUT SMART PUMPS: INTERFACES, AUTOPSIES, AND FUNCTIONALITY ISSUES

Despite the added technology that potentially limits the severity of errors in pump programming, there is little evidence that the designers of smart pumps have applied the science of usability to these devices. The goal of usability science, which draws from the field of human factors engineering, is to drive user-centered design into products.[19,20] That is, such devices as smart pumps need to be designed allowing for the known limitations of human performance. Adherence to the principles of usability often results in intuitive devices that require little training; makes errors difficult if not impossible; and when errors do occur, devices with high degrees of usability prompt easy recognition and recovery from the error.

Unfortunately, commercially available smart pumps demonstrate the same failing of traditional pumps. These include keypads that allow double value entry; displays that are difficult to read from a distance or in a poorly lit room (eg, a patient care environment at night); and significant degrees of cognitive work to correctly program the pump.[21–24] Nearly 15 years ago, Lin and colleagues described evaluation and subsequent redesign of a commercially available pump interface to dramatically reduce errors, promote recovery, and improve speed and ease of use.[21] Despite this important work, infusion devices including expensive smart pumps suffer from poor usability and thus are designed to promote errors.

A second decidedly not smart feature of smart pumps is what can be called their "autopsy" functionality. These devices are outstanding for logging keystrokes, alerts, and actions taken in response to an alert for future review. Unfortunately, this information is kept in the device's memory until it is manually downloaded through direct intervention. As a result, a provider who overrides an alert creates a record that is available for future "autopsy." However, like the proverbial tree falling in the woods with no one to hear it, if the provider using the pump does not recognize the meaning or significance of the alert and proceeds with executing the error, the technology is essentially meaningless in preventing that harm event. Admittedly, analysis of the event may help providers and safety professionals understand the sequence of events that resulted in the adverse event. However, this new insight does nothing for the harmed patient in question. One potential solution to the "autopsy" problem is connecting the pumps through either a wired or wireless network. A networked pump theoretically could be monitored for real-time detection of inappropriate overrides. In the event of an inappropriate override, the individuals detecting the override could contact the end-user clinician and intervene to prevent harm from occurring. One academic center has published their experience with a wireless network of smart pumps but offers no insights into whether or not they are monitoring use to allow real-time safety interventions.[25] There is no available published evidence that networked smart pumps have been used in a real-time detection manner in clinical settings.

Other concerns identified that could be framed as functionality issues of smart pumps include pump weight, battery life, and issues with tubing.[4,26] These factors coupled with inconsistencies between library entries and the provided medications, and medications missing from the library, may all contribute to whether bedside providers elect to use these devices.[27]

THE IMPORTANCE OF END-USER ACCEPTANCE

The Technology Acceptance Model is a group of theories used to explain why end-users may or may not use a given technology. In studies outside health care and a study of acceptance of BCMA in a children's hospital,[26,28] factors that predict acceptance are closely correlated with subsequent use. In the study of the acceptance of BCMA by pediatric nurses, the factors that best predicted whether the nurses accepted the BCMA included the technology's perceived usefulness and the perceived ease of use of the technology. Usefulness amounts to whether the device helps the end-user perform their job. A study of nurses' acceptance of smart pump technology at an adult academic hospital comparing preimplementation perceptions with 1-year postimplementation perceptions revealed generally positive acceptance after 1 year.[29] Specific concerns, however, related to the implementation process, technical factors, and lack of usability. Although nurses' perceptions of pump speed initially worsened, their perceptions returned to baseline by 1 year. However, their perceptions of pump reliability and noise persisted up to 1-year postimplementation. The noise and reliability concerns specifically stemmed from air-in-line alarms and delay-related alarms that disrupted their work. Although these issues may seem negligible to those outside this system, it is precisely this sort of ongoing aggravation that may influence nurses' acceptance and use of the pumps, as predicted by the Technology Acceptance Model.[29]

The issue of end-user acceptance of smart pumps is arguably critical to capitalizing on the devices' potential. As Leape,[30] one of the most respected thought leaders in patient safety, observed in his 2005 editorial, "Finally, as with any new technology, considerable effort is needed to gain acceptance by users and for them to acquire comfort in its use. Nonetheless, properly designed and properly used, it seems likely that 'smart pumps' will save lives."

SMART PUMPS AS A CONTINGENT SAFETY TECHNOLOGY

Although the work of Fanikos, Malashock, and Hoh demonstrate that smart pumps can prevent errors in clinical environments, ultimately the evidence demonstrating that these pumps achieve the desired goal of preventing harm is largely nonexistent. One explanation for the absence of harm prevention data may be because smart pumps could be viewed as contingent safety technologies. That is, the benefit of the technology is almost entirely contingent on everything upstream occurring correctly. Unlike Reason's[31] Swiss cheese model where one distal slice can prevent the alignment of upstream "holes" from reaching a patient, the distal slice of a smart pump has limited benefit if any of the steps in **Fig. 2** are incorrect.

If this concept of a contingent safety technology is correct, then smart pumps may ultimately prove to be a necessary but insufficient component of a system to provide safety medication delivery to children.

SMART PUMPS AND OTHER SAFETY TECHNOLOGIES

It is reasonable that readers might wonder how smart pumps might interact with other safety technologies including CPOE and electronic health records. One potential benefit of networking an electronic health record comprised of CPOE and documentation with smart pumps is autoprogramming of infusion pump. In this setting, the clinician would enter an order that is electronically "pushed" to the smart pump for checking, confirmed by a nurse, and automatically documented. This future integrated medication delivery system sounds promising. However, automation of the complete process has multiple implications. First, this system would presume care starts with an order. However, as Russell and Scanlon[18] hypothesized, much of care actually initiates with a pump change. The large number of discrepancies between orders and infusions in this study begs the question of which is the correct, desired infusion rate: the order or the pump settings? It is unclear that automating the process will eliminate care discrepancies, particularly if changes initiate at the pump. Such unintended consequences require careful exploration before widespread distribution. A second potential benefit of networked smart pumps includes the automated movement of infusion data from the pump to nursing documentation in the electronic health record. Such functionality has the potential to improve nursing efficiency and data accuracy compared with manual charting.

Another major concern is the consequence of tightly coupling the system and removing people from the equation. Although errors are the result of people interacting with less than ideal system components, people also routinely add safety. As evidenced by the need for human airline pilots to take over for autopilots under emergent situations, there may be situations requiring human intervention to avoid harm from failure in the infusion process. Unfortunately, tightly linking the system may make it difficult, if not impossible, for the bedside clinician to understand where a failure is occurring.

Regardless of how smart pumps interact with other safety technologies, it is clear that achieving safe infusion delivery requires consideration from a systems perspective if the devices are to ever live up to their potential.

REFERENCES

1. Hertzel C, Sousa VD. The use of smart pumps for preventing medication errors. J Infus Nurs 2009;32(5):257–67.
2. Carayon P, Schoofs Hundt A, Karsh B-T, et al. Work system design for patient safety: the SEIPS model. Qual Saf Health Care 2006;15:50–8.
3. Fanikos J, Fiumara K, Baroletti S, et al. Impact of smart infusion technology on administration of anticoagulants (unfractionated heparin, argatroban, lepuridin and bivalirudin). Am J Cardiol 2007;99:1002–5.

4. Starenkyj E, Wolfe P, Hoh T, et al. What does your IV smart pump infusion data tell you about your IV clinical practice and patient safety? Stud Health Technol Inform 2009;146:803–4.
5. Malashock C, Shull SS, Gould AD. Effect of smart infusion pumps on medication errors related to infusion device programming. Hosp Pharm 2004;39(5):460–9.
6. Reves JG. "Smart pump" technology reduces errors. Anesthesia Patient Safety Foundation Newsletter; 2003. Available at: http://www.apsf.org/newsletters/html/2003/spring/smartpump.htm. Accessed July 2, 2012.
7. National Patient Safety Foundation announces solutions winner for Janssen Elder care award. National Patient Safety Foundation; 2003. Available at: http://www.npsf.org/updates-news-press/press/national-patient-safety-foundation-announces-solutions-winner-for-janssen-elder-care-award/. Accessed July 2, 2012.
8. Rosenkoetter MM, Bowcutt M, Khasanshina EV, et al. Perceptions of the impact of "smart pumps" on nurses and nursing care provided. J Assoc Vasc Access 2008; 13(2):60–9.
9. Wilson K, Sullivan M. Preventing medication errors with smart infusion technology. Am J Health Syst Pharm 2004;61:177–83.
10. Larsen GY, Parker HB, Cash J, et al. Standard drug concentrations and smart-pump technology reduce continuous-medication-infusion errors in pediatric patients. Pediatrics 2005;116(1):e21–5.
11. Husch M, Sullivan C, Rooney D, et al. Insights from the sharp end of intravenous medication infusion errors: implications for infusion technology. Qual Saf Health Care 2005;14:80–6.
12. Nuckols TK, Bower AG, Paddock SM, et al. Programmable infusion pumps in ICUs: an analysis of corresponding adverse events. J Gen Intern Med 2007; 23(Suppl 1):41–5.
13. Trbovich PL, Pinkney S, Cafazzo JA, et al. The impact of traditional and smart pump infusion technology on nurse medication administration performance in a simulated inpatient unit. Qual Saf Health Care 2010;19:430–4.
14. Rothschild JM, Keohane CA, Cook F, et al. A controlled trial of smart infusion pumps to improved medication safety in critically ill patients. Crit Care Med 2005;33(3):533–9.
15. Schroeder ME, Wolman RL, Wetterneck TB, et al. Tubing misload allows free flow event with smart intravenous infusion pump. Anesthesiology 2006;105(2): 434–5.
16. Smaling J, Holt MA. Integration and automation transform medication administration safety. Health Manag Technol 2005;26(4):18, 20.
17. Manrique-Rodriguez S, Sanchez-Galindo A, Fernandez-Llamazares CM, et al. Smart pump alerts: all that glitters is not gold. Int J Med Inform 2012;81:344–50.
18. Russell RA, Scanlon MC. Discrepancies between medication orders and infusion pump programming in a paediatric intensive care unit. Qual Saf Health Care 2010;19(Suppl 3):i31–5.
19. Karsh B, Scanlon MC. When is a defibrillator not a defibrillator? When it's like a clock radio. The challenge of usability and patient safety in the real world. Ann Emerg Med 2007;50:433–6.
20. Murff HJ, Gosbee JW, Bates DW. Human factors and medical devices. In: Wachter RM, editor. Making health care safer: a critical analysis of patient safety practices. Available at: http://www.ncbi.nlm.nih.gov/books/NBK27000/. Accessed July 3, 2012.
21. Lin L, Isla R, Doniz K, et al. Applying human factors to the design of medical equipment: patient-controlled analgesia. J Clin Monit Comput 1998;14(4):253–63.

22. Brown SL, Bogner MS, Parmentier CM, et al. Human error and patient-controlled analgesia pumps. J Intraven Nurs 1997;20:311–6.
23. Lin L. Human Error in Patient-Controlled Analgesia: Incident Reports and Experimental Evaluation. In: Proceedings of the Human Factors and Ergonomics Society 42nd Annual Meeting. California: Human Factors and Ergonomics Society 1998. p. 1043–47.
24. Scanlon MC, Densmore E, Karsh B. Human factors and pediatric patient safety. Pediatr Clin North Am 2006;53(6):1105–19.
25. Siv-Lee L, Morgan L. Implementation of wireless "intelligent" pump IV infusion technology in a not-for-profit academic hospital setting. Hosp Pharm 2007; 42(9):832–40.
26. Holden RJ, Brown R, Scanlon MC, et al. Modeling nurses' acceptance of bar coded medication administration technology at a pediatric hospital. J Am Med Inform Assoc 2012. [Epub ahead of print].
27. McAlearney AS, Vrontos J, Schneider PJ, et al. Strategic work-arounds to accommodate new technology: the case of smart pumps in hospital care. J Patient Saf 2007;3(2):75–81.
28. Holden RJ, Karsh B. The technology acceptance model: its past and its future in health care. J Biomed Inform 2010;43:159e72.
29. Carayon P, Schoofs Hundt A, Wetterneck TB. Nurses' acceptance of smart IV pump technology. Int J Med Inform 2010;79:401–11.
30. Leape LL. "Smart" pumps: a cautionary tale of human factors engineering. Crit Care Med 2005;33(3):679–80.
31. Reason J. Human error: models and management. BMJ 2000;320:768–70.

Automated Detection of Adverse Events in Children

Valere Lemon, RN, BSN, MBA[a], David C. Stockwell, MD, MBA[b,c,*]

KEYWORDS

- Automated adverse event detection • Incident report • Pediatric • Patient safety
- Adverse event surveillance

KEY POINTS

- Children's National Medical Center has benefited greatly from increased adverse event detection, in particular automated adverse event detection.
- This system has contributed to improved quality of care and cost-effectiveness for patients and families.
- The reduction in adverse events noted can be attributed to the targeted approach provided with the automated trigger tool.
- The current availability of triggers is being broadened with the development of pediatric specific triggers.
- Organizations can collaborate with their electronic health record contractor to design and build an automated trigger tool that best serves their needs and aids in quality improvement efforts.

INTRODUCTION

Hospitals strive to provide safe, efficient, and affordable care in a fast-paced environment and minimize adverse events. Knowledge surrounding adverse events in children remains inadequate. Approximately 70,000 children are harmed yearly because of adverse events, although more than half of these events may be preventable.[1] All patients warrant an atmosphere of safety and comfort while receiving care in our hospitals and outpatient treatment centers. Thus, using innovative methods to detect and reduce or eliminate these adverse events is imperative.

Providing an optimal, safe environment means knowing the vulnerabilities that exist in a system. Only then can an organization begin to provide highly reliable care. Therefore the identification of adverse events or defects in a system is critically important.

[a] Center for Pediatric Informatics, Children's National Medical Center, 111 Michigan Avenue, Washington, DC 20010, USA; [b] Department of Pediatrics, Improvement Science at Children's National Medical Center, Eye Street, Washington, DC 20037, USA; [c] The George Washington University School of Medicine, Washington, DC, USA
* Corresponding author. Division of Critical Care Medicine, Children's National Medical Center, Suite M4800, 111 Michigan Avenue, Northwest, Washington, DC 20010.
E-mail address: dstockwell@childrensnational.org

Pediatr Clin N Am 59 (2012) 1269–1278
http://dx.doi.org/10.1016/j.pcl.2012.08.007
0031-3955/12/$ – see front matter © 2012 Elsevier Inc. All rights reserved.
pediatric.theclinics.com

Creating a streamlined process to identify key trends in adverse events, leading to policy changes and a reduction in harm, is an achievable goal. What follows is a discussion regarding the state of adverse event detection methods to improve active surveillance of these events, based on reporting results from our own institution.

The standard method for identifying adverse events is most often surveillance of the voluntary reporting system of an institution.[2] Because this approach has its flaws, many have attempted to augment detection in numerous ways. When compared with other more structured methods of adverse event detection, namely manual chart review as well as trigger tool methods, voluntary reporting consistently underidentifies events.[3,4] Manual chart review can be resource-intensive because its primary method includes review of the medical record in its entirety. Because many adverse events and their associated triggers are rare, this detection method is often associated with a low yield. Trigger tools, whether manual or automated, have been one of the more popular methods. A trigger tool may be defined as data present in the electronic health record (EHR), or paper chart, that potentially identifies that an adverse event has occurred or could occur. Common examples of such data are documentation of reversal agents such as naloxone or flumazenil in the medical record. The administration of naloxone suggests that the patient has received too much opioid for their needs, an ideal trigger for further investigation. Similarly, the presence of laboratory values that are out of range of normal may be used as a trigger. **Table 1** shows common detection methods used in many pediatric organizations.

There are 2 standard methods of trigger-based adverse event detection system: manual and automated. Manual review is based on evaluation of randomly selected charts, usually a limited number of charts. Here, the reviewer searches for specific triggers in each of those medical records. By definition, this approach is based on a sampling method. By contrast, automated adverse event detection (AAED) is based on the identification of specific triggers in all EHRs for any given period. Rather than a reviewer searching for triggers in a sample of paper-based medical records, for AAED, algorithms are written to automatically identify triggers on a continuous basis. The benefits of this approach are evident. First, once the algorithms have been written, AAED is more time efficient, because each trigger is electronically forwarded to a reviewer. Second, because AAED allows for monitoring all EHRs, an organization likely obtains a more comprehensive understanding of adverse events, both the common and uncommon ones.

METHODS

Beginning in September, 2007, Children's National Medical Center began using the AAED method using specifically designed pediatric triggers. **Box 1** shows a complete list of the current trigger library, determined and maintained by a process using the following criteria:

- The presence of the trigger needs to be electronically identifiable
- The frequency of the trigger is manageable with current resources
- There must be a favorable positive predictive value of detecting an adverse event; the absolute positive predictive value may vary depending on the type of event(s) detected by the trigger (eg, low positive predictive values may be tolerated if the frequency of the trigger is relatively low yet the trigger identifies a high level of harm)
- Anticipated serious level of harm ($\geq$level E on the National Coordinating Council for Medication Error Reporting and Prevention (NCC MERP)) Index for Categorizing Medication Errors (**Table 2**)[5]
- Expected adverse events are not being adequately investigated by other teams within the institution

Table 1
Methods of detection: advantages and disadvantages

Detection Approach	Advantages	Disadvantages
Active surveillance: administrative data	Few resources needed Inexpensive Readily available	Limited identification Real-time clinical intervention not present Requires explicit documentation to ensure coding accuracy
Active surveillance: manual triggers	Substantial identification of events	Substantial resources needed Expensive Real-time clinical intervention is challenging Time-consuming chart reviewer training Real-time intervention limited by time report is generated
Active surveillance: electronic triggers	Substantial identification of events Real-time intervention present Time efficient	Substantial resources required Expensive Requires chart reviewer training Requires some technological sophistication
Active surveillance: technology reports	Inexpensive Few resources needed May detect more potential ADEs than other methods	Some identification of events Real-time clinical intervention is present, but depends on when report is generated Requires some technological sophistication
Active surveillance: direct observation	Real-time intervention is present Identifies more preventable events	Substantial resources required Limited identification of events Focus on medication administration events
Voluntary reporting	Inexpensive All types of events included Minimal resources required	Real-time intervention limited by notification of event Concentrations on ADE administration events Relies on staff member to submit event notification Requires nonpunitive environment and positive safety culture

Substantial and expensive assumes a continuous process and not periodic evaluation.
Abbreviation: ADE, adverse drug event.

Trigger reports are generated daily and subsequently investigated to determine if there had been an adverse event. A full-time clinical reviewer, using the EHR-integrated AAED tool, investigates each AAED trigger within 24 hours of its occurrence. The reviewer first validates that an adverse event occurred by reviewing the details of the trigger in a patient's medical record. If the reviewer determines that the trigger identifies an adverse event, the event is categorized as either preventable or nonpreventable. Furthermore, the adverse events identified are assigned a harm severity score based on the NCC MERP index. If the adverse event results in

---

Box 1
Triggers currently used at Children's National Medical Center

Trigger Report

Medication administration

- Digoxin immune Fab
- Flumazenil
- Naloxone
- Protamine
- Hyaluronidase

Laboratory values

- Hypoglycemia
  - Glucose <40 mg/dL
- Anticoagulation
  - Partial thromboplastin time (PTT) $\geq$140 seconds
  - International normalized ratio (INR) $\geq$6
  - Anti-Xa $\geq$1.5 IU/mL
- Neonatal jaundice
  - Total bilirubin >25 mg/dL
- Acute renal injury
  - Creatinine doubling to at least >0.6 mg/dL

Admission, discharge, transfer

- Transfer to the intensive care unit (ICU) from acute care unit
  - Emphasis on transfer within 12 hours of admission and ICU readmission within 24 hours of initial transfer
- Readmission to acute care unit
  - Within 30 days of discharge

---

a significant level of harm (NCC MERP>E) an incident report is filed and the risk management team is notified. If necessary, unit-based leaders are also immediately notified of any serious adverse events. Monthly reports of all events regardless of severity score are prepared for each inpatient unit, the perioperative area, and emergency department.

Each preventable adverse event, as well as each adverse event for which preventability could not be clearly determined, and all adverse events that resulted in harm to the patient are reviewed and discussed in a hospital-based AAED steering committee. The details surrounding each of these events are extensively discussed and consensus is reached on the reviewer's initial categorization and harm severity scoring. The multidisciplinary steering committee also provides a way to ensure review consistency. Although parents are not currently present in this committee, steps are being taken to include them in the future. The purpose of this system is not to scrutinize providers for errors, rather to identify system flaws, allowing for a safer environment for staff and patients. Routine discussions of these events, stable steering committee membership, and tracking events over time allows a mechanism to detect trends that may not be readily apparent when reviewing events sporadically.

Table 2	
NCC MERP index for categorizing medication errors	
No Error	
A	Circumstances or events that have the capacity to cause error
Error, No Harm	
B	An incident occurred but did not reach the patient
C	An incident occurred that reached the patient but did not cause patient harm
D	An incident occurred that reached the patient and required monitoring to confirm that it resulted in no harm to the patient or required intervention to preclude harm
Error, Harm	
E	An incident occurred that resulted in the need for treatment or intervention and caused temporary patient harm
F	An incident occurred that resulted in initial or prolonged hospitalization and caused temporary patient harm
G	An incident occurred that resulted in permanent patient harm
H	An incident occurred that resulted in a near-death event (eg, anaphylaxis, cardiac arrest)
Error, Death	
I	An incident occurred that resulted in death

RESULTS

Throughout the 4 years of the AAED program, 9143 triggers have been investigated at Children's National Medical Center, of which 2441 (34%) identified adverse events. Only 75 (3%) of those 2441 events were also identified by traditional voluntary reporting (**Table 3**). Of those 2441 adverse events, 552 (19%) were determined to be preventable (see **Table 3**).

Using the criteria outlined earlier, consulting with clinical experts, and evaluating the data collected over a period of time, it was determined that a few of the triggers did not

Table 3			
Trigger frequencies and positive predictive value (PPV): September, 2007 to June, 2012			
Current Triggers	**Total Triggers**	**Adverse Events (PPV of Adverse Events, %)**	**Preventable (PPV of Preventable Adverse Events, %)**
Digibind administration	2	1 (50.0)	0 (0)
Naloxone administration	116	90 (77.6)	36 (40.0)
Protamine administration	74	12 (16.2)	1 (8.3)
Flumazenil administration	11	8 (72.7)	3 (37.5)
Hyaluronidase administration	67	62 (92.5)	32 (51.6)
Glucose <40 mg/dL	163	46 (28.2)	5 (10.9)
PTT ≥140 s	64	36 (56.3)	0 (0)
INR >6.0	3	2 (66.7)	0 (0)
Anti-Xa >1.5 mg/dL	11	9 (81.8)	0 (0)
Creatinine doubling >0.6 mg/dL	809	413 (51.1)	12 (2.9)
Total bilirubin >25 mg/dL	20	3 (15.0)	0 (0)
Transfers to higher level of care	1882	515 (27.4)	113 (21.9)
Total	3222	1197 (37.2)	202 (16.9)

deliver the positive predictive value or level of harm desired and were thus retired from use (**Table 4**). The detailed experience with each AAED trigger is described in the following sections.

Hypoglycemia

The hypoglycemia trigger was originally designated to identify any glucose level less than 50 mg/dL (normal range, 54–117). This trigger led to the identification of a critical issue with insulin-associated high rates of hypoglycemia in the neonatal ICU (NICU).[6] Once the issue was raised with and accepted by NICU leadership, protocol and policy changes were put into effect and a significant decrease in insulin-related adverse events in the NICU was noted. Because over the past 3 years no insulin adverse event with a harm score of F or greater has been noted and in an effort to increase the positive predictive value for adverse events, the glucose trigger value was decreased to 40 mg/dL in January, 2012. Since that time, the monthly volume for this trigger has decreased by 159%.

Anticoagulation

Anticoagulation has been evaluated via a combination of triggers, namely an INR greater than 4 (normal range, 0.86–1.14), Activated PTT (aPTT) greater than 100 seconds (normal range, 24–37.7 seconds), anti-Xa (therapeutic heparin activity) greater than 1.5 IU/mL (normal range, 0.5–1.0 IU/mL), or protamine administration (suggestive of overheparinization). Through the use of these triggers, problems with the application of standing protocols were identified and the need for restructuring and standardization of anticoagulation therapy protocols addressed. Similar to that of the glucose trigger, the lack of events with harm severity F or greater after a significant period of evaluation led to a decision in January, 2012 to modify the aPTT trigger value to more than 139 seconds, and the INR trigger value to more than 6.0.

Opioid and Benzodiazepine Reversal Agents

Monitoring of the antidotes naloxone and flumazenil has led to the identification of a need for operational changes in the Children's National procedural sedation procedures in the ICU. Although no overdosing was noted, the triggers suggested overuse of these medications. Based on review and discussion with the ICU leadership, procedural sedation protocols have been adjusted, encouraging the use of small titratable doses. This intervention has led to a reduction from 1 to 2 events involving oversedation to zero events over the past year. In addition, the use of these medications is

Table 4
Retired trigger frequencies and positive predictive value (PPV): September, 2007 to January, 2012

Retired Triggers	Total Triggers	Adverse Events (PPV of AEs)	Preventable (PPV of Preventable AEs)
Sodium polystyrene sulfonate	86	2 (2.3)	2 (100)
Potassium >6 mEq/L	929	24 (2.5)	11 (45.8)
Glucose <50 mg/dL	4092	958 (2.3)	239 (24.9)
PTT >100 s	894	438 (49.0)	110 (25.1)
INR >4.0	387	73 (18.9)	10 (13.7)
Ionized Ca >1.5 mmol/L	165	20 (12.1)	0 (0)
Total	6166	1442 (23.4)	362 (25.1)

reviewed on an individual case-by-case basis in the sedation committee of the organization's. This strategy allows for a review of institutional sedation processes and active surveillance of high-risk medications.

Creatinine doubling to at least 0.6 mg/dL
Acute renal injury can be identified by monitoring serum creatinine. An AAED trigger that detects serum creatinine levels doubling to at least 0.6 mg/dL allows care teams to proactively investigate the potential impact of nephrotoxic medications, hydration status, or procedures on renal dysfunction. This timely medical record review allows for immediate medication or hydration changes based on the patient's renal function.

Patient transfer to a higher level of care
Rapid response teams (RRTs) have helped achieve reduction of mortality related to codes that occur outside the ICU, with reductions of 18% noted in a 2007 publication.[7] With this particular AAED trigger, every transfer of a patient to one of the ICUs from an acute care unit is considered a transfer to a higher level of care. This AAED trigger completely and consistently identifies codes outside the ICU and transfers to an ICU within 12 hours of admission as well as 24-hour readmissions to one of the ICUs. At Children's National Medical Center, each of these adverse events is consistently reviewed by relevant clinical divisions. This trigger also serves as backup method for capturing RRT calls that involve a transfer to an ICU.

With improved education of the staff of recent transfer-related events and their contributing factors, each inpatient unit receives consistent review of these challenging cases. Issues that can be improved on are relayed to the respective clinical leaders. The goal is to provide earlier intervention and identification of patient decompensation, leading to an earlier assessment by the RRT.

Hospital readmissions
The Affordable Care Act (ACA)[8] has forced institutions to identify causes of unplanned readmissions within 30 days and begin working toward a reduction in these rates. The penalty for noncompliance could be lack of reimbursement for hospitals with worse-than-expected 30-day readmission rates.[9] Targeting issues with readmission populations and implementing change are complex because of the external factors in the patient's home environment that may elicit an illness and cause readmission.

At Children's National Medical Center, administrative data are used within the AAED program to generate a baseline report of readmissions. Assessment of the administrative data confirmed that a reviewer can determine basic demographic trends in gender, race, and diagnosis; however, there are recurrent themes in causes of readmission that can be identified only through in-depth medical record review. In October, 2011, Children's National Medical Center initiated an in-depth review of admissions occurring within 30 days of discharge. Between October, 2011 and April, 2012, 613 readmissions were identified within 30 days of discharge, with 37% of those occurring within 7 days of discharge, and an average of 7.1 readmissions occurring within 30 days per 100 discharges.

Through careful medical record review of each readmission, key readmission trends have been identified, including commonly involved care teams, patient diagnoses, and discharge planning and follow-up. The most common readmission diagnoses within our review period include status asthmaticus, sickle cell disease with vaso-occlusive crisis, immunocompromised patients with fever and indwelling central vascular catheters, status epilepticus, pneumonia, and bronchiolitis.

Common factors leading to readmission that have been identified through medical record review at Children's National Medical Center include: (1) lack of proper teaching/education before discharge; (2) language/education barriers; (3) medication or treatment noncompliance; (4) premature discharge or transfer; (5) lack of outpatient resources (eg, transportation, medication, therapy).

DISCUSSION

The use of an AAED program has added to the safety culture at Children's National Medical Center. One objective confirmation of this finding includes the number of adverse events that have been identified outside the voluntary incident reporting system. The AAED program has added 2441 adverse events over 4 years to help us better understand areas that can be improved with patient care. This system is occurring in an otherwise strong voluntary reporting environment, with more than 6000 of these reports generated each year.

Another measure that indicates the benefit and impact of the AAED program is a 60% decrease in preventable adverse events detected by this automated electronic program over its 4-year history.

The data collected from the daily AAED trigger review result in a monthly generated report. This report is reviewed in an aggregated form in the monthly steering committee. In addition, the data are shared with various committees throughout the organization, including the sedation committee and the anticoagulation task force (**Table 5**). Committee members determine if the adverse events were associated with any breakdown in hospital policy or procedure. As an example, at Children's National Medical Center, proper use of sedative and analgesic reversal agents has been extensively monitored in the sedation committee, and continues to be a monthly

Table 5
Consulting trigger experts and committees

Adverse Event Trigger	Trigger-Specific Experts
Naloxone administration	Sedation committee and PICU, NICU, and CICU leadership
Flumazenil administration	Sedation committee and PICU, NICU, and CICU leadership
Glucose <40 mg/dL	Endocrinology and PICU, NICU, and CICU leadership
Protamine administration	Anticoagulation task force
PTT >139 s	Anticoagulation task force
INR >6.0	Anticoagulation task force
Antifactor Xa >1.5	Anticoagulation task force
Creatinine doubling	Nephrology Radiology (contrast cases)
Bilirubin >25 mg/dL	Neonatology
Digibind administration	Cardiology
Hyaluronidase administration	Nursing infiltrate team
Transfers to the ICU	PICU, NICU, and CICU leadership, emergency department, acute care medical directors as appropriate
Readmissions within 30 days of discharge	Case management, discharge planning committee

Abbreviations: CICU, cardiac ICU; PICU, pediatric ICU.

agenda focus. The assessment of readmissions has also been a focal point within many committees at numerous levels within the institution.

According to van Walraven and colleagues,[10] clinicians are likely to have a higher sense of accountability for readmissions that occur within a shorter time frame, such as within 7 days of discharge. Thus, they are more likely to institute and adhere to practices that would lead to a reduction in these rates. By identifying trends within readmission data, specific associated issues can be targeted to assist unit-based leaders with action plans to reduce service-specific readmissions.

Working closely with payers to identify an effective metric for hospital readmission is imperative. Although a hospital may have a readmission rate that is greater than preferred, careful review may show that it is associated with reduced mortality. Preservation of low mortality has greater importance than reducing the readmission rate in any given patient population.[10] Identifying common issues that lead to readmission is a more useful approach and is more likely to reduce readmission rates that contribute to preventable patient harm.

The use of adverse event data should not be with punitive intention. The primary goal of evaluating adverse event data is the identification of trends that identify processes or procedures that can be altered to improve performance and safety. The use of trigger tools is performed in a similar fashion to that of common cause analysis, by which a theme is identified and validated, and action is taken to diminish the trend.[11] In addition, through the rapport that is built between the members of AAED and hospital leadership, the validity and reliability of the AAED program are strengthened.

SUMMARY

Children's National Medical Center has benefited greatly from increased adverse event detection, in particular AAED. We assert that this system has contributed to improved quality of care and cost-effectiveness for patients and families. The reduction in adverse events noted can be attributed to the targeted approach provided with the automated trigger tool. In our opinion, AAED complements voluntary incident reporting. The current availability of triggers is being broadened with the development of pediatric specific triggers. Organizations can collaborate with their EHR contractor to design and build an automated trigger tool that best serves their needs and aids in quality improvement efforts.

REFERENCES

1. Woods D, Thomas E, Holl J, et al. Adverse events and preventable adverse events in children. Pediatrics 2005;115:155–60.
2. Cullen DJ. The incident reporting system does not detect adverse drug events: a problem for quality improvement. Jt Comm J Qual Improv 1995;21:541.
3. Ferranti J, Horvath MM, Cozart H, et al. Reevaluating the safety profile of pediatrics: a comparison of computerized adverse drug event surveillance and voluntary reporting in the pediatric environment. Pediatrics 2008;121(5):e1201–7.
4. Kilbridge PM, Noirot LA, Reichley RM, et al. Computerized surveillance for adverse drug events in a pediatric hospital. J Am Med Inform Assoc 2009; 16(5):607–12.
5. About medication errors. NCC MERP index for categorizing medication errors. Rockville (MD): National Coordinating Council for Medication Error Reporting and Prevention. 1996 [updated 2001]. p. c1995–2012. Available at: http://www.nccmerp.org/medErrorCatIndex.html. Accessed March 16, 2012.

6. Dickerman MJ, Jacobs BR, Vinodrao H, et al. Recognizing hypoglycemia in children through automated adverse-event detection. Pediatrics 2011;127:e1035–41.

7. Sharek PJ, Parast LM, Leong K, et al. Effect of a rapid response team on hospital-wide mortality and code rates outside the ICU in a Children's Hospital. JAMA 2007;298(19):2267–74.

8. Department of Health and Human Services (US). Patient protection and Affordable Care Act. Final rule and interim final rule. Fed Regist 2012;77(59):e18310–475. Available at: http://www.gpo.gov/fdsys/pkg/FR-2012-03-27/pdf/2012-6125.pdf. Accessed October 3, 2012.

9. Joynt KE, Jha AK. Thirty-day readmissions–truth and consequences. N Engl J Med 2012;366:1366–9.

10. Van Walraven C, Jennings A, Taljaard M, et al. Incidence of potentially avoidable urgent readmissions and their relation to all-cause urgent readmissions. CMAJ 2011;183:e1067–72.

11. Browne AM, Mullen R, Teets J, et al. Common cause analysis: focus on institutional change (assessment). In: Henriksen K, Battles JB, Keyes MA, et al, editors. Advances in patient safety: new directions and alternative approaches, vol. 1. Rockville (MD): Agency for Healthcare Research and Quality; 2008. Available at: http://www.ncbi.nlm.nih.gov/books/NBK43639/. Accessed October 3, 2012.

Is Preventable Harm the Right Patient Safety Metric?

Wallace V. Crandall, MD, J. Terrance Davis, MD,
Richard McClead, MD, Richard J. Brilli, MD, FCCM*

KEYWORDS

- Preventable harm • Harm • Patient harm • Preventable harm index • Patient safety

KEY POINTS

- Given current resources, efforts to reduce patient harm should first focus, where possible, on preventable harm events.
- Studies examining improvements in patient safety and medical error prevention refer to the rate of harm in a given population.
- To compare outcomes between institutions or programs, it is imperative that definitions and detection methods be consistent.
- The count in each harm domain is the number of events (not a rate); therefore, disparate events can be summed to a total that reflects all events of patient harm for any given time period.
- Achieving zero preventable harm forever may not be possible, but it is the only goal that makes sense.

In the 13 years since the Institute of Medicine released its report *To Err is Human*,[1] patient safety has become a focal point of discussion by the public, the government,[2] and health care professionals. Significant but limited progress has occurred in reducing some types of harm such as central line–associated blood stream infections[3–5] and ventilator-associated pneumonias (VAP).[6] However, progress toward comprehensive national efforts to reduce patient harm has been frustratingly slow.[7–9] As such, the Center for Medicare and Medicaid Services began disallowing payment for certain readily identifiable, preventable harm events ("never events")[10,11] and other insurers have followed.

Reducing patient harm is complicated by problems inherent in accurately categorizing, detecting, and measuring harm. This paper summarizes the medical literature attempting to address such challenges, our institution's approach to similar issues,

Nationwide Children's Hospital, The Ohio State University, College of Medicine, 700 Children's Drive, Columbus, OH 43205, USA
* Corresponding author.
E-mail address: rbrilli@nationwidechildrens.org

Pediatr Clin N Am 59 (2012) 1279–1292
http://dx.doi.org/10.1016/j.pcl.2012.09.003
0031-3955/12/$ – see front matter © 2012 Elsevier Inc. All rights reserved.

and the results we have achieved by focusing efforts around a preventable harm index (PHI).[12–15]

CATEGORIZING HARM: WHAT HARM IS "PREVENTABLE"?

A common view is that not all harm is preventable and separating inevitable harm from preventable harm is complex.[16] Given current resources, efforts to reduce patient harm should first focus, where possible, on preventable harm events. Importantly, "preventability" can change over time. For example, VAP in pediatric patients was once considered the "cost of doing intensive care unit business." It is now known that VAP can be effectively eliminated by carefully following a VAP prevention bundle.[6] In the case of VAP, yesterday's inevitable harm has become today's preventable harm. This is likely true of other forms of today's "inevitable harm." Thus, defining what harm is preventable is an iterative process that requires continually challenging the notion of "preventability."

A recent review by Nabhan and colleagues[17] adds clarity about the types of harm that might be preventable and summarizes published report's use of the term "preventable harm." This summary describes 7 themes commonly found in a preventable harm definition; however, 3 are most compelling and common: (1) Presence of an identifiable modifiable cause (cited in 44% of references reviewed), (2) adoption of an intervention or process will prevent future occurrences (cited in 23%), and (3) lack of adherence to guidelines implies preventability (cited in 16%). Furthermore, 50% of the studies that outlined specific harm severity classifications used item 1 above as the operational definition for preventable harm. At Nationwide Children's Hospital, we have adopted a definition for preventable harm that incorporates the principals noted. We believe this definition navigates the complexities between preventable and inevitable harm. Specifically, designation as preventable does not necessarily mean that each occurrence in question was preventable at the time, because this may be impossible to determine. Instead we have chosen to classify *domains of harm* as "preventable" as a call to action to improve patient care. This definition is designed to change the thinking that harm occurrences are expected complications and, to instead see them as challenges to reduce and ultimately eliminate. In some situations, when preventive policies were well known and not followed, or known complications were not adequately prepared for, such events will be adjudicated as preventable.

MEASURING PATIENT HARM

Traditionally, studies examining improvements in patient safety and medical error prevention refer to the rate of harm in a given population. This approach is intended to allow inter-institutional comparison of event rates (benchmarking) and to normalize event frequency according to patient volume or other demographic characteristics. Rate determination offers many challenges,[13] including defining both the number of harm events (the numerator) and the number vulnerable to that harm (the denominator).

Difficulties in determining numbers of harm events (numerator) include variation in event definitions and event detection methods. Little consistency exists in defining harm events. A recent review of 45 studies of adverse drug events (ADEs) yielded 26 different definitions. Consequently, prevalence of drug errors ranges from 2% to 75%.[18] This issue is magnified when studies involve multiple institutions and/or multiple forms of harm, making data comparison between institutions difficult or impossible. Although consistently defining harm event to allow comparison of data is a daunting task, it becomes even more difficult when events such as "failure to diagnose" or near misses are included.[17] Some harm domains are more reliably defined and applied. Specific examples include pressure ulcers (PUs) and hospital-acquired infections. Multi-institutional, regional, and national collaboratives are more often using the National Healthcare Safety Network definitions for hospital-acquired infections or the Wound, Ostomy and Continence Nurses Society Practice Guideline PU definitions.[4,5,19]

Varying detection methodologies can yield different numbers of harm events. Each detection method has limitations. The most common detection method is voluntary reporting or occurrence reporting. Multiple studies document significant underreporting of events, ranging from 2% to 8% of total actual events.[20,21] Retrospective or concurrent chart review is a second detection method frequently combined with occurrence reporting.[22,23] This method is disadvantaged by inconsistency in terminology and in defining what actually constitutes an event, making it difficult to interpret the data. Trigger-based chart review is a third method that looks for specific "occurrences, prompts, or flags found on review of the medical record that 'trigger' further investigation to determine the presence or absence of an actual adverse event."[24] Although global trigger tools find considerably more events than other detection methods and are reasonably reliable,[25] the process is labor intensive. Electronic automation may ultimately improve the usefulness of this methodology.[26] Mandatory reporting of some specific harm events has also been suggested as a method to reduce underreporting of harm events; however, this approach may actually send reporting "underground" owing to fear of reprisal.[27] For certain types of harm, such as hospital-acquired PUs, active surveillance using scheduled rounds can be useful to enhance reporting and detection. Importantly, results depend on the frequency of surveillance rounds (detection methods). For example, weekly "hospital-wide skin rounds" detect many more PUs than quarterly rounds conducted just in intensive care units.

Defining the population vulnerable to harm (denominator) is problematic. For example, for ADEs the denominator might be the total number of patients, the number of patient-days, the number of patients receiving that drug, the number of dispensed doses of all drugs, or the number of dispensed doses of that particular drug.[13] Each denominator definition would yield a different rate for the same numerator. This same challenge exists for patient falls, PUs, and hospital-acquired infections.

To compare outcomes between institutions or programs, it is imperative that definitions and detection methods be consistent; otherwise, such comparisons are not value added. This issue will grow as hospital reimbursement and reputation are linked with harm event rates and as outcomes linked to individual practitioners become public (eg, Pennsylvania and New York).[28,29] To date, public disclosure of harm and outcomes data has had minimal impact.[30,31] As will be discussed subsequently, the PHI obviates some of these concerns.[15]

PATIENT SAFETY INDICATORS: A PRACTICAL MEASURE OF HARM?

The Patient Safety Indicator (PSI) is a recently described composite measure of patient harm. The Agency for Healthcare Research and Quality developed a list of indicators, including patterns of diagnoses and/or procedures, that suggest that a potentially preventable adverse event may have occurred.[32] The PSIs were developed through literature review, clinical input from physician groups, and empiric testing. This composite system can help hospitals to identify admissions or groups of admissions that might include populations at increased risk for preventable harm. Not surprisingly, hospitalizations that contain a PSI, as a group, have excess mortality, lengths of stay, and cost compared with those hospitalizations without a PSI.[33] The PSIs do not lend themselves to tracking specific types of harm reduction over time and suffer from many of the problems associated with harm data derived from administrative sources.[27,34]

THE PHI: A DIFFERENT TYPE OF HARM METRIC

In 2010, we described the use of a patient harm metric that does not involve a denominator: The PHI.[15] This metric has several important features that make it particularly useful. First, the PHI sums (aggregates) individual events of harm and as such closely tracks numbers of patients harmed. Because the PHI uses only numbers of events, there is no denominator; therefore, it is not an event rate. This makes the number more personal (how many children are injured), more understandable, and more motivational. For example, a rate of 0.1 ADEs per 1000 dispensed doses seems reasonably low; however, at Nationwide Children's hospital, it represents more than 125 patients per year who had an ADE. A focus on actual patients harmed rather than rates can inspire staff and leaders to make the changes necessary to reduce the numbers of such events.

At Nationwide Children's hospital, preventable harm is tracked in 8 separate domains (**Table 1**). All harm events are adjudicated as preventable using the harm definition previously described. Further, we have adopted internally consistent definitions for each harm domain based on national or regional publications where available. These domains of harm may not represent all hospital harm and other hospitals could choose to use additional domains as long as internal consistency of harm definitions and case identification is maintained. For all domains of harm, our event detection system includes voluntary event reporting, trigger tools, customer feedback including complaints and grievances, and active surveillance (PUs in particular). Total hospital-acquired infections are the sum of all hospital-acquired infections including central line associated blood stream infections, VAPs, catheter-associated urinary tract infections, and surgical site infections. ADEs for PHI purposes focus on severity levels 4 through 9 (D-I) as defined by the National Coordinating Council for Medication Error Reporting and Prevention.[35] Our version of a rapid response team, the Assessment Consultation Team–preventable codes include any respiratory, cardiac, or cardiopulmonary arrest occurring outside the ICUs, the perioperative area, or the emergency department and are deemed preventable if detectable deterioration occurred before the event and an Assessment Consultation Team consult was not activated before

Table 1 PHI template	
PHI	**2012**
Total hospital-acquired infections	n
Total ADEs	n
Assessment Consultation Team preventable codes	n
Surgical complications	n
Total serious falls	n
Hospital acquired PUs	n
Miscellaneous harm	n
Total serious safety events	n
Annual sum	Sum n's

the code. A multidisciplinary Code Blue Committee reviews and adjudicates each event. Postoperative complications include (1) unplanned returns to the operating room within 7 days of operation without death and (2) unanticipated death anytime during the hospital stay. Not all operative complications are preventable. To determine preventability, the following questions must be answered: (1) Is the event a known complication? and (2) Were all prevention steps followed? If yes answers these questions, then the event may not be preventable. Previously unknown complications are not considered preventable. Serious preventable falls are those that result in injury (eg, laceration, fracture) or require additional radiologic imaging (eg, simple x-ray or computed tomography). Developmental falls are excluded. PUs include grades 2 through 4 as defined by the Wound, Ostomy and Continence Nurses Society.[19,36] Serious safety events (SSEs) are defined as variations from best or expected practice that reach the patient and are followed by serious harm up to and including death. "Serious harm" is defined as at least "moderate temporary harm" using specific criteria defined by our consultants, Healthcare Performance Improvement, LLC.[37] SSEs are counted once. For, example if a surgical complication rises to the level of an SSE, it is listed in the tally for surgical complications and SSEs, but counts only once in the PHI total.

The count in each harm domain is the number of events (not a rate); therefore, disparate events can be summed to a total that reflects all events of patient harm for any given time period. As we began our safety journey that number was large, and served as a robust motivational call to action. We believe this would apply to most hospitals as they begin a safety campaign to reduce preventable harm.

The PHI is primarily intended as an internal, hospital-specific metric. As a result, harm definitions must be precise (if possible) and internally consistent within 1 institution or system of related hospitals. However, because the PHI is not intended for cross-hospital comparisons, it is not necessary to achieve consensus on definitions between hospitals. The PHI as an internally consistent, hospital-specific metric should be linked to a commitment by each hospital that uses it, to drive the PHI over time to as close to zero as possible. Whether "zero" is attainable, even for individual domains of harm, remains controversial[38,39]; however, many now agree that unless the health care industry and hospital systems have "zero" as an aspirational goal, we will never know what is achievable.

Although the PHI was not originally envisioned for comparison between hospitals, it is now being used as a measure of aggregate harm reduction among collaborating hospitals. Groups of hospitals working together using improvement science methods, sharing best practices, and adopting common harm domain definitions, can create regional, state, or even National Harm Indices that can be used as the global measure of harm reduction across large and disparate populations. Variations of the PHI have now been adopted by the Ohio Children's Hospitals Solutions for Patient Safety, a statewide collaborative of all 8 Ohio children's hospitals, with planned national expansion with an additional 50 children's hospitals.[40]

THE VALUE AND CHALLENGE OF TRANSPARENCY

Once preventable harm metrics have been selected and event detection is consistent, the obvious next step is to use those data to improve outcomes. However, there is often concern regarding the risk associated with disclosure of quality improvement (QI) activities (especially preventable harm metrics), specifically regarding how and with whom the information can be shared. The use of these data internally within an organization is rarely problematic; data generated under the umbrella of QI statutes are generally not discoverable in malpractice suits.[41,42] In most hospitals, such peer-protected QI work has been ongoing for some time and has received broad legal protection. Sharing of QI outcomes, although possibly more challenging from a legal perspective, is in fact quite important in an environment wherein sharing of data between institutions ("all teach, all learn") can facilitate rapid spread of best practices, potentially achieving optimal outcomes more quickly for a larger group of patients.

The release of information regarding harm outside of the internal QI process is referred to as "transparency," and may take 2 forms. At the individual level, transparency means openly disclosing errors and harm to patients and families. There is evidence that this disclosure minimizes damage to the doctor–patient relationship and may decrease litigation.[43,44] At an organizational level, transparency includes public reporting of metrics such as mortality, complication rates, or harm events. The conventional wisdom is that transparency can be a powerful tool to accelerate change, and there are some studies supporting this view,[45] although others differ.[46] Increasingly hospitals are posting outcome metrics on their external websites, including data regarding various types of patient harm (eg, ADE and VAP rates). Although the public may pay little attention to these data,[27,30] hospital personnel often do, and are motivated to improve.

Although the potential for transparency to accelerate and motivate change may be considerable, some risks exist. The risks generally fall into 2 categories: Legal and reputational. The legal risk is that once a specific type of harm is defined as "preventable," the hospital or individual may be judged liable as "preventable implies admission of liability." Therefore, if it could be determined from public data that a specific patient suffered preventable harm, it could be argued that the hospital has admitted culpability by adjudicating the event as preventable. Data presented as overall rates, such as ADEs and VAPs, are unlikely to result in litigation as it is impossible to garner individual patient data from aggregate rates. However, when SSE or PHI data are posted, it is theoretically possible for a plaintiff's attorney to link his or her client's event to those data. This concept remains untested. The reputational risk associated with transparency is related to failing to meet expectations of patients and families. This could occur if, through public reporting of outcomes or harm data, public opinion for individual hospitals declines owing to perceived poor quality of care. However, we would argue that as improvement begins to occur and rates of harm decrease, the hospital may actually be viewed in a favorable light for its open and honest reporting of events and, more important, for having a proactive plan for harm prevention.

NATIONWIDE CHILDREN'S HOSPITAL'S EXPERIENCE WITH THE PHI AND SAFETY TRANSFORMATION

At Nationwide Children's Hospital, the focused patient safety journey began in earnest in late 2008, in close alliance with the board of directors. An overarching strategic vision was developed and enacted. The PHI concept was developed, harm domain definitions codified, and harm event detection methods were refined (eg, can't fix what you don't look for and measure). When fully developed, the sheer magnitude of the PHI was a clear "call to action," resulting in a publically announced goal to "eliminate preventable harm by the end of 2013." This "call" resulted in a robust safety campaign dubbed Zero Hero—the "Zero" pertaining to the goal, and the "Hero" pertaining to everyone working toward this goal is a hero to their patients and it will take a heroic hospital effort to achieve zero.

A 2-pronged approach was pursued: (1) Establish patient safety and high reliability practices as core values and (2) greatly increase the quality infrastructure such that multiple multidisciplinary microsystem based teams could focus simultaneously on all harm domains.

To improve the safety culture and achieve highly reliable performance, Nationwide Children's Hospital partnered with an external consultant (HPI, LLC).[37] A retrospective common cause analysis of 3 years of SSEs was conducted and safety practices to address and prevent the underlying causes of these events were implemented. Safety practice implementation methods included (1) 3-hour training sessions for all 8000 employees, termed "Zero Hero Basic Training"; (2) additional 2-hour training sessions for managers and physician-leaders on "Leadership Methods" designed to reinforce basic safety practices conducted for 600 identified hospital leaders; and (3) training for several hundred "Safety Coaches," who monitor for and reinforce the proper use of the safety practices. Thus far, safety coaches have reported over 90,000 observations; that is, catching people doing the right thing and calling it out, or coaching if they observe a deficit.

To facilitate the organization's safety and quality transformation, the QI department workforce was tripled, recruiting QI experts predominantly from industry. Each is responsible for the QI efforts of 1–3 microsystems and co-lead nearly all QI projects (>100 currently active) with a physician and/or nurse from the respective microsystem. A common improvement methodology was chosen—the Institute for Healthcare Improvement Model for Improvement (eg, Aim, Key Driver Diagrams, rapid cycle Plan-Do-Study-Acts, and statistical process control charts [Shewart charts]).[47] To establish a critical mass of individuals trained in the science of improvement, we initially sent 48 individuals including physicians, nurses, and quality analysts to the Intermountain Institute for Healthcare Delivery in Salt Lake City, Utah. In 2011 Nationwide Children's launched a QI science course, "Quality Improvement Essentials," with the goal to train more than 150 leaders, including all physician section and department chiefs.

The Safety Attitudes Questionnaire (SAQ) Survey by Pascal Metrics[48] is used by Nationwide Children's Hospital to measure institutional safety culture, because studies have demonstrated a link between the SAQ safety and teamwork climate and clinical outcomes.[49–53] Whole-hospital safety surveys were conducted in 2009 and 2011. The SAQ scores were compared before (2009) and after Zero Hero program implementation (2011). **Fig. 1** demonstrates a significant increase in overall safety climate score and **Fig. 2** shows an increase in the number of units within our hospital above the 50th percentile in safety opinion scores. The SAQ will be repeated in 2013.

Three core measures are used to assess the effectiveness of the hospital improvement work: The PHI, the SSER (SSEs per 10,000 adjusted patient-days), and Hospital Mortality Rate (unadjusted and severity adjusted). **Fig. 3** shows PHI results. The increase in the PHI after the start of the Zero Hero program results from increased reporting and detection of adverse events (**Fig. 4**), an important first step in improving outcomes by creating a culture of "safe reporting." To date there has been a 45% decrease in PHI compared with the 2010 peak. Because overall event reporting has remained high (see **Fig. 4**), detection methods have been strengthened, and event definitions are unchanged, the PHI decrease likely reflects a real change in outcomes. **Fig. 5** depicts a significant and sustained 85% drop in the SSER, decreasing from 1 event every 11 days to 1 event every 122 days. Last, **Figs. 6** and **7** depict hospital mortality rates since 2000. In **Fig. 6**, the most recent mortality data points (2010–2011) represent special cause mortality rate decrease and coincide with the period of full Zero Hero campaign implementation. Further, **Fig. 7** depicts severity adjusted mortality (Pediatric Health Information System-administrative database from 43 not-for-profit, tertiary care pediatric hospitals in the United States; these hospitals are affiliated with the Child Health Corporation of America) compared with unadjusted

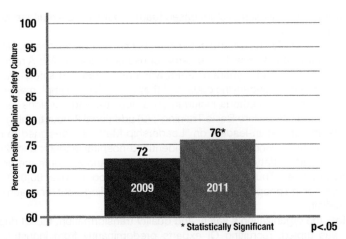

Fig. 1. Safety opinion scores from the Safety Attitudes Questionnaire administered in 2009, before the Zero Hero Program and in 2011, 6 months after completion of the Zero Hero Basic Training.

rates since 2000. Severity adjusted mortality for 2009 to 2011 is significantly lower (P<.0001) compared with severity adjusted mortality for 2000 to 2008. We believe these metrics, taken together, suggest that the Zero Hero safety program is effective and although our hospital has not yet eliminated preventable harm, we believe there is substantial progress toward that goal.

During this safety journey (2008–present), Nationwide Children's Hospital has incrementally increased internal and external transparency. This increased transparency was intended to motivate the organization to achieve the best possible results by creating a sense of both internal and external accountability and to provide all hospital staff with real time awareness of current progress. Therefore beginning in July 2008, the hospital began posting 6 quality metrics on the Internet quality site (eg, ADE rates, hospital-acquired infection rates). In September 2009, coinciding with the Zero Hero Program launch, the hospital began posting on the Intranet (firewall-protected internal Web site) the "Days Since Last SSE," followed in January 2010 with postings of all PHI data. Because the PHI represented actual harm events and not rates, there was concern about possible legal repercussions. None has occurred thus far. To our

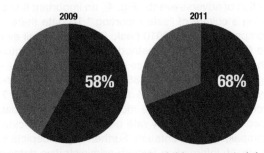

Fig. 2. Percent of 117 hospital units at Nationwide Children's Hospital that were at or above the 50th percentile score for Safety Opinion in the Pascal Metrics national database in 2009 versus 2011.

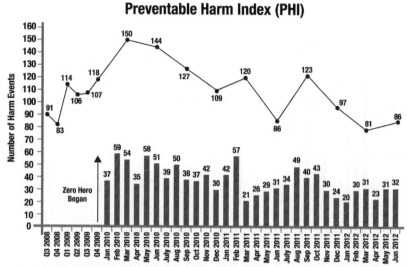

Fig. 3. PHI for 2008 through the second quarter of 2012.

knowledge, in November 2011 Nationwide Children's Hospital became the first in the country to post the hospital SSER on the Internet quality Web site (external site). Based on Internet hits it seems this information is of interest to the health care safety community; however, it has (to date) drawn little public interest.

IS PHI THE RIGHT METRIC?

No single metric can adequately represent the safety record of a hospital or group of hospitals, and each metric has strengths and weaknesses, as discussed.[2,13] However, despite the limitations of available measures and in contrast with Noble and Pronovost's 2010 statement that "it is not yet possible to monitor improvement in patient safety or measurably prove reduction in harm,"[27] we believe our data demonstrate

Fig. 4. Event reports: 2009 to present.

Fig. 5. Nationwide Children's Hospital SSER: 2009 average days between SSE was 11 days; currently, it is 122 days. The black line is 12-month rolling average of SSERs/10,000 adjusted patient-days.

improvement across a broad array of safety-related metrics and the aggregated PHI helps to document that improvement, at least in this institution.

Of the metrics we have deployed, the PHI has provided significant motivation to improve because of its simplicity and ease of understanding throughout the hospital. The PHI represents actual harm events rather than a more nebulous rate, and because it is never acceptable to harm a child, the PHI requires little explanation and minimal

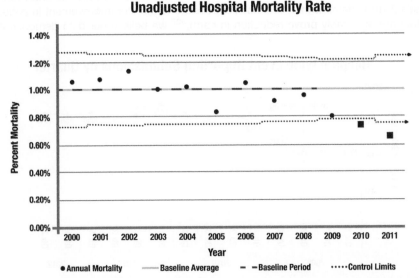

Fig. 6. The black squares represent special cause variation and significantly lower mortality rate.

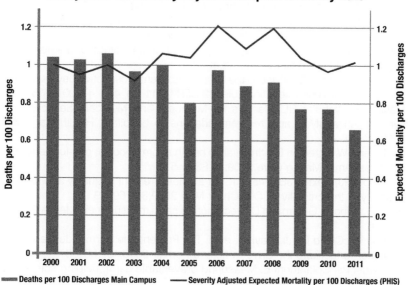

Unadjusted vs. Severity Adjusted Hospital Mortality Rate

▬▬ Deaths per 100 Discharges Main Campus   ▬▬ Severity Adjusted Expected Mortality per 100 Discharges (PHIS)

Fig. 7. The risk-adjusted mortality rate for 2009 through 2011 is significantly lower compared with the risk adjusted mortality rate from 2000 to 2008 (*P*<.0001).

"context" discussion (we either harmed a child or we did not). It is, therefore, simple to unite behind and strive for a goal of zero preventable harm. It is our view that the combination of internal consistency in defining, detecting, and reporting aggregated preventable harm (the PHI) and setting an ambitious public goal of zero harm, that has allowed rapid improvement.

Although we realize that achieving zero preventable harm forever may not be possible, we believe it is the only goal that makes sense. Denham and others advocate applying that principle to hospital-acquired infections.[38,39] We believe that zero must be the only goal for all preventable harm.

REFERENCES

1. Kohn LT, Corrigan JM, Donaldson MS, editors. To err is human: building a safer health system. In: Kohn L, Corrigan J, Donaldson M, editors. Washington (DC): National Academy Press; 1999. p. 26–48.
2. Pronovost PJ, Goeschel CA. Viewing healthcare delivery as a science: challenges, benefits, and policy implications. Health Serv Res 2010;45:1508–22.
3. Miller M, Niedner M, Huskins C, et al. Reducing PICU central line-associated blood stream infections: 3-year results. Pediatrics 2011;128:e1077–83.
4. Lipitz-Snyderman A, Steinwachs D, Needham DM, et al. Impact of a statewide intensive care unit quality improvement initiative on hospital mortality and length of stay: retrospective comparative analysis. BMJ 2011;342:d219.
5. Miller MM, Griswold M, Harris M, et al. Decreasing catheter-associated bloodstream infections: NACHRI's quality transformation efforts. Pediatrics 2010;125:205–13.
6. Bigham M, Amato R, Bondurrant P, et al. Ventilator-associated pneumonia in the pediatric ICU: characterizing the problem and implementing a sustainable solution. J Pediatr 2009;154:582–7.

7. Landrigan CP, Parry GJ, Bones CB, et al. Temporal trends in rates of patient harm resulting from medical care. N Engl J Med 2010;363:2124–33.
8. Sharek PJ, Classen D. The incidence of adverse events and medical error in pediatrics. Pediatr Clin North Am 2006;53:1067–77.
9. Leape L, Berwick D, Clancy C, et al. Transforming healthcare: a safety imperative. Qual Saf Health Care 2009;18:424–8.
10. Medicare Program. Changes to the hospital inpatient prospective payment systems and fiscal year 2008 rates: final rule. 42 CFR § 411–13, 489. 47200–4718 (2007).
11. Mattie AS, Webster BL. Centers for Medicare and Medicaid Services' "never events." An analysis and recommendations to hospitals. Health Care Manag 2008;27:338–49.
12. Glickman SW, Peterson ED. Innovative health reform models: pay-for-performance initiatives. Am J Manag Care 2009;15:S300–5.
13. Pronovost PJ, Sexton JB, Pham JC, et al. Measurement of quality and assurance of safety in the critically ill. Clin Chest Med 2009;30:169–79.
14. Parry G, Cline A, Goldmann D. Deciphering harm measurement. JAMA 2012;307:2155–6.
15. Brilli RJ, McClead RE Jr, Davis T, et al. The Preventable Harm Index: an effective motivator to facilitate the drive to zero. J Pediatr 2010;157:681–3.
16. Pronovost PJ, Colantuoni E. Measuring preventable harm; helping science keep pace with policy. JAMA 2009;301:1273–5.
17. Nabhan M, Elraiyah TB, Brown DR, et al. What is preventable harm in healthcare? A systematic review of definitions. BMC Health Serv Res 2012;12:128.
18. Lisby M, Nielsen LP, Brock B, et al. How are medication errors defined? A systematic literature review of definitions and characteristics. Int J Qual Health Care 2010;22:507–18.
19. Wound, Ostomy, Continence Nurses Society. Guideline for prevention and management of pressure ulcers. Mount Laurel (NJ): WOCN Clinical Practice Guideline; 2010.
20. Sharek PJ, Horbar JD, Mason W, et al. Adverse events in the neonatal intensive care unit: development, testing, and findings of a NICU-focused trigger tool to identify harm in North American NICUs. Pediatrics 2006;118:1332–40.
21. Rozich JD, Haraden CR, Resar RK. Adverse drug event trigger tool: a practical methodology for measuring medication related harm. Qual Saf Health Care 2003;12:194–200.
22. Thomas EJ, Studdert DM, Burstin HR, et al. Incidence and types of adverse events and negligent care in Utah and Colorado. Med Care 2000;38:261–71.
23. Kaushal R, Bates DW, Landrigan C, et al. Medication errors and adverse drug events in pediatric patients. JAMA 2001;285:2114–20.
24. Resar RK, Rozich JD, Classen DC. Methodology and rationale for the measurement of harm with trigger tools. Qual Saf Health Care 2003;12:39–45.
25. Naessens JM, O'Byrne TJ, Johnson MG, et al. Measuring hospital adverse events: assessing inter-rater reliability and trigger performance of the Global Trigger Tool. Int J Qual Health Care 2010;22:266–74.
26. Dickerman MJ, Jacobs BR, Vinodrao H, et al. Recognizing hypoglycemia in children through automated adverse-event detection. Pediatrics 2011;127:e1035–41.
27. Noble DJ, Pronovost PJ. Underreporting of patient safety incidents reduces health care's ability to quantify and accurately measure harm reduction. J Patient Saf 2010;6:247–50.
28. Pennsylvania Health Care Cost Containment Council. Cardiac Surgery in Pennsylvania 2008-2009. Available at: http://www.phc4.org/reports/cabg/09/download.htm. Accessed August 20, 2012.

29. Adult Cardiac Surgery in New York State 2007-2009. NY State Department of Health. 2012. Available at: http://www.health.ny.gov/statistics/diseases/cardiovascular/heart_disease/docs/2007-2009_adult_cardiac_surgery.pdf. Accessed August 20, 2012.

30. Epstein AJ. Do cardiac surgery report cards reduce mortality? Med Care Res Rev 2006;63:403–26.

31. Ryan AM, Nallamothu BK, Dimick JB. Medicare's public reporting initiative on hospital quality had modest or no impact on mortality from three key conditions. Health Aff 2012;31:585–92.

32. Agency for Healthcare Research and Quality. Guide to patient safety indicators. Version 2.1 Rev 3. 2005. Available at: http://www.qualityindicators.ahrq.gov/Modules/psi_overview.aspx. Accessed June 29, 2012.

33. Rivard PE, Luther SL, Christiansen CL, et al. Using patient safety indicators to estimate the impact of potential adverse events on outcomes. Med Care Res Rev 2008;65:67.

34. Isaac T, Jha AK. Are patient safety indicators related to widely used measures of hospital quality? J Gen Intern Med 2008;23:1373–8.

35. National Coordinating Council for Medication Error Reporting and Prevention (NCC MERP). NCC MERP index for categorizing medication errors. 2001. Available at: http://www.nccmerp.org/pdf/indexColor2001-06-12.pdf. Accessed July 5, 2012.

36. National Pressure Ulcer Advisory Panel. Pressure ulcer category/staging illustrations. Available at: http://www.npuap.org/pr2.htm. Accessed July 5, 2012.

37. Healthcare Performance Improvement, LLC. HPI: innovative solutions in healthcare performance. Available at: http://hpiresults.com. Accessed July 5, 2012.

38. Denham CR, Angood P, Berwick D, et al. The chasing zero department: making idealized design a reality. J Patient Saf 2009;5:210–5.

39. Denham CR, Angood P, Berwick D, et al. Chasing zero: can reality meet the rhetoric? J Patient Saf 2009;5:216–22.

40. Solutions for Patient Safety. Our vision: To make Ohio the safest place in the nation for children's health care. Available at: http://solutionsforpatientsafety.org/. Accessed June 28, 2012.

41. Howard J, Levy F, Mareiniss DP, et al. New legal protections for reporting patient errors under the Patient Safety and Quality Improvement Act: a review of the medical literature and analysis. J Patient Saf 2010;6:147–52.

42. Department of Health and Human Services. Patient Safety and Quality Improvement; final rule (42 CFR Part 3), November 21, 2008. Fed Reg 2008;73(226):70731–814. Available at: http://www.pso.ahrq.gov/regulations/fnlrule01.pdf. Accessed April 20, 2011.

43. Griffen FD. The impact of transparency on patient safety and liability. Bull Am Coll Surg 2008;93:19–23.

44. Straumanis JP. Disclosure of medical error: is it worth the risk? Pediatr Crit Care Med 2007;8:S38–43.

45. Carey JS, Danielsen B, Junnod F, et al. The California cardiac surgery and intervention project: evolution of a public reporting program. Am Surg 2006;72:978–83.

46. Werner RM, Konetzka T, Kruse GB. Impact of public reporting on unreported quality of care. Health Serv Res 2009;44:379–98.

47. Langley GL, Nolan KM, Nolan TW, et al. The improvement guide: a practical approach to enhancing organizational performance. 2nd edition. San Francisco: Jossey-Bass; 2009.

48. Pascal Metrics, Inc. Bringing data to life to save lives. Available at: http://www.pascalmetrics.com. Accessed October 5, 2012.

49. Pronovost PJ, Berenholtz SM, Goeschel C, et al. Improving patient safety in intensive care units in Michigan. J Crit Care 2008;23:207–21.
50. Halligan M, Zecevic A. Safety culture in healthcare: a review of concepts, dimensions, measures and progress. BMJ Qual Saf 2011;20:338–43.
51. Huang DT, Clermont G, Kong L, et al. Intensive care unit safety culture and outcomes: a US multicenter study. Int J Qual Health Care 2010;22:151–61.
52. Pettker CM, Thung SF, Norwitz ER, et al. Impact of a comprehensive patient safety strategy on obstetric adverse events. Am J Obstet Gynecol 2009;200: 492.e1–8.
53. Sexton JB, Berenholtz SM, Goeschel CA, et al. Assessing and improving safety climate in a large cohort of intensive care units. Crit Care Med 2011;39:934–8.

Reducing Mortality Related to Adverse Events in Children

Andrew Y. Shin, MD[a,b,*], Christopher A. Longhurst, MD, MS[c,d],
Paul J. Sharek, MD, MPH[b,d]

KEYWORDS

- Pediatrics • Mortality • Adverse events • Patient safety

KEY POINTS

- Mortality in children can be significantly reduced through the prevention of avoidable adverse events.
- The Institute for Healthcare Improvement's 100,000 Lives Campaign to reduce adverse events associated with mortality in the adult population is only partly applicable to the pediatric population.
- Innovative research, such as reducing diagnostic errors and errors related to communication, shows early promise but remains largely understudied.

Since the publication of 2 landmark reports on medical errors and health care quality by the Institute of Medicine (IOM),[1,2] preventing adverse events has become a national priority. In *To Err is Human: Building a Safer Healthcare System*, the IOM concluded that between 44,000 and 98,000 Americans die each year as a result of medical errors.[1] For comparison, even when using the lower estimate, deaths attributable to medical errors exceed those from motor vehicle accidents (43,458), breast cancer (42,297), and illicit drug use (17,000).[1] Subsequent reports with improved detection methodologies have suggested that the incidence of medically related adverse events may be an underestimation.[3–7] These studies, and several others with similar findings, effectively launched the patient safety movement in the United States and around the world.

In response, the Institute for Healthcare Improvement (IHI) embarked on a nation-wide venture called the "100,000 Lives Campaign" to significantly reduce mortality

[a] Division of Cardiology, Department of Pediatrics, Stanford University School of Medicine, 750 Welch Road, Suite #305, Palo Alto, CA 94304, USA; [b] Center for Quality and Clinical Effectiveness, Lucile Packard Children's Hospital, 725 Welch Road, Palo Alto, CA 94304, USA; [c] Division of Systems Medicine, Department of Pediatrics, Stanford University School of Medicine, 4100 Bohannon Drive, Menlo Park, CA 94025, USA; [d] Division of General Pediatrics, Department of Pediatrics, Stanford University School of Medicine, 700 Welch Road, Palo Alto, CA 94304, USA
* Corresponding author. Division of Cardiology, Department of Pediatrics, 750 Welch Road, Suite #305, Palo Alto, CA 94070.
E-mail address: drewshin@stanford.edu

Pediatr Clin N Am 59 (2012) 1293–1306
http://dx.doi.org/10.1016/j.pcl.2012.09.002
0031-3955/12/$ – see front matter © 2012 Elsevier Inc. All rights reserved.

related to avoidable adverse events in American hospitals.[8] The initiative articulated an agenda that uses an evidence-based approach to operationally standardize care in 6 clinical areas among the enrolled estimated 2300 of the United States' 6000 hospitals. Although not without controversy regarding the campaign's interpretation of results,[9] the IHI announced that, after 18 months, the campaign had successfully reached its goal by nationally preventing more than 120,000 avoidable deaths in hospitals across the United States during the 18-month intervention time frame. However, important statistical and methodological uncertainty has obliged IHI leadership to be skeptical in attributing mortality reduction to campaign efforts alone.[10]

Given the unique circumstantial and physiologic differences between pediatric and adult resuscitation and mortality, the "natural fit" of the IHI's 6 interventions for pediatrics is uncertain. Nearly a decade after the results were published, the specific impact of the IHI's 100,000 Lives Campaign on the pediatric population has not been systematically summarized or studied. This article analyzes the impact of the individual elements of the IHI's 100,000 Lives Campaign as it relates to pediatric caregivers and patients, as well as discusses additional interventions with evidence of their potential to systematically reduce mortality related to adverse events in pediatrics (**Table 1**).

THE 6 INTERVENTIONS OF THE CAMPAIGN PLATFORM

The enrolled institutions committed to reduce the number of avoidable deaths by implementing one or more of the following 6 interventions that comprise the IHI's campaign platform: (1) Deploy rapid response teams (RRTs) to bring skilled resources to the bedside of any patient at the first sign of decline and potentially facilitating transfer to an intensive care unit (ICU) where rapid resuscitation efforts are more likely to be successful. (2) Prevent adverse drug events (ADEs) by reconciling medications at all transitions in care. (3) Deliver reliable evidence-based care for acute myocardial infarction (given the pediatric focus of this article, this intervention will not be discussed). (4) Prevent central-line–associated bloodstream infections (CLABSIs) by applying a bundle of evidence-based practices based on guidelines issued by the

Table 1
Evidence of interventions associated with mortality reduction related to adverse events in children

	Intervention	Relative Strength for Mortality Reduction in Children	Relative Strength of Evidence in Children
IHI 100,000 Lives Campaign	Rapid response team	Strong	Good evidence
	ADE prevention	Intermediate	Good evidence
	CLABSI prevention	Strong	Good evidence
	Evidence-based care for acute myocardial infarction	Not applicable	Not applicable
	Surgical site infection prevention	Weak	Limited studies available
	Ventilator-associated pneumonia prevention	Weak	Limited studies available
Other	CPOE & clinical decision support systems	Unknown	Limited studies available
	Diagnosis error prevention	Unknown	Minimal evidence
	Standardized communication	Unknown	Minimal evidence
	Raising culture of safety	Unknown	Minimal evidence

Centers for Disease Control and Prevention (CDC). (5) Prevent surgical site infections (SSIs) by implementing a bundle of evidence-based practices issued by the CDC. (6) Prevent ventilator-associated pneumonia (VAP) by implementing a bundle of evidence-based practices including a 30° elevation of the head of the bed, daily sedation "vacations," and daily readiness-to-wean assessments. These interventions were largely chosen based on wide acceptance and consensus in the medical community, strong evidentiary support in the adult medical literature, and relative ease of institutional implementation to address problems that are common and widespread.

Rapid Response Teams

Survival rates of all pediatric inpatients after cardiopulmonary arrest are poor,[11–13] with just 34% surviving 24 hours, 27% surviving to discharge,[12] and 15% surviving 1 year.[13] Surviving a code outside of the pediatric ICU is similarly improbable, with just 33% of pediatric patients with an arrest outside of the ICU surviving to discharge.[11,12] The concept of an ICU-trained multidisciplinary team to respond to "pre-arresting" deteriorating patients not in the ICU was developed in response to research that revealed that both adult and pediatric patients often have evidence of physiologic decline several hours before cardiopulmonary arrest.[11,14–18] Although the concept of and rationale for RRT programs are sound, the recommendation made by the IHI to implement RRTs as a strategy to decrease nationwide in-hospital mortality has not been without debate. Systematic reviews have cited mixed, contradictory, or inconclusive evidence as arguments for further research before decreeing RRTs standard care.[19–24] To date, there continues to be controversy on the effectiveness of RRTs on adult hospital-wide mortality.

In pediatrics, there are a few studies that describe the effect of RRTs on mortality and other patient outcomes. The first studies initially did not demonstrate a meaningful decrease in total hospital mortality after implementation of an RRT.[25,26] Both study designs were limited in their short time frame of the postintervention period (12 months and 8 months, respectively), potentially contributing to an underestimation of RRT programs on mortality by premature analysis. Subsequently, however, Sharek and colleagues,[27] demonstrated in a cohort study that the implementation of an RRT was statistically associated with an 18% decrease in hospital-wide mortality rate, bringing the preintervention monthly mortality rate of 1.01 deaths per 100 discharges to 0.83 deaths per 100 discharges. In the same study, the rate of codes outside of the ICU per 1000 eligible patient-days decreased by 71.2% after RRT implementation. The study controlled for potential bias by secular trends by using longer time frames for preintervention and postintervention periods (18-month postintervention period) and demonstrated similarities in characteristics and case mix complexity between the control and intervention populations. Since then, ensuing studies have shown consistent findings. In a cohort study by Tibballs and colleagues,[25] implementation of a medical emergency team in a free-standing children's hospital was associated with a significant decline in total hospital deaths from 4.38 to 2.8 per 1000 admissions (risk ratio [RR], 0.65; 95% confidence interval [CI], 0.57–0.75; $P<.0001$). In the same study, survivability from cardiac arrest increased from 7 of 20 patients to 17 of 23 (RR, 2.11; 95% CI, 1.11–4.02; $P = .01$). Hanson and colleagues[28] demonstrated a reduction in the rate of non-ICU cardiac arrests with a risk reduction of 0.35 (95% CI, 0–1.24; $P = .125$) associated with RRT implementation. In the first large multicenter study of RRTs in pediatrics, Kotsakis and colleagues[29] developed, implemented, and examined a standardized rapid response system across 4 pediatric academic centers in Ontario, Canada. Using a prospective observational design, analysis of more than 110,000 hospital admissions and more than 14,000 pediatric ICU admissions during a 4-year study period revealed significant decreases in code blue events (defined as actual and near cardiopulmonary arrests) with a risk reduction ratio of 0.71 (95% CI, 0.61–0.83; P<.0001). The study also demonstrated a significant decrease in mortality rate in patients who were readmitted to the ICU with a risk reduction ratio of 0.43 (95% CI, 0.17–0.99; P<.05).

There are several potential reasons for discrepancies between outcomes when implementing RRTs in adult versus pediatric inpatient populations. First, the cause and pathophysiology of pediatric respiratory and cardiopulmonary arrests differ from that of adults.[13,30,31] Consequently, the parameters for activating an RRT are likely to reflect the epidemiologic differences between adult and pediatric prearrest physiologies. Second, unique adult protocols and time-sensitive response teams for unique adult crisis situations such as coronary insufficiency syndromes, heart failure, and stroke may contribute to the dilution of a mortality benefit of adult RRTs. Finally, higher prevalence of do-not-resuscitate orders in adults compared with pediatrics may be an important confounder for interpreting adult RRT outcomes. With the advent of better methodologies to evaluate rapid response systems[32] and improved sensitivity in early warning indicators,[33] there is potential for RRTs to be increasingly valuable in preventing pediatric mortality.

Adverse Drug Events

The available data on the incidence of medication errors suggest that prescribing, dispensing, and administering medications are error-prone processes in pediatrics.[34–43] The published estimates of medication errors causing harm (ADE rates) in pediatrics are few[34,39] compared with those of adults.[44–49] There is a demonstrable relationship between ADEs and mortality in adults,[45,47,49,50] whereas the evidence of ADEs as an important contributor to pediatric mortality is sparse. Kaushal[34] reported ADE rates in children in inpatient wards at 2 urban teaching hospitals to be 2.3 per 100 admissions (26 events), of which 5 (19%) were classified as preventable, with 2 (10%) categorized as fatal or life threatening. Holdsworth[39] measured an ADE rate in pediatric inpatients of 6 per 100 admissions (76 events), with 46 (61%) classified as preventable and 8 (11%) classified as life threatening. Takata and colleagues,[51] using the rigorous trigger tool methodology pioneered by the IHI, identified rates of 11.1 ADEs per 100 admissions in 14 children's hospitals across the United States. Of the 107 ADEs identified in 960 total charts, none were classified as fatal or life threatening. Overall, at present, there is little evidence suggesting that ADEs are substantial contributors to mortality in the hospitalized pediatric population.

The prevention of ADEs and implementation of computerized order entry systems (CPOEs) have merged as parallel priorities for many institutions. Most evaluations of CPOEs and ADEs in adult and pediatric settings have focused on measuring intermediate outcomes (eg, prescribing errors, rule violations, and compliance)[52–54] until Holdsworth[39] demonstrated that the implementation of a CPOE was associated with a risk reduction of preventable ADEs of 0.56 (95% CI, 0.34–0.91) in the inpatient pediatric population. The impact on mortality was not studied. In the first study to demonstrate reductions in pediatric mortality rates with implementation of a CPOE, Longhurst and colleagues[55] reported a 20% decrease (1.008–0.716 deaths per 100 discharges per month) in the mean monthly adjusted mortality rate after CPOE implementation (95% CI, 0.8%–40%; P = .03) during 18 months. In this report, introduction of the CPOE was shown to improve medication turnaround times by 19% and 5% in the solid organ transplant unit and pediatric ICU, respectively, a finding that other investigators have previously argued as the most proximate cause of CPOE-related mortality changes.[54,56–59] The investigators noted that ADE rates were low before and after the CPOE implementation and likely not an important contributor to the shift in mortality.

Central-Line–Associated Bloodstream Infections

CLABSIs are common health care-associated infections and result in increases in length of stay, morbidity, and mortality in adult and pediatric patients.[60–68] Each year in the United States, it is estimated that CLABSIs result in approximately 31,000 deaths.[69] Wenzel and Edmond[70] calculated that nosocomial bloodstream infections represented the eighth leading cause of death in the United States. In response, the CDC has issued evidence-based guidelines that articulate many essentials of care shown to reduce the risk of CLABSIs.[71] Preventing CLABSIs has been the focus of substantial pediatric research and quality improvement efforts.[65,66,68,72–76] In a New York quality improvement collaborative among 18 neonatal and pediatric ICUs, Schulman and colleagues[77] demonstrated a 67% statewide decline in CLABSI rates (6.4–2.1/1000 central-line days, P<.0005) with the standardization of central-line insertion and maintenance practice. In a similar California collaborative of 13 regional neonatal ICUs, Wirtschafter and colleagues[78] demonstrated a 25% reduction in CLABSIs from 4.32 to 3.22 per 1000 central-line days. Bizzarro and colleagues[79] used the evidenced-based recommendations by the CDC to reduce CLABSIs from 8.4 to 1.7 per 1000 central-line days (adjusted rate ratio, 0.19 [95% CI, 0.08–0.45]) in a neonatal ICU. In 2010, the National Association of Children's Hospitals and Related Institutions (NACHRI) structured a collaboration of 29 pediatric ICUs and described the reduction of CLABSIs by 43% (5.4–3.1/1000 central-line days) through the collective use of insertion and maintenance bundles.[80] Finally, in an extended 3-year postintervention report,[81] the NACHRI quality transformation effort realized a decrease in CLABSI rate of 56% or 5.2 to 2.3 CLABSIs per 1000 central-line days (rate ratio, 0.44 [95% CI, 0.37–0.53]; P<.0001). The authors estimated that greater than 900 CLABSIs were prevented, avoiding greater than 100 mortalities in 29 pediatric ICUs during the 3-year study period, and more than 65 pediatric ICUs have since joined the collaborative.[82] CLABSIs have captured the nation as a preventable complication that contributes prominently to pediatric mortality. Future efforts should focus on continued implementation of the best-practice bundles of care in central-line management and further research to improve bundle elements that can prevent CLABSIs altogether.

Surgical Site Infections

In a 1999 report by the National Nosocomial Infections Surveillance (NNIS) system, SSIs were considered the third most frequently reported nosocomial infections accounting for 14% to 16% of all nosocomial infections among hospitalized adults and children.[83,84] Moreover, they were the most common nosocomial infection among surgical patients and deaths among patients with SSIs; 77% were related to infection, and the majority (93%) were serious infections involving organs or spaces accessed during surgery.[84] However, most of the epidemiologic reviews from broad national surveillance systems are more than a decade old[62,69] and do not capture the impact resulting from improved care practices since 2002. There are only a few US studies published that specifically address the problem of SSIs in children and even fewer pediatric studies that attempt to quantify the relationship between pediatric SSI and mortality. Published SSI rates after sternotomy for pediatric cardiac surgery range from 2.3% to 5%.[85–87] In a prospective multicenter study by Horwitz and colleagues,[88] the incidence of wound infection in a general pediatric surgical population was 4.4% in the 30 postoperative days among 846 patients within 3 pediatric institutions in Texas.

Ryckman and colleagues[89] demonstrated reductions in pediatric SSI rates from 1.5 to 0.54 per 100 procedure-days (64% reduction) in a single center study using established adult evidence-based bundles with pediatric-based modifications. However, influence on clinical outcome, including mortality, was not analyzed. Since then, many studies have better characterized pediatric SSIs[85,87,90–92] but are limited in design with only a few controlled studies. Most studies use a comparative before–after structure with inadequate control for secular trends. In short, it remains unclear whether successful SSI prevention efforts in the pediatric inpatient population has and/or will result in significant impact on mortality.

Ventilator-Associated Pneumonias

In adults, VAP is a frequent hospital acquired infection that is considered an important quality-of-care indicator based on multiple reports that link it to attributable mortality.[69,93–95] Although the accuracy of the association has been controversial,[96,97] systematic reviews have estimated the attributable mortality rate to range between 3% and 17%.[98,99] Because VAP is considered the most common nosocomial infection in critically ill adults,[100–103] preventing it has emerged as an important component to the IHI's campaign. VAP is considered the second most common nosocomial infection in pediatric ICUs in the United States.[62,104] In 2004, the NNIS system of the CDC reported a mean VAP rate of 2.9/1000 ventilator days for 52 participating US pediatric ICUs.[105] Unfortunately, the characteristics, associated risk factors, and outcomes of pediatric VAP are less established compared with the adult population. In a 2009 prospective, observational study, Srinivasan and colleagues[106] reported VAP to be significantly associated with a greater need for mechanical ventilation, longer intensive care length of stay, and higher hospital costs. The investigators reported an association with increased absolute hospital mortality (10.5% vs 2.4%, $P = .56$), but given the limitation of the small sample size, they failed to demonstrate statistical significance. Apisarnthanarak and coworkers[107] reported high rates of VAP demonstrated prospectively in a cohort study of neonates with birth weight less than 2000 g (6.5/1000 ventilator days for patients with an estimated gestational age [EGA] <28 weeks and 4/1000 ventilator days for EGA ≥28 weeks). In this study, VAP was an independent predictor of mortality (adjusted odds ratio, 3.4; 95% CI, 1.2–12.3) and prominent in extremely preterm neonates who stayed in the neonatal ICU for at least 30 days (RR, 8.0; 95% CI, 1.9–35; $P<.001$). Because of the paucity of epidemiologic and outcome studies on pediatric VAP, there are no reports, to date, that describe effective shifts in VAP rates or outcome using evidence-based guidelines issued by the CDC,[108] the American Thoracic Society, and/or the Infectious Diseases Society of America.[109]

BEYOND THE 100,000 LIVES CAMPAIGN

The 2000 IOM report, *To Err is Human*, represented a significant tipping point that vaulted patient safety as a national health policy issue resulting in new legislation to further outcome research. Recent research on interventions outside of the 6 identified in the 100,000 Lives Campaign has shown noteworthy promise. First, CPOE and clinical decision support systems have been shown to be significantly associated with a reduction in institutional mortality rates in a quaternary children's hospital,[55] independent of the well-established association with ADE prevention.[34,52] Second, efforts targeting the systematic reduction of diagnosis errors[110–113] have recently shown promise in reducing preventable harm. In a multisite survey of pediatricians, Singh and colleagues[114] determined that diagnostic errors occurred commonly and that nearly half of respondents reported patient harm as a result of these errors. Schiff and Bates[115] hypothesize that electronic health records and clinical decision support systems can play a vital role in reducing the frequency of diagnostic errors. Third, there is increasing evidence that standardizing communication, particularly at transitions in patient care, can prevent medical errors that lead to high-severity adverse events. In 2004, a Sentinel Alert issued by the Joint Commission reported that most cases of perinatal death and injury share communication failures as the root cause.[116] In an example of improved communication resulting in improved outcome, Agarwal and colleagues[117] reported that a structured handover processes was associated with a decrease in postoperative complications (24% vs 12%, $P<.001$) in a pediatric cardiovascular ICU. Finally, early evidence exists linking multidisciplinary teamwork and culture of safety to decreased preventable harm and mortality.[118–120] Muething and colleagues[121] described a bundle of interventions including an error-prevention training program, explicit patient safety oversight, and transparent feedback mechanisms, which were associated with a significant reduction in serious safety events from a mean of 0.9 to 0.3 per 10,000 adjusted patient-days ($P<.0001$). This intervention was importantly associated with an increase in the institution's perceived culture of safety.

SUMMARY

Since the IHI's announcement and launch of the 100,000 Lives Campaign, preventing medical adverse events to reduce avoidable mortality has emerged as a central focus for health care providers, institutions, regulators, insurance companies, and the patients themselves. Evidence-based interventions targeting the 6 interventions in the campaign have been associated with a substantial reduction in preventable hospital deaths in the United States. The generalizability of the IHI's campaign to the pediatric population is only partly applicable. Pediatric experiences with RRTs and preventing central-line infections parallel the published experience of adults, with continuing promise to significantly reduce preventable pediatric mortality. The severity of ADEs seems to be less in pediatrics compared with adults, although better detection methodologies continue to be built. Finally, the risk factors and outcomes of pediatric SSIs and VAP are comparatively understudied; thus, the extent of preventable mortality from decreasing the frequency of these 2 hospital acquired infections in the pediatric population is currently unknown. Other systematic interventions deserving particular attention for future study include CPOE and clinical decision support systems, the systematic reduction of diagnosis errors, standardized communication particularly at the time of transitions of care, and improved institutional culture of safety. Future efforts should focus on developing and refining "pediatric planks" that can be used to target the highest risk populations and highest risk classes of preventable adverse events in neonates and children.

REFERENCES

1. Committee on Quality of Health Care in America, Institute of Medicine. In: Kohn LT, Corrigan JM, Donaldson MS, editors. To err is human: building a safer health system. Washington, DC: The National Academies Press; 2000.
2. Committee on Quality of Health Care in America, Institute of Medicine. Crossing the quality chasm: a new health system for the 21st century. Washington DC: The National Academies Press; 2001.
3. Nebeker JR, Hoffman JM, Weir CR, et al. High rates of adverse drug events in a highly computerized hospital. Arch Intern Med 2005;165:1111–6.

4. Sharek PJ, Horbar JD, Mason W, et al. Adverse events in the neonatal intensive care unit: development, testing, and findings of an NICU-focused trigger tool to identify harm in North American NICUs. Pediatrics 2006;118:1332–40.

5. Resar RK, Rozich JD, Classen D. Methodology and rationale for the measurement of harm with trigger tools. Qual Saf Health Care 2003;12(Suppl 2): ii39–45.

6. Rozich JD, Haraden CR, Resar RK. Adverse drug event trigger tool: a practical methodology for measuring medication related harm. Qual Saf Health Care 2003;12:194–200.

7. Resar RK, Rozich JD, Simmonds T, et al. A trigger tool to identify adverse events in the intensive care unit. Jt Comm J Qual Patient Saf 2006;32:585–90.

8. Berwick DM. The 100 000 lives campaign: setting a goal and a deadline for improving health care quality. JAMA 2006;295:324–7.

9. Wachter RM, Pronovost PJ. The 100,000 lives campaign: a scientific and policy review. Jt Comm J Qual Patient Saf 2006;32:621–7.

10. Berwick DM, Hackbarth AD, McCannon CJ. IHI replies to 'the 100,000 lives campaign: a scientific and policy review'. Jt Comm J Qual Patient Saf 2006; 32:628–33.

11. Young KD, Seidel JS. Pediatric cardiopulmonary resuscitation: a collective review. Ann Emerg Med 1999;33:195–205.

12. Nadkarni VM, Larkin GL, Peberdy MA, et al. First documented rhythm and clinical outcome from in-hospital cardiac arrest among children and adults. JAMA 2006;295:50–7.

13. Reis AG, Nadkarni V, Perondi MB, et al. A prospective investigation into the epidemiology of in-hospital pediatric cardiopulmonary resuscitation using the international Utstein reporting style. Pediatrics 2002;109:200–9.

14. Buist MD, Moore GE, Bernard SA, et al. Effects of a medical emergency team on reduction of incidence of and mortality from unexpected cardiac arrests in hospital: preliminary study. BMJ 2002;324:387–90.

15. Hillman KM, Bristow PJ, Chey T, et al. Antecedents to hospital deaths. Intern Med J 2001;31:343–8.

16. Schein RM, Hazday N, Pena M, et al. Clinical antecedents to in-hospital cardiopulmonary arrest. Chest 1990;98:1388–92.

17. Franklin C, Mathew J. Developing strategies to prevent inhospital cardiac arrest: analyzing responses of physicians and nurses in the hours before the event. Crit Care Med 1994;22:244–7.

18. Guidelines 2000 for cardiopulmonary resuscitation and emergency cardiovascular care. Part 9: pediatric basic life support. The American Heart Association in collaboration with the International Liaison Committee on Resuscitation. Circulation 2000;102:I253–90.

19. Bellomo R, Goldsmith D, Uchino S, et al. A prospective before-and-after trial of a medical emergency team. Med J Aust 2003;179:283–7.

20. Rothschild JM, Woolf S, Finn KM, et al. A controlled trial of a rapid response system in an academic medical center. Jt Comm J Qual Patient Saf 2008;34: 417–25, 365.

21. Hillman K, Chen J, Cretikos M, et al. Introduction of the medical emergency team (MET) system: a cluster-randomised controlled trial. Lancet 2005;365: 2091–7.

22. Priestley G, Watson W, Rashidian A, et al. Introducing critical care outreach: a ward-randomised trial of phased introduction in a general hospital. Intensive Care Med 2004;30:1398–404.

23. Bristow PJ, Hillman KM, Chey T, et al. Rates of in-hospital arrests, deaths and intensive care admissions: the effect of a medical emergency team. Med J Aust 2000;173:236–40.
24. Chan PS, Khalid A, Longmore LS, et al. Hospital-wide code rates and mortality before and after implementation of a rapid response team. JAMA 2008;300: 2506–13.
25. Tibballs J, Kinney S, Duke T, et al. Reduction of paediatric in-patient cardiac arrest and death with a medical emergency team: preliminary results. Arch Dis Child 2005;90:1148–52.
26. Brilli RJ, Gibson R, Luria JW, et al. Implementation of a medical emergency team in a large pediatric teaching hospital prevents respiratory and cardiopulmonary arrests outside the intensive care unit. Pediatr Crit Care Med 2007;8:236–46 [quiz: 247].
27. Sharek PJ, Parast LM, Leong K, et al. Effect of a rapid response team on hospital-wide mortality and code rates outside the ICU in a Children's Hospital. JAMA 2007;298:2267–74.
28. Hanson CC, Randolph GD, Erickson JA, et al. A reduction in cardiac arrests and duration of clinical instability after implementation of a paediatric rapid response system. Qual Saf Health Care 2009;18:500–4.
29. Kotsakis A, Lobos A-T, Parshuram C, et al. Implementation of a multicenter rapid response system in pediatric academic hospitals is effective. Pediatrics 2011; 128:72–8.
30. Topjian AA, Nadkarni VM, Berg RA. Cardiopulmonary resuscitation in children. Curr Opin Crit Care 2009;15:203–8.
31. Jacobs I, Nadkarni V, Bahr J, et al. Cardiac arrest and cardiopulmonary resuscitation outcome reports update and simplification of the Utstein templates for resuscitation registries: a statement for healthcare professionals from a task force of the International Liaison Committee on Resuscitation (American Heart Association, European Resuscitation Council, Australian Resuscitation Council, New Zealand Resuscitation Council, Heart and Stroke Foundation of Canada, InterAmerican Heart Foundation, Resuscitation Councils of Southern Africa). Circulation 2004;110:3385–97.
32. Bonafide CP, Roberts KE, Priestley MA, et al. Development of a pragmatic measure for evaluating and optimizing rapid response systems. Pediatrics 2012;129:e874–81.
33. Akre M, Finkelstein M, Erickson M, et al. Sensitivity of the pediatric early warning score to identify patient deterioration. Pediatrics 2010;125:e763–9.
34. Kaushal R. Medication errors and adverse drug events in pediatric inpatients. JAMA 2001;285:2114–20.
35. Kozer E, Scolnik D, Macpherson A, et al. Variables associated with medication errors in pediatric emergency medicine. Pediatrics 2002;110:737–42.
36. Frey B, Buettiker V, Hug MI, et al. Does critical incident reporting contribute to medication error prevention? Eur J Pediatr 2002;161:594–9.
37. King WJ, Paice N, Rangrej J, et al. The effect of computerized physician order entry on medication errors and adverse drug events in pediatric inpatients. Pediatrics 2003;112:506–9.
38. Cimino MA, Kirschbaum MS, Brodsky L, et al. Assessing medication prescribing errors in pediatric intensive care units. Pediatr Crit Care Med 2004;5: 124–32.
39. Holdsworth MT. Incidence and impact of adverse drug events in pediatric inpatients. Arch Pediatr Adolesc Med 2003;157:60.

40. Kaushal R, Jaggi T, Walsh K, et al. Pediatric medication errors: what do we know? What gaps remain? Ambul Pediatr 2004;4:73–81.

41. Ghaleb MA, Barber N, Franklin BD, et al. The incidence and nature of prescribing and medication administration errors in paediatric inpatients. Arch Dis Child 2010;95:113–8.

42. Ghaleb MA, Barber N, Franklin BD, et al. Systematic review of medication errors in pediatric patients. Ann Pharmacother 2006;40:1766–76.

43. Miller MR, Robinson KA, Lubomski LH, et al. Medication errors in paediatric care: a systematic review of epidemiology and an evaluation of evidence supporting reduction strategy recommendations. Qual Saf Health Care 2007;16:116–26.

44. Brennan TA, Leape LL, Laird NM, et al. Incidence of adverse events and negligence in hospitalized patients. Results of the Harvard Medical Practice Study I. N Engl J Med 1991;324:370–6.

45. Bates DW, Cullen DJ, Laird N, et al. Incidence of adverse drug events and potential adverse drug events. Implications for prevention. ADE Prevention Study Group. JAMA 1995;274:29–34.

46. Bates DW, Boyle DL, Vander Vliet MB, et al. Relationship between medication errors and adverse drug events. J Gen Intern Med 1995;10:199–205.

47. Classen DC, Pestotnik SL, Evans RS, et al. Adverse drug events in hospitalized patients: excess length of stay, extra costs, and attributable mortality. JAMA 1997;277:301–6.

48. Classen DC, Pestotnik SL, Evans RS, et al. Computerized surveillance of adverse drug events in hospital patients. 1991. Qual Saf Health Care 2005;14:221–5 [discussion: 225–6].

49. Lazarou J. Incidence of adverse drug reactions in hospitalized patients: a meta-analysis of prospective studies. JAMA 1998;279:1200–5.

50. Bates DW, Spell N, Cullen DJ, et al. The costs of adverse drug events in hospitalized patients. Adverse Drug Events Prevention Study Group. JAMA 1997;277:307–11.

51. Takata GS, Mason W, Taketomo C, et al. Development, testing, and findings of a pediatric-focused trigger tool to identify medication-related harm in US children's hospitals. Pediatrics 2008;121:e927–35.

52. Fortescue EB, Kaushal R, Landrigan CP, et al. Prioritizing strategies for preventing medication errors and adverse drug events in pediatric inpatients. Pediatrics 2003;111:722–9.

53. Potts AL, Barr FE, Gregory DF, et al. Computerized physician order entry and medication errors in a pediatric critical care unit. Pediatrics 2004;113:59–63.

54. van Rosse F, Maat B, Rademaker CMA, et al. The effect of computerized physician order entry on medication prescription errors and clinical outcome in pediatric and intensive care: a systematic review. Pediatrics 2009;123:1184–90.

55. Longhurst CA, Parast L, Sandborg CI, et al. Decrease in hospital-wide mortality rate after implementation of a commercially sold computerized physician order entry system. Pediatrics 2010;126:14–21.

56. Han YY, Carcillo JA, Venkataraman ST, et al. Unexpected increased mortality after implementation of a commercially sold computerized physician order entry system. Pediatrics 2005;116:1506–12.

57. Longhurst C, Sharek P, Hahn J, et al. Perceived increase in mortality after process and policy changes implemented with computerized physician order entry. Pediatrics 2006;117:1450–1 [author reply: 1455–6].

GD, Bates DW. Can electronic clinical documentation help prevent diag-
errors? N Engl J Med 2010;362:1066–9.

l event alert issue 30–July 21, 2004. Preventing infant death and injury
delivery. Adv Neonatal Care 2004;4:180–1.

l HS, Saville BR, Slayton JM, et al. Standardized postoperative handover
s improves outcomes in the intensive care unit: a model for operational
ability and improved team performance. Crit Care Med 2012;40:
5.

RE, Khanna K, Sorra J, et al. Exploring relationships between hospital
safety culture and adverse events. J Patient Saf 2010;6:226–32.

B. On the journey to a culture of patient safety. Healthc Q 2008;11:

s J, Schrooten W, Klazinga NS, et al. Improving patient safety culture. Int
h Care Qual Assur 2010;23:489–506.

g SE, Goudie A, Schoettker PJ, et al. Quality improvement initiative to
serious safety events and improve patient safety culture. Pediatrics
ttp://dx.doi.org/10.1542/peds.2011-3566.

58. Sittig DF, Ash JS, Zhang J, et al. Lessons from 'Unexpected increased mortality after implementation of a commercially sold computerized physician order entry system'. Pediatrics 2006;118:797–801.

59. Ammenwerth E, Talmon J, Ash JS, et al. Impact of CPOE on mortality rates–contradictory findings, important messages. Methods Inf Med 2006;45:586–93.

60. Siempos II, Kopterides P, Tsangaris I, et al. Impact of catheter-related blood-stream infections on the mortality of critically ill patients: a meta-analysis. Crit Care Med 2009;37:2283–9.

61. Burke JP. Infection control - a problem for patient safety. N Engl J Med 2003;348:651–6.

62. Richards MJ, Edwards JR, Culver DH, et al. Nosocomial infections in pediatric intensive care units in the United States. National Nosocomial Infections Surveillance System. Pediatrics 1999;103:e39.

63. Pittet D, Tarara D, Wenzel RP. Nosocomial bloodstream infection in critically ill patients. Excess length of stay, extra costs, and attributable mortality. JAMA 1994;271:1598–601.

64. Pittet D, Wenzel RP. Nosocomial bloodstream infections. Secular trends in rates, mortality, and contribution to total hospital deaths. Arch Intern Med 1995;155:1177–84.

65. Urrea M, Pons M, Serra M, et al. Prospective incidence study of noso-comial infections in a pediatric intensive care unit. Pediatr Infect Dis J 2003;22:490–4.

66. Yogaraj JS, Elward AM, Fraser VJ. Rate, risk factors, and outcomes of nosoco-mial primary bloodstream infection in pediatric intensive care unit patients. Pediatrics 2002;110:481–5.

67. Wisplinghoff H, Seifert H, Tallent SM, et al. Nosocomial bloodstream infections in pediatric patients in United States hospitals: epidemiology, clinical features and susceptibilities. Pediatr Infect Dis J 2003;22:686–91.

68. Elward AM, Hollenbeak CS, Warren DK, et al. Attributable cost of nosocomial primary bloodstream infection in pediatric intensive care unit patients. Pediatrics 2005;115:868–72.

69. Klevens RM, Edwards JR, Richards CL, et al. Estimating Health Care-Associated Infections and Deaths in U.S. Hospitals, 2002. Public Health Rep 2007;122:160–6.

70. Wenzel RP, Edmond MB. The impact of hospital-acquired bloodstream infec-tions. Emerg Infect Dis 2001;7:174–7.

71. O'Grady NP, Alexander M, Dellinger EP, et al. Guidelines for the prevention of intravascular catheter-related infections. Centers for Disease Control and Prevention. MMWR Recomm Rep 2002;51:1–29.

72. Grohskopf LA, Sinkowitz-Cochran RL, Garrett DO, et al. A national point-prevalence survey of pediatric intensive care unit-acquired infections in the United States. J Pediatr 2002;140:432–8.

73. Odetola FO, Moler FW, Dechert RE, et al. Nosocomial catheter-related bloodstream infections in a pediatric intensive care unit: risk and rates asso-ciated with various intravascular technologies. Pediatr Crit Care Med 2003;4:432–6.

74. Aly H, Herson V, Duncan A, et al. Is bloodstream infection preventable among premature infants? A tale of two cities. Pediatrics 2005;115:1513–8.

75. Pronovost P, Needham D, Berenholtz S, et al. An intervention to decrease catheter-related bloodstream infections in the ICU. N Engl J Med 2006;355:2725–32.

76. Nowak JE, Brilli RJ, Lake MR, et al. Reducing catheter-associated bloodstream infections in the pediatric intensive care unit: business case for quality improvement. Pediatr Crit Care Med 2010;11:579–87.

77. Schulman J, Stricof R, Stevens TP, et al. Statewide NICU central-line-associated bloodstream infection rates decline after bundles and checklists. Pediatrics 2011;127:436–44.

78. Wirtschafter, DD, Pettit J, Kurtin P, et al. A statewide quality improvement collaborative to reduce neonatal central line-associated blood stream infections. J Perinatol 2010;30:170–81.

79. Bizzarro MJ, Sabo B, Noonan M, et al. A quality improvement initiative to reduce central line–associated bloodstream infections in a neonatal intensive care unit. Infect Control Hosp Epidemiol 2010;31:241–8.

80. Miller MR, Griswold M, Harris JM, et al. Decreasing PICU catheter-associated bloodstream infections: NACHRI's quality transformation efforts. Pediatrics 2010;125:206–13.

81. Miller MR, Niedner MF, Huskins WC, et al. Reducing PICU central line–associated bloodstream infections: 3-year results. Pediatrics 2011;128:e1077–83.

82. NACHRI PICU CLA-BSI Collaborative Teams: Phase 1,2, and 3. Available at: http://www.childrenshospitals.net/AM/Template.cfm?Section=Search3&template=/CM/HTMLDisplay.cfm&ContentID=55358. Accessed October 4, 2012.

83. Emori TG, Gaynes RP. An overview of nosocomial infections, including the role of the microbiology laboratory. Clin Microbiol Rev 1993;6:428–42.

84. Mangram AJ, Horan TC, Michele L, et al. Guideline for prevention of surgical site infection, 1999. Infect Control Hosp Epidemiol 1999;20:250–80.

85. Nateghian A, Taylor G, Robinson JL. Risk factors for surgical site infections following open-heart surgery in a Canadian pediatric population. Am J Infect Control 2004;32:397–401.

86. Allpress AL, Rosenthal GL, Goodrich KM, et al. Risk factors for surgical site infections after pediatric cardiovascular surgery. Pediatr Infect Dis J 2004;23:231–4.

87. Mehta PA, Cunningham CK, Colella CB, et al. Risk factors for sternal wound and other infections in pediatric cardiac surgery patients. Pediatr Infect Dis J 2000;19:1000–4.

88. Horwitz JR, Chwals WJ, Doski JJ, et al. Pediatric wound infections: a prospective multicenter study. Ann Surg 1998;227:553–8.

89. Ryckman FC, Schoettker PJ, Hays KR, et al. Reducing surgical site infections at a pediatric academic medical center. Jt Comm J Qual Patient Saf 2009;35:192–8.

90. Woodward CS, Son M, Calhoon J, et al. Sternal wound infections in pediatric congenital cardiac surgery: a survey of incidence and preventative practice. Ann Thorac Surg 2011;91:799–804.

91. Tortoriello TA, Friedman JD, McKenzie ED, et al. Mediastinitis after pediatric cardiac surgery: a 15-year experience at a single institution. Ann Thorac Surg 2003;76:1655–60.

92. Durandy Y. Mediastinitis in pediatric cardiac surgery: prevention, diagnosis and treatment. World J Cardiol 2010;2:391–8.

93. Umscheid CA, Mitchell MD, Doshi JA, et al. Estimating the proportion of healthcare-associated infections that are reasonably preventable and the related mortality and costs. Infect Control Hosp Epidemiol 2011;32:101–14.

94. Bekaert M, Timsit J-F, Vansteelandt S, et al. Attributable mortality of ventilator-associated pneumonia: a reappraisal using causal analysis. Am J Respir Crit Care Med 2011;184:1133–9.

95. Safdar N, Dezfulian C, Collard HR, et al. C of ventilator-associated pneumonia: a syst 33:2184–93.

96. Carlet J. Dying from or with a nosocomial p Crit Care Med 2001;29:2392–4.

97. Muscedere J. Ventilator-associated pneum continues. Crit Care Med 2009;37:2845–6.

98. Melsen WG, Rovers MM, Bonten MJ. Ve mortality: a systematic review of observat 37:2709–18.

99. Melsen WG, Rovers MM, Koeman M, et al. of ventilator-associated pneumonia from Care Med 2011;39:2736–42.

100. Bonten MJ, Kollef MH, Hall JB. Risk factors from epidemiology to patient management.

101. Vallés J, Mesalles E, Mariscal D, et al. acquired pneumonia requiring ICU admis 1981–8.

102. Diaz O, Diaz E, Rello J. Risk factors for p Infect Dis Clin North Am 2003;17:697–705.

103. Leu HS, Kaiser DL, Mori M, et al. Hospita mortality and morbidity. Am J Epidemiol 19

104. Gaynes RP, Edwards JR, Jarvis WR, et neonates in high-risk nurseries in the Unite tions Surveillance System. Pediatrics 1996;

105. National Nosocomial Infections Surveillance tions surveillance (NNIS) system report, through June 2004, issued October 2004. /

106. Srinivasan R, Asselin J, Gildengorin G, et associated pneumonia in children. Pediatri

107. Apisarnthanarak A, Holzmann-Pazgal G, H pneumonia in extremely preterm neonates characteristics, risk factors, and outcomes.

108. Tablan OC, Anderson LJ, Besser R, et al. G associated pneumonia, 2003: recommendati tion Control Practices Advisory Committee. N

109. Resar R, Pronovost P, Haraden C, et al. U: ventilator care processes and reduce v Comm J Qual Patient Saf 2005;31:243–8.

110. Graber M. Diagnostic errors in medicine: a Patient Saf 2005;31:106–13.

11. Diagnosing Diagnosis Errors: Lessons fro Project - Advances in Patient Safety: From F 2: Concepts and Methodology) - NCBI Bool nlm.nih.gov/books/NBK20492/. Accessed (Wachter RM. Why diagnostic errors don't done about them. Health Aff (Millwood) 20 Newman-Toker DE, Pronovost PJ. Diagnost safety. JAMA 2009;301:1060–2. ingh H, Thomas EJ, Wilson L, et al. Error: multisite survey. Pediatrics 2010;126:70–9

115. Schiff nostic

116. Sentin during

117. Agarw proce: sustai 2109–

118. Mardc patien

119. Tiesse 58–63

120. Helling J Hea

121. Mueth reduce 2012.

Standardization of Case Reviews (Morbidity and Mortality Rounds) Promotes Patient Safety

Jayant K. Deshpande, MD, MPH[a],*, Patricia G. Throop, BSN, CPHQ[b],
Jennifer M. Slayton, RN, MSN[b]

KEYWORDS

- Safety • Quality • Improvement • Morbidity • Mortality • M&M

KEY POINTS

- The morbidity and mortality (M&M) conference is a well-recognized and long-standing tradition in medical practice. From its inception, this discussion has been an improvement tool for physician practice, meant to address and identify ways to reduce the recurrence of medical error.
- Involving other members of the health care team and including discussion of systems issues can make the M&M conference an effective means of impacting the quality and safety of patient care and patient care processes.
- A standardized, consistent approach to the case reviews enhances patient safety and quality improvement because it provides a means to understand factors contributing to an adverse event or near miss, to formulate a plan to improve, and to track the impact of change made in practice or process.
- Fostering forthright, nonjudgmental case discussion allows participants to overcome their fear of accusation and criticism and focus on improvement.
- A standard way of identifying potential system failures by participants, empowering workgroups to address specific systems-based problems, and regular follow-up can result in improved patient safety and care.

INTRODUCTION

The morbidity and mortality (M&M) conference is a forum common to most medical specialties in which clinicians discuss medical error and adverse events. The M&M conference became a regular feature of clinical practice and a major part of physician

Disclosure: The authors have no conflicts of interest or any relationship with a commercial company that has a direct financial interest in the subject matter or materials discussed in the article or with a company making a competing product.
[a] Departments of Pediatrics and Anesthesiology, Arkansas Children's Hospital and The University of Arkansas for Medical Sciences, 1 Children's Way, Slot 301, Little Rock, AR 72202-3591, USA; [b] Performance Management and Improvement, Monroe Carell Jr Children's Hospital at Vanderbilt, 2200 Children's Way, S- 2410, Nashville, TN 37202-9900, USA
* Corresponding author.
E-mail address: jdeshpande@uams.edu

Pediatr Clin N Am 59 (2012) 1307–1315
http://dx.doi.org/10.1016/j.pcl.2012.08.002
0031-3955/12/$ – see front matter © 2012 Published by Elsevier Inc.

education early in the twentieth century, following the publication of the Flexner report on medical education and the creation of the American College of Surgeons.[1,2]

Early in the twentieth century, Dr E.A. Codman, a surgeon at the Massachusetts General Hospital, introduced the end result system to improve clinical practice and reduce medical error.[3,4] As part of this system, Codman developed the concept of what he termed "the end result card," to document a patient's symptoms, clinical diagnosis, treatment plans, complications, final diagnosis, and annually updated outcome. A detailed analysis of the cause was recorded for any case with an adverse event.[3] Codman promoted the ideas of open acknowledgment of the end results, publishing results of the reviews, and establishing committees empowered to correct errors that were identified. Despite early intense opposition from physicians, Codman's work influenced the standardization of hospital practices by the American College of Surgeons in 1916.[5] Twenty years later, the Philadelphia County Medical Society established the Anesthesia Mortality Committee, an early precursor of the M&M conference. Its objective was to facilitate discussion and to share knowledge about fatalities secondary to anesthesia, and "other interesting anesthetic situations." The committee was a multi-institutional physician review group that aimed to improve the standards of care. The Committee name later was changed to the Anesthesia Study Commission (ASC) and its purview included not just a review of fatalities but also other clinical issues that impacted patient outcome. Anesthesiologists, surgeons, and internists representing a variety of institutions composed the ASC and the meetings were open to "all physicians, residents and interns… as well as numerous nonresident visitors."[6] The commission generated periodic public reports of its activities. In a 1945 review and a follow-up report in 1947, Ruth[6] and Ruth and colleagues[7] reported that at least two-thirds of fatalities reviewed were classified as preventable and that the commission's conclusions often differed from the causes of death included on death reports. This early experience has affected how M&M conferences are conducted to the present day. From the beginning, the M&M conference has had a twofold purpose: education and system improvement. The ASC was founded to improve anesthesia practice through an open review of cases in which medical errors were likely to be found. Meetings were held monthly, and error was confronted directly albeit anonymously. Ruth outlines an inherent conflict in the Committee's discussions between the educational goals and a fear of incrimination on the part of participants. This strain is relevant even today.[4]

In a report of the experience with a system-wide M&M conference at Vanderbilt,[8] it was noted that the M&M conference has evolved primarily into a forum for education and a venue to discuss "fascinomas" or interesting cases. The Accreditation Council for Graduate Medical Education (ACGME), has made the conference a required component of surgical resident training following a format similar to that used by the ASC.[9] The M&M conference also is common practice among internal medicine, pediatrics and other training programs. The format of the conference varies tremendously among academic programs, and the goals of the conference often are not clearly defined.[4] Cases commonly are selected because of their educational interest or potential teaching value and may not include discussion of adverse or nonroutine events.[10,11] Biddle[12] analyzed the topics discussed at one hospital's anesthesia M&M conferences.[12] He found that most involved neither morbidity nor mortality, with the bulk classified as educational. A cross-sectional review by Pierluissi and colleagues[11] of the internal medicine M&M conference found that there was little time for discussion of error, with most of the discussion time spent on case presentation and guest speaker commentary.[11] The investigators pointed out that it is important to discuss adverse events and medical errors. Open discussion promotes

23. Bristow PJ, Hillman KM, Chey T, et al. Rates of in-hospital arrests, deaths and intensive care admissions: the effect of a medical emergency team. Med J Aust 2000;173:236–40.

24. Chan PS, Khalid A, Longmore LS, et al. Hospital-wide code rates and mortality before and after implementation of a rapid response team. JAMA 2008;300: 2506–13.

25. Tibballs J, Kinney S, Duke T, et al. Reduction of paediatric in-patient cardiac arrest and death with a medical emergency team: preliminary results. Arch Dis Child 2005;90:1148–52.

26. Brilli RJ, Gibson R, Luria JW, et al. Implementation of a medical emergency team in a large pediatric teaching hospital prevents respiratory and cardiopulmonary arrests outside the intensive care unit. Pediatr Crit Care Med 2007;8:236–46 [quiz: 247].

27. Sharek PJ, Parast LM, Leong K, et al. Effect of a rapid response team on hospital-wide mortality and code rates outside the ICU in a Children's Hospital. JAMA 2007;298:2267–74.

28. Hanson CC, Randolph GD, Erickson JA, et al. A reduction in cardiac arrests and duration of clinical instability after implementation of a paediatric rapid response system. Qual Saf Health Care 2009;18:500–4.

29. Kotsakis A, Lobos A-T, Parshuram C, et al. Implementation of a multicenter rapid response system in pediatric academic hospitals is effective. Pediatrics 2011; 128:72–8.

30. Topjian AA, Nadkarni VM, Berg RA. Cardiopulmonary resuscitation in children. Curr Opin Crit Care 2009;15:203–8.

31. Jacobs I, Nadkarni V, Bahr J, et al. Cardiac arrest and cardiopulmonary resuscitation outcome reports update and simplification of the Utstein templates for resuscitation registries: a statement for healthcare professionals from a task force of the International Liaison Committee on Resuscitation (American Heart Association, European Resuscitation Council, Australian Resuscitation Council, New Zealand Resuscitation Council, Heart and Stroke Foundation of Canada, InterAmerican Heart Foundation, Resuscitation Councils of Southern Africa). Circulation 2004;110:3385–97.

32. Bonafide CP, Roberts KE, Priestley MA, et al. Development of a pragmatic measure for evaluating and optimizing rapid response systems. Pediatrics 2012;129:e874–81.

33. Akre M, Finkelstein M, Erickson M, et al. Sensitivity of the pediatric early warning score to identify patient deterioration. Pediatrics 2010;125:e763–9.

34. Kaushal R. Medication errors and adverse drug events in pediatric inpatients. JAMA 2001;285:2114–20.

35. Kozer E, Scolnik D, Macpherson A, et al. Variables associated with medication errors in pediatric emergency medicine. Pediatrics 2002;110:737–42.

36. Frey B, Buettiker V, Hug MI, et al. Does critical incident reporting contribute to medication error prevention? Eur J Pediatr 2002;161:594–9.

37. King WJ, Paice N, Rangrej J, et al. The effect of computerized physician order entry on medication errors and adverse drug events in pediatric inpatients. Pediatrics 2003;112:506–9.

38. Cimino MA, Kirschbaum MS, Brodsky L, et al. Assessing medication prescribing errors in pediatric intensive care units. Pediatr Crit Care Med 2004;5: 124–32.

39. Holdsworth MT. Incidence and impact of adverse drug events in pediatric inpatients. Arch Pediatr Adolesc Med 2003;157:60.

40. Kaushal R, Jaggi T, Walsh K, et al. Pediatric medication errors: what do we know? What gaps remain? Ambul Pediatr 2004;4:73–81.

41. Ghaleb MA, Barber N, Franklin BD, et al. The incidence and nature of prescribing and medication administration errors in paediatric inpatients. Arch Dis Child 2010;95:113–8.

42. Ghaleb MA, Barber N, Franklin BD, et al. Systematic review of medication errors in pediatric patients. Ann Pharmacother 2006;40:1766–76.

43. Miller MR, Robinson KA, Lubomski LH, et al. Medication errors in paediatric care: a systematic review of epidemiology and an evaluation of evidence supporting reduction strategy recommendations. Qual Saf Health Care 2007;16: 116–26.

44. Brennan TA, Leape LL, Laird NM, et al. Incidence of adverse events and negligence in hospitalized patients. Results of the Harvard Medical Practice Study I. N Engl J Med 1991;324:370–6.

45. Bates DW, Cullen DJ, Laird N, et al. Incidence of adverse drug events and potential adverse drug events. Implications for prevention. ADE Prevention Study Group. JAMA 1995;274:29–34.

46. Bates DW, Boyle DL, Vander Vliet MB, et al. Relationship between medication errors and adverse drug events. J Gen Intern Med 1995;10:199–205.

47. Classen DC, Pestotnik SL, Evans RS, et al. Adverse drug events in hospitalized patients: excess length of stay, extra costs, and attributable mortality. JAMA 1997;277:301–6.

48. Classen DC, Pestotnik SL, Evans RS, et al. Computerized surveillance of adverse drug events in hospital patients. 1991. Qual Saf Health Care 2005; 14:221–5 [discussion: 225–6].

49. Lazarou J. Incidence of adverse drug reactions in hospitalized patients: a meta-analysis of prospective studies. JAMA 1998;279:1200–5.

50. Bates DW, Spell N, Cullen DJ, et al. The costs of adverse drug events in hospitalized patients. Adverse Drug Events Prevention Study Group. JAMA 1997;277: 307–11.

51. Takata GS, Mason W, Taketomo C, et al. Development, testing, and findings of a pediatric-focused trigger tool to identify medication-related harm in US children's hospitals. Pediatrics 2008;121:e927–35.

52. Fortescue EB, Kaushal R, Landrigan CP, et al. Prioritizing strategies for preventing medication errors and adverse drug events in pediatric inpatients. Pediatrics 2003;111:722–9.

53. Potts AL, Barr FE, Gregory DF, et al. Computerized physician order entry and medication errors in a pediatric critical care unit. Pediatrics 2004;113: 59–63.

54. van Rosse F, Maat B, Rademaker CMA, et al. The effect of computerized physician order entry on medication prescription errors and clinical outcome in pediatric and intensive care: a systematic review. Pediatrics 2009;123:1184–90.

55. Longhurst CA, Parast L, Sandborg CI, et al. Decrease in hospital-wide mortality rate after implementation of a commercially sold computerized physician order entry system. Pediatrics 2010;126:14–21.

56. Han YY, Carcillo JA, Venkataraman ST, et al. Unexpected increased mortality after implementation of a commercially sold computerized physician order entry system. Pediatrics 2005;116:1506–12.

57. Longhurst C, Sharek P, Hahn J, et al. Perceived increase in mortality after process and policy changes implemented with computerized physician order entry. Pediatrics 2006;117:1450–1 [author reply: 1455–6].

58. Sittig DF, Ash JS, Zhang J, et al. Lessons from 'Unexpected increased mortality after implementation of a commercially sold computerized physician order entry system'. Pediatrics 2006;118:797–801.

59. Ammenwerth E, Talmon J, Ash JS, et al. Impact of CPOE on mortality rates–contradictory findings, important messages. Methods Inf Med 2006;45:586–93.

60. Siempos II, Kopterides P, Tsangaris I, et al. Impact of catheter-related bloodstream infections on the mortality of critically ill patients: a meta-analysis. Crit Care Med 2009;37:2283–9.

61. Burke JP. Infection control - a problem for patient safety. N Engl J Med 2003;348: 651–6.

62. Richards MJ, Edwards JR, Culver DH, et al. Nosocomial infections in pediatric intensive care units in the United States. National Nosocomial Infections Surveillance System. Pediatrics 1999;103:e39.

63. Pittet D, Tarara D, Wenzel RP. Nosocomial bloodstream infection in critically ill patients. Excess length of stay, extra costs, and attributable mortality. JAMA 1994;271:1598–601.

64. Pittet D, Wenzel RP. Nosocomial bloodstream infections. Secular trends in rates, mortality, and contribution to total hospital deaths. Arch Intern Med 1995;155: 1177–84.

65. Urrea M, Pons M, Serra M, et al. Prospective incidence study of nosocomial infections in a pediatric intensive care unit. Pediatr Infect Dis J 2003; 22:490–4.

66. Yogaraj JS, Elward AM, Fraser VJ. Rate, risk factors, and outcomes of nosocomial primary bloodstream infection in pediatric intensive care unit patients. Pediatrics 2002;110:481–5.

67. Wisplinghoff H, Seifert H, Tallent SM, et al. Nosocomial bloodstream infections in pediatric patients in United States hospitals: epidemiology, clinical features and susceptibilities. Pediatr Infect Dis J 2003;22:686–91.

68. Elward AM, Hollenbeak CS, Warren DK, et al. Attributable cost of nosocomial primary bloodstream infection in pediatric intensive care unit patients. Pediatrics 2005;115:868–72.

69. Klevens RM, Edwards JR, Richards CL, et al. Estimating Health Care-Associated Infections and Deaths in U.S. Hospitals, 2002. Public Health Rep 2007;122:160–6.

70. Wenzel RP, Edmond MB. The impact of hospital-acquired bloodstream infections. Emerg Infect Dis 2001;7:174–7.

71. O'Grady NP, Alexander M, Dellinger EP, et al. Guidelines for the prevention of intravascular catheter-related infections. Centers for Disease Control and Prevention. MMWR Recomm Rep 2002;51:1–29.

72. Grohskopf LA, Sinkowitz-Cochran RL, Garrett DO, et al. A national point-prevalence survey of pediatric intensive care unit-acquired infections in the United States. J Pediatr 2002;140:432–8.

73. Odetola FO, Moler FW, Dechert RE, et al. Nosocomial catheter-related bloodstream infections in a pediatric intensive care unit: risk and rates associated with various intravascular technologies. Pediatr Crit Care Med 2003; 4:432–6.

74. Aly H, Herson V, Duncan A, et al. Is bloodstream infection preventable among premature infants? A tale of two cities. Pediatrics 2005;115:1513–8.

75. Pronovost P, Needham D, Berenholtz S, et al. An intervention to decrease catheter-related bloodstream infections in the ICU. N Engl J Med 2006;355: 2725–32.

76. Nowak JE, Brilli RJ, Lake MR, et al. Reducing catheter-associated bloodstream infections in the pediatric intensive care unit: business case for quality improvement. Pediatr Crit Care Med 2010;11:579–87.

77. Schulman J, Stricof R, Stevens TP, et al. Statewide NICU central-line-associated bloodstream infection rates decline after bundles and checklists. Pediatrics 2011;127:436–44.

78. Wirtschafter, DD, Pettit J, Kurtin P, et al. A statewide quality improvement collaborative to reduce neonatal central line-associated blood stream infections. J Perinatol 2010;30:170–81.

79. Bizzarro MJ, Sabo B, Noonan M, et al. A quality improvement initiative to reduce central line–associated bloodstream infections in a neonatal intensive care unit. Infect Control Hosp Epidemiol 2010;31:241–8.

80. Miller MR, Griswold M, Harris JM, et al. Decreasing PICU catheter-associated bloodstream infections: NACHRI's quality transformation efforts. Pediatrics 2010;125:206–13.

81. Miller MR, Niedner MF, Huskins WC, et al. Reducing PICU central line–associated bloodstream infections: 3-year results. Pediatrics 2011;128:e1077–83.

82. NACHRI PICU CLA-BSI Collaborative Teams: Phase 1,2, and 3. Available at: http://www.childrenshospitals.net/AM/Template.cfm?Section=Search3&template=/CM/HTMLDisplay.cfm&ContentID=55358. Accessed October 4, 2012.

83. Emori TG, Gaynes RP. An overview of nosocomial infections, including the role of the microbiology laboratory. Clin Microbiol Rev 1993;6:428–42.

84. Mangram AJ, Horan TC, Michele L, et al. Guideline for prevention of surgical site infection, 1999. Infect Control Hosp Epidemiol 1999;20:250–80.

85. Nateghian A, Taylor G, Robinson JL. Risk factors for surgical site infections following open-heart surgery in a Canadian pediatric population. Am J Infect Control 2004;32:397–401.

86. Allpress AL, Rosenthal GL, Goodrich KM, et al. Risk factors for surgical site infections after pediatric cardiovascular surgery. Pediatr Infect Dis J 2004;23:231–4.

87. Mehta PA, Cunningham CK, Colella CB, et al. Risk factors for sternal wound and other infections in pediatric cardiac surgery patients. Pediatr Infect Dis J 2000;19:1000–4.

88. Horwitz JR, Chwals WJ, Doski JJ, et al. Pediatric wound infections: a prospective multicenter study. Ann Surg 1998;227:553–8.

89. Ryckman FC, Schoettker PJ, Hays KR, et al. Reducing surgical site infections at a pediatric academic medical center. Jt Comm J Qual Patient Saf 2009;35:192–8.

90. Woodward CS, Son M, Calhoon J, et al. Sternal wound infections in pediatric congenital cardiac surgery: a survey of incidence and preventative practice. Ann Thorac Surg 2011;91:799–804.

91. Tortoriello TA, Friedman JD, McKenzie ED, et al. Mediastinitis after pediatric cardiac surgery: a 15-year experience at a single institution. Ann Thorac Surg 2003;76:1655–60.

92. Durandy Y. Mediastinitis in pediatric cardiac surgery: prevention, diagnosis and treatment. World J Cardiol 2010;2:391–8.

93. Umscheid CA, Mitchell MD, Doshi JA, et al. Estimating the proportion of healthcare-associated infections that are reasonably preventable and the related mortality and costs. Infect Control Hosp Epidemiol 2011;32:101–14.

94. Bekaert M, Timsit J-F, Vansteelandt S, et al. Attributable mortality of ventilator-associated pneumonia: a reappraisal using causal analysis. Am J Respir Crit Care Med 2011;184:1133–9.

95. Safdar N, Dezfulian C, Collard HR, et al. Clinical and economic consequences of ventilator-associated pneumonia: a systematic review. Crit Care Med 2005; 33:2184–93.

96. Carlet J. Dying from or with a nosocomial pneumonia in the intensive care unit? Crit Care Med 2001;29:2392–4.

97. Muscedere J. Ventilator-associated pneumonia and mortality: the controversy continues. Crit Care Med 2009;37:2845–6.

98. Melsen WG, Rovers MM, Bonten MJ. Ventilator-associated pneumonia and mortality: a systematic review of observational studies. Crit Care Med 2009; 37:2709–18.

99. Melsen WG, Rovers MM, Koeman M, et al. Estimating the attributable mortality of ventilator-associated pneumonia from randomized prevention studies. Crit Care Med 2011;39:2736–42.

100. Bonten MJ, Kollef MH, Hall JB. Risk factors for ventilator-associated pneumonia: from epidemiology to patient management. Clin Infect Dis 2004;38:1141–9.

101. Vallés J, Mesalles E, Mariscal D, et al. A 7-year study of severe hospital-acquired pneumonia requiring ICU admission. Intensive Care Med 2003;29: 1981–8.

102. Diaz O, Diaz E, Rello J. Risk factors for pneumonia in the intubated patient. Infect Dis Clin North Am 2003;17:697–705.

103. Leu HS, Kaiser DL, Mori M, et al. Hospital-acquired pneumonia. Attributable mortality and morbidity. Am J Epidemiol 1989;129:1258–67.

104. Gaynes RP, Edwards JR, Jarvis WR, et al. Nosocomial infections among neonates in high-risk nurseries in the United States. National Nosocomial Infections Surveillance System. Pediatrics 1996;98:357–61.

105. National Nosocomial Infections Surveillance System. National nosocomial infections surveillance (NNIS) system report, data summary from January 1992 through June 2004, issued October 2004. Am J Infect Control 2004;32:470–85.

106. Srinivasan R, Asselin J, Gildengorin G, et al. A prospective study of ventilator-associated pneumonia in children. Pediatrics 2009;123:1108–15.

107. Apisarnthanarak A, Holzmann-Pazgal G, Hamvas A, et al. Ventilator-associated pneumonia in extremely preterm neonates in a neonatal intensive care unit: characteristics, risk factors, and outcomes. Pediatrics 2003;112:1283–9.

108. Tablan OC, Anderson LJ, Besser R, et al. Guidelines for preventing health-care–associated pneumonia, 2003: recommendations of CDC and the Healthcare Infection Control Practices Advisory Committee. MMWR Recomm Rep 2004;53:1–36.

109. Resar R, Pronovost P, Haraden C, et al. Using a bundle approach to improve ventilator care processes and reduce ventilator-associated pneumonia. Jt Comm J Qual Patient Saf 2005;31:243–8.

110. Graber M. Diagnostic errors in medicine: a case of neglect. Jt Comm J Qual Patient Saf 2005;31:106–13.

111. Diagnosing Diagnosis Errors: Lessons from a Multi-institutional Collaborative Project - Advances in Patient Safety: From Research to Implementation (Volume 2: Concepts and Methodology) - NCBI Bookshelf. Available at: http://www.ncbi.nlm.nih.gov/books/NBK20492/. Accessed October 4, 2012.

112. Wachter RM. Why diagnostic errors don't get any respect–and what can be done about them. Health Aff (Millwood) 2010;29:1605–10.

113. Newman-Toker DE, Pronovost PJ. Diagnostic errors–the next frontier for patient safety. JAMA 2009;301:1060–2.

114. Singh H, Thomas EJ, Wilson L, et al. Errors of diagnosis in pediatric practice: a multisite survey. Pediatrics 2010;126:70–9.

115. Schiff GD, Bates DW. Can electronic clinical documentation help prevent diagnostic errors? N Engl J Med 2010;362:1066–9.
116. Sentinel event alert issue 30–July 21, 2004. Preventing infant death and injury during delivery. Adv Neonatal Care 2004;4:180–1.
117. Agarwal HS, Saville BR, Slayton JM, et al. Standardized postoperative handover process improves outcomes in the intensive care unit: a model for operational sustainability and improved team performance. Crit Care Med 2012;40: 2109–15.
118. Mardon RE, Khanna K, Sorra J, et al. Exploring relationships between hospital patient safety culture and adverse events. J Patient Saf 2010;6:226–32.
119. Tiessen B. On the journey to a culture of patient safety. Healthc Q 2008;11: 58–63.
120. Hellings J, Schrooten W, Klazinga NS, et al. Improving patient safety culture. Int J Health Care Qual Assur 2010;23:489–506.
121. Muething SE, Goudie A, Schoettker PJ, et al. Quality improvement initiative to reduce serious safety events and improve patient safety culture. Pediatrics 2012. http://dx.doi.org/10.1542/peds.2011-3566.

learning, which can lead to reduced errors and increased safety. Focusing the discussion on improving the system of care minimizes individual defensiveness and the mistaken belief that an error will not recur if the "culprit" is identified and appropriately managed. Individuals participating in an open, nonjudgmental exchange of ideas contribute to improving the system and advancing safety. In the United States, the ACGME has recognized that physician trainees need to develop competency in six major areas to become effective physicians.[13] Based on published and ongoing experience, the authors believe that a forthright discussion of adverse events, which includes accountability for any necessary follow-up improvement actions, enhances learning in all six areas. Patient care is improved because the system of care is made safer. Discussion of contributing factors, including those that are patient-specific and disease-specific, along with a better understanding of how other factors contribute to a good or adverse outcome increases medical knowledge. Nonjudgmental, forthright discussions among physicians and other members of the health care team about adverse events should improve interpersonal communication and professionalism. Analyzing patient outcomes (practice-based learning) and understanding how the system of care affects patient outcome (systems-based practice) allows physicians and others to learn together.

Frequently, when error is discussed in an M&M conference, the focus is on an unexpected occurrence instead of understanding the processes of care that contributed to the error.[10] Trainees attending the conference frequently think that the purpose of the discussion is to assign blame for an error instead of to improve patient safety.[10,14] Systems-based issues are rarely identified and, often, there is not enough time allowed to discuss specific interventions to improve patient care across systems of care. The authors surmise that this occurs for several reasons. Physicians, nurses, and other health care workers have been trained in a strong culture of intense personal accountability that focuses on individual responsibility for both positive and negative patient outcomes. Even though Codman introduced the end result system nearly 100 years ago, the emphasis on improvement has evolved to identifying individual error and shortcoming that, when corrected, should result in better patient outcome. Yet over the course of the twentieth century, health care has changed from the care of a patient by an individual doctor or nurse at home to care provided by doctors, nurses, and others within a system. Organizations which accredit institutions (eg, The Joint Commission, the ACGME) and certify individual physicians as specialists (eg, American Board of Medical Specialties and its component Boards) have been established with the notion of assuring the public of a level of quality. Training physicians and other health care workers in practice-based learning and systems-based practice has been emphasized only in the last decade or so. The authors expect that, although individual accountability will remain a major component of M&M conferences, these discussions will also include a reasoned assessment of systems issues.

THE STRUCTURED M&M CONFERENCE PROMOTES SAFETY AND QUALITY IMPROVEMENT

The near ubiquitous presence of the M&M conference in physician culture and, increasingly, in other fields, such as nursing, makes the conference a natural and opportune forum in which to conduct case-based discussions with the purpose of improving patient safety and quality of care.

In 2008, the initial 2-year experience at the Monroe Carell, Jr Children's Hospital at Vanderbilt using the M&M conference for systems improvement was published.[8] The renamed MM&I (morbidity, mortality, and improvement) conference was adopted as part of the institution's formal peer review and quality improvement processes. This experience is briefly summarized here.

Cases for discussion are selected by a multidisciplinary and interdisciplinary Mortality Review Task Force and include all deaths, patient injuries that caused prolonged or permanent damage, and near-miss situations. Pediatric resident trainees serve as conference coordinators, with guidance from physicians experienced in quality and safety principles. One case (or a set of similar cases) is selected because of the potential for involvement of system-wide problems or issues that affect more than one patient care population or single hospital unit.

Details of the case preparation and presentation at M&M conference are published elsewhere.[8] All clinical faculty and staff are invited to attend the conference. Health care providers involved with the case receive a special invitation to participate in the conference. In addition, subspecialists are invited to comment on specific aspects of the case. As part of the institution's peer review and quality improvement processes, the MM&I discussion is considered privileged and confidential. As institutional experience has grown during the past few years, the MM&I conference has evolved from its original 75 minutes to the current 60-minute format outlined in **Table 1**. Throughout the discussion, a cause-and-effect or fishbone diagram (Ishikawa diagram[15]; **Fig. 1**) is used to identify specific factors that might have contributed to the adverse outcome in the case. The cause-and-effect diagram is a standard process improvement tool for facilitating identification of potential failure points.

These factors are assigned to one of six broad categories: people, procedure, equipment, environment, policy, and other. All participants have an opportunity to identify systems-based issues and recommend potential solutions. After these issues are identified, the discussion leader (an experienced attending physician who is a safety and improvement champion) selects the key contributing factors that need to be addressed. An action plan is created. The action plan identifies a concise intervention, assigns accountability (including completion target timeframes), and tracks the status of implementation. The progress from each workgroup that is assigned

Table 1
General format of the 60-minute Vanderbilt morbidity, mortality, and improvement conference

MM&I Conference Outline	Time Allotted	Participants
Opening: Reminder of systems-based approach and confidentiality	2 min	Leader
Review of task force progress from prior conferences	5 min	MM&I task force
Case presentation (timeline format)	10 min	Resident leaders
Brief literature review relevant to case in question	5 min	Resident leaders
Identification of key issues leading to undesired outcome	20 min	All participants
Identification of workgroups to address the key issues	10 min	MM&I task force
Reminder of confidentiality	2 min	Leader
Evaluation of conference	5 min	Leader

Adapted from Deis JN, Smith KM, Warren MD, et al. Transforming the Morbidity and Mortality Conference into an instrument for system-wide improvement. In: Henriksen K, Battles JB, Keyes MA, et al, editors. Advances in patient safety: new directions and alternative approaches. Rockville (MD): Agency for Healthcare Research and Quality; 2008.

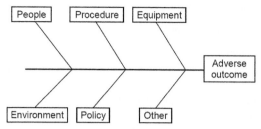

Fig. 1. Fishbone (Ishikawa) diagram used to organize and understand factors contributing to an adverse event.

project accountability is presented at subsequent conferences. Both medical and surgical cases are represented. Other types of cases may be selected based on undesirable outcomes not typically addressed in traditional M&M conferences, such as prolonged medical care with poor prognosis.

During the discussion, conference participants identify potential leading contributors that may have caused the adverse or near-miss event. Inadequate or incomplete communication among members of the health care team was the most common contributing factor, cited in over 60% of the cases in the 2008 report.[8] During the 2 years covered by the report, conferences had an average of 88 participants per session (range 62–115). Attendees included faculty and resident physicians, community physicians, medical students, nurses, pharmacists, respiratory therapists, case managers, social workers, and senior hospital administrators. The attendance at the MM&I conferences has grown to over 125 participants. To allow broad participation from different disciplines and individuals, the conference is moderated by an experienced physician champion.

There are some limitations of the initial experience at Vanderbilt.[8] It was noted that, "While the MM&I has led to several process improvements at our institution, these process changes have not yet been rigorously evaluated to determine their effects on patient safety, morbidity, and mortality. Our current study is largely a qualitative study that focuses on the MM&I process at our institution." Overall, "the structured hospital-wide MM&I conference is an effective way to engage multiple members of the health care team in a discussion of adverse outcomes while collaboratively focusing on potential systems-based improvements in patient care and safety. Nonjudgmental case discussion helps overcome the individual's fear of accusation and criticism, which can stifle honest exchange of information and hinder improvement initiatives. Identification of potential system failures by participants, empowerment of workgroups to address specific systems-based problems, and transparent accountability for regular follow-up can lead to improved patient safety."[8]

Szostek and colleagues[16] modified the M&M conference of an academic medicine department, introducing a structured case audit to impact system improvement (**Box 1**). The investigators' audit tools included the fishbone diagram, mind map, and systems walk (**Table 2**). The investigators conducted a cross-sectional study of all internal medicine residents at Mayo Clinic Rochester in 2007 to determine whether a structured systems-oriented audit increased the residents' awareness of systems issues in health care. Improvements in systems and patient care outcomes were assessed by reviewing the systems audits between 2006 and 2008. The investigators concluded that their standardized systems audit was an effective way to increase residents' awareness of health care systems and meaningfully contribute to institutional quality improvement initiatives. In addition, the investigators report that their systems audit has "transformed their M&M to a conference in which adverse outcomes are

---

Box 1
The six steps of systems audit used at Mayo Clinic

1. Review all documentation relating to the case and identify all health care providers involved
2. Interview stakeholders, including those who directly provided care and those involved in the system
3. Use a quality improvement tool (eg, fishbone diagram, mind map, systems walk) to conduct a root-cause analysis
4. Determine overall cost of care and cost of the adverse outcome
5. Identify a systems issue that contributed to the outcome
6. Propose systems-level interventions and prioritize based on effort-yield projections

From Szostek JH, Wieland ML, Loertscher LL, et al. A systems approach to morbidity and mortality conference. Am J Med 2010;123(7):663–8; with permission.

---

critically examined from a systems perspective." They further report that a significant culture shift has occurred in their program because medical error and adverse events are now openly discussed with less stigma or individual "shame and blame."

Similarly, investigators in the United Kingdom assessed the impact of a standardized process for reviewing mortality in a British hospital. Higginson and colleagues[17] introduced the structured process into selective clinical care groups in the hospital while allowing others to continue their customary format for discussions. Before the intervention, the investigators observed M&M conference meetings and conducted semistructured interviews with meeting chairs. They then introduced a structured mortality review process into three clinical specialties over a 12-month period. The impact on meetings and on health care workers was assessed using a qualitative analysis. The investigators reported that "the introduction of the standardised [sic] mortality review process strengthened these processes. Clinicians supported its inclusion into M&M meetings and managers and board members saw that a standardised trust-wide process offered greater levels of assurance." The researchers concluded that using a standardized process for M&C conferences "can improve accountability of mortality data and support quality improvement without compromising professional learning…"

The structured M&M conference has benefits for nonclinical members of the health care team, as well as for clinicians. Schwarz and colleagues[18] reported that such conferences can be vehicles for significant systems improvement. The investigators

---

Table 2
System audit tools used at Mayo Clinic

Fishbone Diagram	Mind Map	Systems Walk
A cause-and-effect diagram. The "head" of the fish represents the adverse outcome or systems problem and the "bones" represent contributing factors. (see **Fig. 1**)	A diagram representing relationships between a systems problem and its root causes. The adverse outcome or problem is typically depicted in the center with contributing factors branching outward to multiple levels.	A diagram depicting the stepwise sequence of elements in a system, similar to a flow chart. Often used to identify unnecessary or redundant steps in a process.

From Szostek JH, Wieland ML, Loertscher LL, et al. A systems approach to morbidity and mortality conference. Am J Med 2010;123(7):663–8; with permission.

introduced "a morbidity and mortality conference (M&M) quality improvement initiative that aims to facilitate structured analysis of patient care and identify barriers to providing quality care, which can subsequently be improved." Clinical and nonclinical staff was included in the teams "conducting root-cause analyses of health care delivery at their hospital. Weekly conferences focus on seven domains of causal analysis: operations, supply chain, equipment, personnel, outreach, societal, and structural. Each conference focuses on assessing the care provided, and identifying ways in which services can be improved in the future." The investigators found that the staff impression of the M&M conference was quite favorable. Staff took active part in identifying opportunities for improvement. The involvement of nonclinicians and clinicians made "the adapted M&M conference…a simple, feasible tool for quality improvement [even] in resource-limited settings."[18]

Traditional M&M conferences often lack the key elements recommended by widely accepted medical analysis models such as Root Cause Analysis.[19] As a result, M&M conferences may have a limited ability to help caregivers learn from medical incidents and improve patient safety and quality of care. Berenholtz and colleagues[20] found that structured assessment of information discussed during M&M conference using "a defect tool" developed by the investigators to analyze errors enhances learning by trainees. Fellows in surgical critical care at Johns Hopkins Hospital were required to complete a defect project during their fellowship. Defects were defined as any clinical or operational events that should not happen again. Fellows were asked to identify a defect, select a faculty mentor, and assemble an interdisciplinary team to complete the learning from a defect tool.[21] Fellows participated in monthly discussion to report on progress and receive feedback meant help them advance on the project. Berenholtz and colleagues[20] report that combining the defect tool with M&M conferences enhances learning because this allows "eliciting input from all staff involved in the incident, using a structured framework to investigate all underlying contributing factors, and assigning responsibility for management and follow-up on recommendations." The investigators noted that finding mentors with experience in systems-based practice and practice-based learning can be challenging. The authors believe that the shortage of mentors will improve because, since the 2006 publication by Pronovost and colleagues,[21] a variety of opportunities have become available for institutions to develop such expertise. For example, fellowship training focused on quality improvement and patient safety now is available in several institutions, faculty training is available at various academic institutions through degree and nondegree programs, and the Institute for Healthcare Improvement offers both concentrate in-person and online training through which individuals can acquire the necessary knowledge and tools.

The authors could not find patient outcome measures (ie, actual reduction in medical errors or an increase in patient safety) directly attributable either to the traditional M&M conference or the various revised M&M conferences discussed previously. However, the revised M&M conference has been shown to impact the culture of safety in a hospital. For example, Szekendi, and colleagues[22] evaluated their experience at Northwestern Memorial Hospital on the impact of a structured multidisciplinary M&M conference, which their hospital implemented in 2003. The investigators analyzed the results of their staff's responses on the Hospital Survey on Patient Safety Culture, developed by the Agency for Healthcare Research and Quality, which was administered in 2004, 2006, and 2008. They report that "significant improvements have been achieved in multiple domains, including 'hospital management support for patient safety,' 'feedback and communication about error,' and 'nonpunitive response to error.'" There remains a need for further investigation to determine the precise impact of M&M conferences on specific patient outcomes.

SUMMARY

The M&M conference is a well-recognized and long-standing tradition in medical practice. From its inception, this discussion has been an improvement tool for physician practice, meant to address and identify ways to reduce the recurrence of medical error. Involving other members of the health care team and including discussion of systems issues can make the M&M conference an effective means of affecting the quality and safety of patient care and patient care processes. A standardized, consistent approach to the case reviews enhances patient safety and quality improvement because it provides a means to understand factors contributing to an adverse event or near miss, to formulate a plan to improve, and to track the affect of change made in practice or process. Fostering forthright, nonjudgmental case discussion allows participants to overcome their fear of accusation and criticism and focus on improvement. A standard way of identifying potential system failures by participants, empowering workgroups to address specific systems-based problems, and regular follow-up can result in improved patient safety and care.

REFERENCES

1. Proceedings of Conference on Hospital Standardization. Joint Session of Committee on Standards. Bull Am Coll Surg 1917;3:1.
2. Flexner A. Medical education in the United States and Canada. From the Carnegie Foundation for the Advancement of Teaching, Bulletin Number Four, 1910. Bull World Health Organ 2002;80(7):594–602. Available at: http://www.ncbi.nlm.nih.gov/pmc/articles/PMC2567554/pdf/12163926.pdf. Accessed October 5, 2012.
3. Codman EA. A study in hospital efficiency. Boston: privately printed. Available at: http://www.jameslindlibrary.org/illustrating/records/a-study-in-hospital-efficiency/images.pdf. Accessed October 5, 2012.
4. Orlander JD. The morbidity and mortality conference: the delicate nature of learning from error. Acad Med 2002;77:1001–6.
5. Lempcke PA. Evolution of the medical audit. JAMA 1967;199(8):543–55.
6. Ruth HS. Anesthesia study commissions. JAMA 1945;127:514–7.
7. Ruth HS, Haugen FP, Grove DD. Anesthesia Study Commissions: findings of eleven years' activity. JAMA 1947;135(14):881–4.
8. Deis JN, Smith KM, Warren MD, et al. Transforming the morbidity and mortality conference into an instrument for system-wide improvement. In: Henriksen K, Battles JB, Keyes MA, et al, editors. Advances in patient safety: new directions and alternative approaches. Rockville (MD): Agency for Healthcare Research and Quality; 2008. Available at: http://www.ncbi.nlm.nih.gov/books/NBK43710/. Accessed October 5, 2012.
9. ACGME Program requirements for graduate medical education in surgery. Chicago: Accreditation Council for Graduate Medical Education; 2008. Available at: http://www.acgme.org/acWebsite/downloads/RRC_progReq/440_general_surgery_01012008_07012012.pdf. Accessed August 18, 2012.
10. Hamby LS. Using prospective outcomes data to improve morbidity and mortality conferences. Curr Surg 2000;57:384–8.
11. Pierluissi E, Fischer MA, Campbell AR, et al. Discussion of medical errors in morbidity and mortality conferences. JAMA 2003;290:2838–42.
12. Biddle C. Investigating the nature of the morbidity and mortality conference. Acad Med 1990;65:420.

13. ACGME general competencies and outcomes assessment for designated institutional officials. Available at: http://www.acgme.org/acWebsite/irc/irc_competencies.asp. Accessed August 17, 2012.
14. Harbison SP, Regehr G. Faculty and resident opinions regarding the role of morbidity and mortality conference. Am J Surg 1999;177:136–9.
15. Plsek PE, Onnias A. Cause-effect diagrams. Quality improvement tools. 2nd edition. Wilton (CT): Juran Institute, Inc; 1994.
16. Szostek JH, Wieland ML, Loertscher LL, et al. A systems approach to morbidity and mortality conference. Am J Med 2010;123(7):663–8.
17. Higginson J, Walters R, Fulop N. Mortality and morbidity meetings: an untapped resource for improving the governance of patient safety? BMJ Qual Saf 2012;21: 576–85.
18. Schwarz D, Schwarz R, Gauchan B, et al. Implementing a systems-oriented morbidity and mortality conference in remote rural Nepal for quality improvement. BMJ Qual Saf 2011;20(12):1082–8.
19. Aboumatar HJ, Blackledge CG, Dickson C, et al. A descriptive study of morbidity and mortality conferences and their conformity to medical incident analysis models: results of the Morbidity and Mortality Conference Improvement Study, phase 1. Am J Med Qual 2007;22:232–8.
20. Berenholtz SM, Hartsell TL, Pronovost PJ. Learning from defects to enhance morbidity and mortality conferences. Am J Med Qual 2009;24:192–5.
21. Pronovost PJ, Holzmueller CG, Martinez E, et al. A practical tool to learn from defects in patient care. Jt Comm J Qual Patient Saf 2006;32:102–8.
22. Szekendi MK, Barnard C, Creamer J, et al. Using patient safety morbidity and mortality conferences to promote transparency and a culture of safety. Jt Comm J Qual Patient Saf 2010;36(1):3–9.

Sleep Science, Schedules, and Safety in Hospitals

Challenges and Solutions for Pediatric Providers

Glenn Rosenbluth, MD[a],*, Christopher P. Landrigan, MD, MPH[b,c,d]

KEYWORDS

- Duty hours • Residents and fellows • Sleep science • Patient safety • Medical errors

KEY POINTS

- Sleep deprivation remains an important factor contributing to medical errors.
- Physicians working extended-duration shifts as well as excessive cumulative hours show a decline in cognitive performance and are more likely to commit medical errors.
- Schedule changes that do not reduce total cumulative hours have not consistently resulted in improvements in patient safety or patient care measures.
- Sleep science research can guide schedule interventions to improve patient care and safety.

INTRODUCTION

During the past decade, increased attention has been paid to the number of hours worked by medical trainees (ie, residents and fellows).[1,2] Before 2003, no regulations existed in the United States regarding the frequency, duration, or total number of hours that trainees could work. However, in response to early literature demonstrating the adverse effects of sleep deprivation on resident-physicians' ability to interpret medical tests,[3] in the 1970s to 1990s, many programs began reducing the frequency of in-house calls—extended shifts lasting between 24 and 40 hours—from every other night call (q2) to every third night (q3) or every fourth night (q4), with 8- to 12-hour day shifts occurring on the days between the extended shifts. As these changes were implemented, there were cries from many experienced physicians extolling the virtues

[a] Division of Hospital Medicine, Department of Pediatrics, UCSF Benioff Children's Hospital, University of California San Francisco School of Medicine, 505 Parnassus Avenue, Box 0110, San Francisco, CA 94143-0110, USA; [b] Division of General Pediatrics, Department of Medicine, Harvard Medical School, Children's Hospital Boston, Enders 1, 300 Longwood Avenue, Boston, MA 02115, USA; [c] Harvard Work Hours, Health, and Safety Group, Division of Sleep Medicine, Department of Medicine, Harvard Medical School, Brigham and Women's Hospital, 221 Longwood Avenue BLI 438, Boston, MA 02115, USA; [d] Division of Sleep Medicine, Harvard Medical School, 401 Park Drive, 2nd Floor East, Boston, MA 02215, USA
* Corresponding author.
E-mail address: rosenbluthg@peds.ucsf.edu

Pediatr Clin N Am 59 (2012) 1317–1328
http://dx.doi.org/10.1016/j.pcl.2012.09.001
0031-3955/12/$ – see front matter © 2012 Elsevier Inc. All rights reserved.

of long hours in the hospital. A commonly heard mantra was, "the only problem with q2 call is all of the cases you miss on your night off."

In the 1990s, based on the available evidence regarding the effects of fatigue on performance, European governments endorsed the European Working Time Directive, which currently restricts all workers, including health care trainees and experienced physicians, to a maximum of 13 consecutive hours and 48 total hours of work per week.[4] All time spent in the hospital by physicians counts toward this limit.

In the United States, some reductions in trainee work hours have followed, reflecting a greater understanding of sleep cycles and sleep health, with a particular focus on reducing medical errors due to sleep deprivation. Initial modest limits for all residents and fellows advanced by the Accreditation Council for Graduate Medical Education (ACGME) in 2003[5] were followed by a more substantive limiting of hours for interns (first-year residents), in particular in 2011.[2]

This article reviews the impact of sleep on overall performance, discusses the context and progress of duty hours regulations as an approach to decreasing fatigue, reviews associations of duty hour changes with medical errors, and provides recommendations for optimizing duty hours in health care settings.

SLEEP SCIENCE AND PERFORMANCE

Human beings, including physicians, are biologically wired to have sleep–wake cycles that correspond to day and night. Circadian rhythms, which are controlled by an endogenous pacemaker in the hypothalamus, drive alertness during the day and sleepiness during the night.[6] The rhythms can respond to external influences to reflect changing external schedules (eg, traveling across time zones), but such adjustments take days to weeks depending on the degree of change required.

Independent of the impairments in performance that are induced by working at night (when the circadian system is promoting sleep), sleep deprivation also can impair performance.[7] Sleep deprivation is known to impair many aspects of human functioning, including many that are essential to the practice of medicine (eg, cognitive performance, memory, and fine motor skills). Meta-analysis has shown that clinical performance and vigilance are particularly impaired by sleep deprivation.[8] The impairment of cognitive functioning has been compared to alcohol intoxication, and research has shown that the cognitive performance decline after 17 hours of wakefulness mirrors a blood alcohol concentration (BAC) of approximately 0.05%.[9]

Chronic low levels of sleep deprivation also impair performance. After 2 weeks of getting only 6 hours of sleep, psychomotor performance impairments are equivalent to those seen in subjects who are awake for 24 hours continuously.[10] Recent research has demonstrated that when chronic sleep deprivation compounds acute sleep deprivation and circadian misalignment, performance is far worse than that which is induced by any of these 3 factors alone (**Fig. 1**).[11]

As a consequence of each of these factors, shift work, even of limited duration, affects sleep. A shift worker is defined as "anyone who works extended-duration shifts and other variable and nonstandard hours, including workers who work late into the night or start working very early in the morning."[12] Using this definition, virtually all trainees in all fields of medicine will be considered shift workers for some part of their careers. Shift work leads to circadian misalignment and decreased sleep. When an individual remains awake for more than 24 hours continuously, acute sleep deprivation compounds the sensation of "jet lag" caused by working at an adverse circadian phase. In addition, sleep the following day is often limited and of poor quality, as the circadian system promotes wakefulness by day.[13]

Length of time on sleep-wake schedule (weeks)

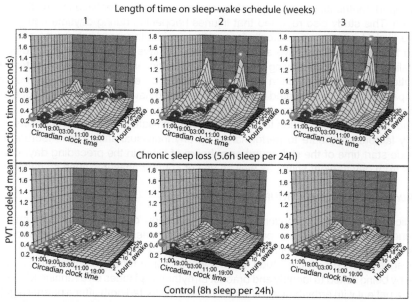

Fig. 1. Chronic sleep loss during 3 weeks (*upper panel*) progressively degrades reaction time, particularly during periods of circadian misalignment and acute sleep deprivation, compared with chronically well-rested subjects (*lower panel*). (*From* Cohen DA, Wang W, Wyatt JK, et al. Uncovering residual effects of chronic sleep loss on human performance. Sci Transl Med 2010;2(14):14ra13; with permission.)

It is also important to recognize that shift work is dangerous to the individual who is working, with multiple studies reporting that shift work may contribute to health problems, including increasing the risk of motor vehicle crashes,[14] obesity, cardiovascular disease, and cancer.[12] Based on the strength of this evidence, the International Agency for Research on Cancer concluded that shift work is "probably carcinogenic" to humans.[15]

SLEEP DEPRIVATION AND PHYSICIAN PERFORMANCE

Physicians are in no way immune to the performance effects of sleep deprivation. In a study of pediatric residents, researchers evaluated task performance in residents at the end of a month of light call (4-week daytime clinic rotations averaging 44 hours per week, with limited night work) compared with residents at the end of a month of heavy call (intensive care unit [ICU] rotations with q4-q5 call, averaging 80 to 90 hours per week).[16] Residents on the light call rotation were also tested with alcohol ingestion to a level of 0.04% to 0.05% BAC, for comparison with residents on heavy call who were alcohol-free. Measurements included reaction time, lapses, omission errors, as well as off-road events in a driving simulator. These psychomotor tasks are similar to tasks that a trainee might be expected to engage in as part of daily patient care or returning home after completing patient care. Overall, performance was comparable between the group on the heavy call month with placebo and the light call month with alcohol intoxication.

Physicians who are fatigued are at a higher risk for on-the-job accidental injuries as well. Percutaneous injuries (eg, needle-stick lacerations), although overall rare, are twice as common during nighttime hours compared with daytime.[17] When asked to self-report contributing factors, physicians most commonly identified fatigue and inattention. This study also reported that injuries happening during daytime hours were more likely to occur on postcall days, when residents were likely to be suffering from fatigue. Residents have also been shown to have a higher risk of nodding off or falling asleep while driving or stopping in traffic as the number of extended-duration shifts increases each month.[14] As would be expected based on the data comparing them to intoxicated residents,[16] they also have an increased risk of motor vehicle accidents following extended-duration shifts.

There is limited information to guide the maximum safe duration of work shifts, and many factors contribute to performance on any individual shift. These factors may include start time of the shift, number of hours of sleep in the preceding day, transitions from day to night shifts, as well as use of countermeasures such as caffeine.

EARLY STUDIES OF DUTY HOURS AND ERRORS

Medical errors affecting patients are more common during months with multiple extended-duration shifts, compared with those with none.[18] The first study associating fatigue with poor performance by medical trainees was done by Friedman and colleagues[3] in 1971. In this study, interns were given a modified sustained attention task by being asked to identify and bracket arrhythmic episodes on a running EKG strip from a patient with arrhythmias. All subjects were evaluated both after a normal night of sleep (mean 7.0 hours sleep) and after completing a 24-hour shift (mean 1.8 hours sleep). The subjects made almost twice as many errors after the prolonged shifts.

Subsequent studies have likewise found that residents working 24 hours or more are more prone to errors across a range of neurocognitive and clinical tasks. A meta-analysis of 60 such studies found that resident performance across a range of clinical tasks dropped nearly 2 standard deviations below baseline rested performance following 24 hours of acute sleep deprivation (**Fig. 2**).[8]

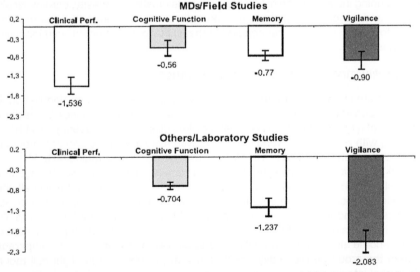

Fig. 2. Effect of short-term sleep loss on performance by type of subject and type of study. The graph shows average effect size corrected for measurement error and standard error of the corrected effect sizes. (*From* Philibert I. Sleep loss and performance in residents and nonphysicians: a meta-analytic examination. Sleep 2005;28(11):1397; with permission.)

In an early intervention study from 1991, patients cared for by internal medicine residents working on a shift schedule showed improvement in length of stay and decreased likelihood of a medication error after work hour reduction.[19]

2003 ACGME GUIDELINES

Before 2003, there were no national limits in the United States on resident duty hours. In the face of mounting public pressure and accumulating evidence regarding the hazards of long work hours, the ACGME released duty hours requirements[5] in 2003, which applied to all accredited training programs. These requirements had 4 major components: (1) duty hours were limited to 80 hours per week, averaged over a 4-week period (inclusive of all in-house call activities); (2) 1 day in 7 must be free from all educational and clinical responsibilities, averaged over a 4-week period, inclusive of call; (3) a 10-hour rest period was required between all daily duty periods and after in-house call; and (4) extended-duration shifts were limited to a maximum of 30 hours of continuous on-site duties. The 30-hour shift was further subdivided as follows: after the first 24 hours, no new patients could be evaluated and treated by the trainee; the final 6 hours were for continuing care of current patients as well as handoffs of care.

STUDIES OF THE 2003 DUTY HOUR STANDARDS

Most studies evaluating the effects of the 2003 standards as a whole have found that they resulted in little if any change in patient-related outcomes. Three large retrospective national cohort studies found that in teaching hospitals as compared with nonteaching hospitals, mortality remained unchanged for surgical patients and minimally improved or unchanged for medical patients.[20–22] One large study[23] examined changes after the elimination of extended-duration shifts for residents, with additional coverage provided by nocturnists (hospital-based attending physicians who primarily provide care at night). The investigators reported improvement in some patient care measures but no improvement in readmission rates, adverse medication interactions, and mortality. The study did not report a decrease in total resident hours, noting only that all residents were within the 80-hour limits.

Other studies have shown improved compliance with guidelines for quality prescribing of discharge medications, reduced mean length of stay and decreased 6-month mortality,[24] and improved perceived quality of care by nurses and patients[25] after transitioning to ACGME-compliant schedules.

One reason for the limited effectiveness of the ACGME's 2003 standards is that in most programs, they led to modest reductions in actual work hours or improvements in sleep, as most programs were at baseline not far from the ACGME's new requirements. Nationwide, work hours decreased by only 5% to 6% after implementation of the standards, and sleep improved only 22 minutes per night[26]; in a tricenter pediatric study, work and sleep hours did not improve at all.[27]

INTERVENTION STUDIES: ELIMINATING SHIFTS EXCEEDING 16 HOURS

In contrast to the studies on the effects of the ACGME's limits, studies evaluating the effects of interventions that went beyond the ACGME's requirements and eliminated shifts exceeding 16 hours have basically shown that patient safety and quality of care improved.

A prospective, randomized, controlled trial[28] examined the rates of medical errors by interns working in ICU settings and compared interns working a standard q3 schedule with 30-hour call shifts to those working an intervention schedule, which limited shift length to a maximum of 16 hours and reduced the total number of hours worked per week from 77 to 81 down to 60 to 63. Medical errors were detected by trained physician observers, voluntary reporting, chart review, and computerized event-detection monitor.

In this study, the interns working the traditional schedule made 36% more medical errors than those on the intervention schedule (136 vs 100 per 1000 patient-days, P<.001). They made 28% more errors that were intercepted before reaching the patients (70 vs 55 per 1000 patient-days, P = .02) and 57% more nonintercepted errors (errors that reached the patients) (45 vs 29 per 1000 patient-days, P<.001). The rates of serious medical errors in which interns were not involved revealed no significant differences between the groups. Medication errors were the most common type of serious medical errors noted when comparing both resident groups (129 per 1000 patient-days vs 75 in the intervention group, P = .03). However, it was the diagnostic errors that showed the greatest relative difference between the traditional and intervention groups (19 vs 3.3 per 1000 patient-days, P<.001).

A series of single-center cohort studies have likewise demonstrated improvements in patient safety measures after elimination or reduction of shifts more than 16 hours.[19,23,29,30] Overall, in a systematic review of the literature, Levine and colleagues[31] found that 7 of 11 studies that evaluated the effects of reducing or eliminating shifts more than 16 hours on patient safety or quality of care found statistically significant improvements; the remaining 4 showed no change, with no studies showing decreases in quality or safety. Of 7 studies that eliminated (as opposed to reduced) shifts exceeding 16 hours, 6 showed statistically significant improvements in safety or quality of care.

US DATA REGARDING THE HAZARDS OF EXTENDED SHIFTS

The Harvard Work Hours Health and Safety Group's national resident cohort study has identified strong links between residents' extended shifts and risks to their own safety and that of their patients. Using a Web-based survey of first-year residents (n = 2737), Barger and colleagues[18] noted that the rate of self-reported medical errors increased with increasing frequency of extended-duration shifts. There was at least one medical error at baseline in 3.8% of months with no extended-duration shifts. A dose escalation was seen, with at least one medical error in 9.8% of the months with 1 to 4 extended-duration shifts, and in 16% of the months with 5 or more extended-duration shifts.

Taken a step further to look at patient harms resulting from these errors, the trend persists. Preventable adverse outcomes had an increased odds ratio of 8.7 (95% CI, 3.4–22) during months with 1 to 4 extended-duration shifts and 7.0 (95% CI, 3.4–11) during months with greater than 5 extended-duration shifts. Significant medical errors that were not self-reported as fatigue-related were also more common in the months with the most extended-duration shifts. In this study, rates of inattention were also strongly associated with the number of extended-duration shifts worked. The rate of falling asleep during a surgery was 7.3% during months with greater than 5 extended-duration shifts, and the frequency of falling asleep during rounds with the attending physician were as high at 15% during these months.

A standard q4 rotation would include 7 to 8 extended-duration shifts, and a q3 call month could include as many as 10 extended-duration shifts. Therefore, the potential for medical errors, preventable adverse outcomes, and general inattention resulting in other provider-level and patient-level complications may be even higher than those reported in this study. This research provided the most substantial contributions to the mounting evidence of the benefits of eliminating extended-duration shifts and decreasing total work hours.

REDUCTIONS IN FREQUENCY OF CALL ARE NOT SUFFICIENT

Studies that simply reduced the frequency of call (while maintaining extended-duration call shifts) have not shown significant impacts on patient safety or quality measures. One retrospective study[32] measured complication rates and mortality rates at a single level 1 trauma center (as defined by the American College of Surgeons, "provides comprehensive service") with more than 11,000 patients. They decreased the call frequency from once every 4.8 days to once every 6.4 days (averaged) and found no change in the outcomes. This call frequency is less frequent than commonly used. Other studies on decreased frequency of extended-duration call also did not document changes in complications,[33] mortality rates,[33] or the number of errors made.[34] One study was identified in which a decrease in the total number of call shifts was associated with a decrease in mortality for trauma and emergency surgical patients.[29] This study, like the others, was a before-and-after intervention study, with limited ability to control for other factors. All the above-mentioned studies included extended-duration shifts of up to 30 hours in their intervention groups.

Schedule adaptations have variable impacts, and can lead to unexpected and unintended outcomes. At least one study[35] found a longer length of stay for patients after implementing a short call system. The term "short call" may actually be a misnomer. Short call generally refers to a shift that may be 4 to 6 hours longer than a traditional duty hour shift but is not an overnight in-house call. This common scheduling adjustment after the 2003 duty hours has not been shown to be safer for patients.

CHANGING PERCEPTIONS AND CULTURE

Perceptions within the medical community regarding sleep deprivation and its effects on performance have evolved as the science has evolved. Self-awareness is common among residents, perhaps because of the increased education mandated by the ACGME. In one recent study[36] of residents' experiences with and perceptions of adverse events, medical errors, and causation, the investigators reported that residents in programs with overall reduced hours were significantly less likely to report work situations, including "working too many hours," as a potential cause of preventable adverse events and medical errors. An increasing percentage of pediatric residents in particular now support duty hour limits, and a minority would even be willing to extend residency in order to reduce weekly work hours.[37]

INSTITUTE OF MEDICINE AND ACGME

In 2009, the US Congress and the Agency for Healthcare Research and Quality called upon the Institute of Medicine (IOM) to evaluate ways in which the residency work environment might be redesigned to enhance patient safety. The IOM appointed the Committee on Optimizing Graduate Medical Trainee (Resident) Hours and Work Schedules to Improve Patient Safety. This committee reviewed the extensive and growing body of evidence related to residents' work schedules, sleep deprivation, performance degradation, and medical errors in the context of the educational training environment. Among the many recommendations in the final report[1] were a limit of 16 hours continuous in-house duty unless protected time was provided for a 5-hour nap, a limit of 4 consecutive night shifts, and increased requirements for time off (10 hours off after a regular daytime duty period, 12 hours off after night duty, 14 hours off after an extended duty period and not return earlier than 6 AM the next day).

The ACGME responded to the IOM report by instituting additional limitations on duty hours, which became effective July 2011.[2] The ACGME applied the 16-hour shift limitation only to first-year trainees, and more senior trainees were limited to 28 hours. They added an option for extending these shifts for those directly involved in the care of a single patient. Consecutive night shifts were limited to a maximum of 6 rather than 4. Rest periods were shortened to a minimum of 8 hours after a standard shift (with a recommendation that they be not less than 10 hours) but increased to 14 hours minimum after a 24-hour shift. In addition, there was a provision that upper-level residents could have breaks shorter than 8 hours to participate in patient care.

PRACTICAL APPROACHES TO OPTIMIZING SHIFT SCHEDULES

In the face of the new guidelines, residency and fellowship programs have been challenged to make adjustments to their residents' schedules. Work schedules may be assigned for a variety of reasons ranging from individual preferences for clustering versus spreading out shifts, minimum staffing needs, and maximizing the number of hours an individual can work under specific guidelines. Sleep science can provide a great deal of guidance on optimizing shift schedules to decrease the likelihood of fatigue while caring for patients.

In considering the effects of residents' work schedules on performance, it is important to consider the effects of acute and chronic sleep deprivation and circadian misalignment. Often, only residents' 24- or 30-hour shifts are considered when thinking about resident sleep deprivation and performance. In reality, the decreased nightly sleep that may come with the standard 12- to 16-hour workdays and circadian factors compound the impairment due to extended shifts. Pragmatic hospital coverage issues also come into play; particularly of concern is the fact that the nadir of performance occurs between 3 AM and 6 AM. These hours correspond to times when physicians are likely to be covering larger-than-usual caseloads due to cross-coverage and also less likely to have direct supervision immediately available.

A common recommendation is to avoid consecutive nights on duty because most individuals cannot get adequate sleep between night shifts to make up the sleep debt,[38] and therefore they become chronically sleep deprived. Although some trainees may believe that working more consecutive nights enables them to function more effectively, data from other shift workers[13] suggest that after a night shift workers generally do not get adequate sleep during the day so the sleep debt grows in the short term. Having a full 24-hour period off after working a night shift can be extremely important. Night shift workers should also be strongly encouraged to take a strategic nap before starting their first night shift.[38] If this is not done, the first night shift is likely to result in at least 24 hours of continuous wakefulness.

With appropriate shift schedule design and planning, residents can increase their sleep before working shifts.[39] In a study comparing a group of interns working a shift schedule designed based on sleep science (intervention) with a group working a standard call schedule (control), those in the intervention group slept significantly more (45.9 vs 51.7 hours per week, $P<.001$) and had increased sleep before starting a night shift.[40] Thirty-one percent of work hours were preceded by 4 or fewer hours of sleep in the preceding 24 hours during the control schedule, as compared with 13% during the intervention schedule. Attention failures were also measured in this study using continuous electrooculography to detect slow eye movements correlated with polysomnography. These failures were significantly less common among interns working the intervention schedule as compared with the traditional schedule (**Fig. 3**).

A recent study also showed that among pediatric residents in a ward setting, eliminating extended shifts led to a greatly reduced percentage of work hours that were preceded by no or limited sleep.[41]

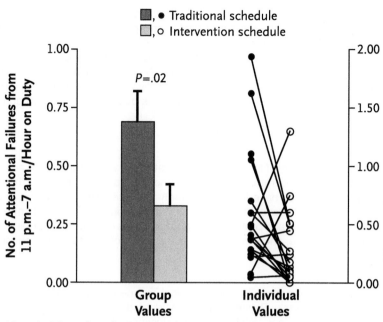

Fig. 3. Mean (+SE) number of attentional failures among the 20 interns as a group and individually while working overnight (11 PM to 7 AM) during the Traditional Schedule and the Intervention Schedule. (*From* Lockley SW, Cronin JW, Evans EE, et al. Effect of reducing interns' weekly work hours on sleep and attentional failures. N Engl J Med 2004;351(18):1835; with permission.)

The precise design of new work schedules, however, is critical to their success. A recent study of pediatrics residents who transitioned from a q4 call system with extended-duration shifts (maximum 30 hours) to a schedule with primarily day and night teams, although including one extended-duration shift of 27 to 28 hours,[42] found that sleep did not improve. In this study, residents working the shift schedule worked approximately 1.5 fewer hours each day. However, rather than sleeping more, mean nightly sleep time (self-reported) decreased by approximately 2 hours, which may have been the result of decreased nighttime coverage on the new schedule as well as the fact that the string of night shifts was preceded by a shift of more than 24 hours. This study demonstrates that schedule changes do not always result in their intended outcomes, and careful planning of schedules is essential to achieve the goals of improved sleep for the provider and as a result improved patient safety. If insufficient personnel are available to keep workloads appropriate as work hour interventions are implemented, the risk of a failed intervention is high.

SHIFT WORK AND HANDOFFS

As shift work becomes more prevalent, increased attention is being paid to handoffs. In a study by Jagsi and colleagues,[36] residents attributed a large proportion of medical errors to poor handoffs. Across all groups, between 58% and 65% of residents reported that poor handoffs contributed "to a great extent" or "to some extent" to errors in patient care. There was no change in this before or after the implementation of the 2003 guidelines, although the frequency of handoffs is likely to have increased.

The I-PASS (IIPE-PRIS Accelerating Safe Sign-outs) study[43] is a large multicenter project designed to study the impact of implementing a resident handoff bundle on resident work flow, experience, and rates of medical errors. The multiinstitutional design will create opportunities to investigate how shift work may affect rates of medical errors while working under the 2011 ACGME requirements. Such studies of handoff and teamwork interventions become critically important as shifts are reduced nationwide and coordination of day and night teams becomes essential to quality of care around the clock.

SUMMARY

In sum, a compelling body of literature demonstrates that sleep deprivation adversely affects health care provider (resident) performance and patient safety. Furthermore, initial intervention studies have found that safety improves with elimination of shifts greater than 16 hours. However, designing new schedules in such a way as to maximize sleep, optimize handoffs, and protect medical education is complex and requires careful planning, persistence, and investment of sufficient resources to ensure success.

REFERENCES

1. Committee on Optimizing Graduate Medical Trainee (Resident) Hours and Work Schedules to Improve Patient Safety. Resident duty hours: enhancing sleep, supervision, and safety. Washington, DC: Institute of Medicine of the National Academies; 2009.
2. Accreditation Council for Graduate Medical Education. Common program requirements. 2011. Available at: http://www.acgme.org/acWebsite/dutyHours/dh_dutyhoursCommonPR07012007.pdf. Accessed November 28, 2011.
3. Friedman RC, Bigger JT, Kornfeld DS. The intern and sleep loss. N Engl J Med 1971;285(4):201–3.
4. British Medical Association. Time's Up. A guide on the EWTD for junior doctors. London: BMA publications unit; 2005.
5. Accreditation Council for Graduate Medical Education. Statement of justification/impact for the final approval of common standards related to resident duty hours. 2002. Available at: http://www.acgme.org/acWebsite/dutyHours/dh_impactStatement.pdf. Accessed April 20, 2011.
6. Czeisler CA, Weitzman E, Moore-Ede MC, et al. Human sleep: its duration and organization depend on its circadian phase. Science 1980;210(4475):1264–7.
7. Koslowsky M, Babkoff H. Meta-analysis of the relationship between total sleep deprivation and performance. Chronobiol Int 1992;9(2):132–6.
8. Philibert I. Sleep loss and performance in residents and nonphysicians: a meta-analytic examination. Sleep 2005;28(11):1392–402.
9. Dawson D, Reid K. Fatigue, alcohol and performance impairment. Nature 1997; 388(6639):235.
10. Van Dongen HP, Maislin G, Mullington JM, et al. The cumulative cost of additional wakefulness: dose-response effects on neurobehavioral functions and sleep physiology from chronic sleep restriction and total sleep deprivation. Sleep 2003;26(2):117–26.
11. Cohen DA, Wang W, Wyatt JK, et al. Uncovering residual effects of chronic sleep loss on human performance. Sci Transl Med 2010;2(14):14ra13.
12. Barger LK, Lockley SW, Rajaratnam SM, et al. Neurobehavioral, health, and safety consequences associated with shift work in safety-sensitive professions. Curr Neurol Neurosci Rep 2009;9(2):155–64.

13. Vidacek S, Kaliterna L, Radosevic-Vidacek B, et al. Productivity on a weekly rotating shift system: circadian adjustment and sleep deprivation effects? Ergonomics 1986;29(12):1583–90.
14. Barger LK, Cade BE, Ayas NT, et al. Extended work shifts and the risk of motor vehicle crashes among interns. N Engl J Med 2005;352(2):125–34.
15. International Agency for Research on Cancer. IARC monographs programme finds cancer hazards associated with shiftwork, painting and firefighting. 2007. Available at: http://www.iarc.fr/en/media-centre/pr/2007/pr180.html. Accessed July 31, 2012.
16. Arnedt JT, Owens J, Crouch M, et al. Neurobehavioral performance of residents after heavy night call vs after alcohol ingestion. JAMA 2005;294(9):1025–33.
17. Ayas NT, Barger LK, Cade BE, et al. Extended work duration and the risk of self-reported percutaneous injuries in interns. JAMA 2006;296(9):1055–62.
18. Barger LK, Ayas NT, Cade BE, et al. Impact of extended-duration shifts on medical errors, adverse events, and attentional failures. PLoS Med 2006;3(12):e487.
19. Gottlieb DJ, Parenti CM, Peterson CA, et al. Effect of a change in house staff work schedule on resource utilization and patient care. Arch Intern Med 1991;151(10):2065–70.
20. Volpp KG, Rosen AK, Rosenbaum PR, et al. Mortality among patients in VA hospitals in the first 2 years following ACGME resident duty hour reform. JAMA 2007;298(9):984–92.
21. Volpp KG, Rosen AK, Rosenbaum PR, et al. Mortality among hospitalized Medicare beneficiaries in the first 2 years following ACGME resident duty hour reform. JAMA 2007;298(9):975–83.
22. Shetty KD, Bhattacharya J. Changes in hospital mortality associated with residency work-hour regulations. Ann Intern Med 2007;147(2):73–80.
23. Horwitz LI, Kosiborod M, Lin Z, et al. Changes in outcomes for internal medicine inpatients after work-hour regulations. Ann Intern Med 2007;147(2):97–103.
24. Bhavsar J, Montgomery D, Li J, et al. Impact of duty hours restrictions on quality of care and clinical outcomes. Am J Med 2007;120(11):968–74.
25. Goldstein MJ, Kim E, Widmann WD, et al. A 360 degrees evaluation of a night-float system for general surgery: a response to mandated work-hours reduction. Curr Surg 2004;61(5):445–51.
26. Landrigan CP, Barger LK, Cade BE, et al. Interns' compliance with Accreditation Council for Graduate Medical Education work-hour limits. JAMA 2006;296(9):1063–70.
27. Landrigan CP, Fahrenkopf AM, Lewin D, et al. Effects of the Accreditation Council for Graduate Medical Education duty hour limits on sleep, work hours, and safety. Pediatrics 2008;122(2):250–8.
28. Landrigan CP, Rothschild JM, Cronin JW, et al. Effect of reducing interns' work hours on serious medical errors in intensive care units. N Engl J Med 2004;351(18):1838–48.
29. Malangoni MA, Como JJ, Mancuso C, et al. Life after 80 hours: the impact of resident work hours mandates on trauma and emergency experience and work effort for senior residents and faculty. J Trauma 2005;58(4):758–61 [discussion: 761–2].
30. Mann FA, Danz PL. The night stalker effect: quality improvements with a dedicated night-call rotation. Invest Radiol 1993;28(1):92–6.
31. Levine AC, Adusumilli J, Landrigan CP. Effects of reducing or eliminating resident work shifts over 16 hours: a systematic review. Sleep 2010;33(8):1043–53.
32. de Virgilio C, Yaghoubian A, Lewis RJ, et al. The 80-hour resident workweek does not adversely affect patient outcomes or resident education. Curr Surg 2006;63(6):435–9 [discussion: 440].

33. Hutter MM, Kellogg KC, Ferguson CM, et al. The impact of the 80-hour resident workweek on surgical residents and attending surgeons. Ann Surg 2006;243(6): 864–71 [discussion: 871–5].

34. Sawyer RG, Tribble CG, Newberg DS, et al. Intern call schedules and their relationship to sleep, operating room participation, stress, and satisfaction. Surgery 1999;126(2):337–42.

35. Schuberth JL, Elasy TA, Butler J, et al. Effect of short call admission on length of stay and quality of care for acute decompensated heart failure. Circulation 2008; 117(20):2637–44.

36. Jagsi R, Weinstein DF, Shapiro J, et al. The Accreditation Council for Graduate Medical Education's limits on residents' work hours and patient safety. A study of resident experiences and perceptions before and after hours reductions. Arch Intern Med 2008;168(5):493–500.

37. Gordon MB, Sectish TC, Elliott MN, et al. Pediatric residents' perspectives on reducing work hours and lengthening residency: a national survey. Pediatrics 2012;130(1):99–107.

38. Landrigan CP, Czeisler CA, Barger LK, et al. Effective implementation of work-hour limits and systemic improvements. Jt Comm J Qual Patient Saf 2007; 33(Suppl 11):19–29.

39. Lockley SW, Barger LK, Ayas NT, et al. Effects of health care provider work hours and sleep deprivation on safety and performance. Jt Comm J Qual Patient Saf 2007;33(Suppl 11):7–18.

40. Lockley SW, Cronin JW, Evans EE, et al. Effect of reducing interns' weekly work hours on sleep and attentional failures. N Engl J Med 2004;351(18):1829–37.

41. Auger KA, Landrigan CP, Gonzalez Del Rey JA, et al. Better rested, but more stressed? Evidence of the effects of resident work hour restrictions. Acad Pediatr 2012;12(4):335–43.

42. Chua KP, Gordon MB, Sectish T, et al. Effects of a night-team system on resident sleep and work hours. Pediatrics 2011;128(6):1142–7.

43. Sectish TC, Starmer AJ, Landrigan CP, et al. Establishing a multisite education and research project requires leadership, expertise, collaboration, and an important aim. Pediatrics 2010;126(4):619–22.

The Emerging Role of Simulation Education to Achieve Patient Safety
Translating Deliberate Practice and Debriefing to Save Lives

Sharon Griswold, MD, MPH[a], Srikala Ponnuru, MD[a],
Akira Nishisaki, MD, MSCE[b,c], Demian Szyld, MD[d],
Moira Davenport, MD[e], Ellen S. Deutsch, MD[b],
Vinay Nadkarni, MD, MS[b,c,*]

KEYWORDS

- Patient safety • Simulation • Deliberate practice • Competence
- Operational performance • Patient outcomes

KEY POINTS

- The time-honored apprenticeship model may not be the most optimal and effective way to train clinicians.
- There is now good evidence that simulation training improves individual and team performance, specifically self-confidence, knowledge, and operational performance on manikins.
- Emerging evidence supports that deliberate practice, procedural simulation, and debriefing can improve operational performance in clinical settings and can result in safer patient and population/system outcomes in selected settings.
- Ultimately, a few studies suggest that this improvement can translate into safer and more efficient care for patients, providers, and systems.

Drs Griswold-Theodorson, Ponnuru, Davenport, Deutsch, and Szyld have no potential conflicts of interest to disclose. Dr Nishisaki receives funding from the AHRQ RO3-1HS021583-01 grant: Evaluating safety and quality of tracheal intubation in pediatric ICUs and the Center of Excellence Grant (PI-Nadkarni), Laerdal Foundation for Acute Care Medicine (nonprofit), Science of Simulation Education, Implementation, and Dissemination. Dr Nadkarni receives funding from, or participates in, the following studies: NIH/NHLBI, 1U01HL094345-01 (PI-Moler), THAPCA Trials—Therapeutic Hypothermia After Pediatric Cardiac Arrest; NIH/NHLBI, 1UO1 (co-PI Agus, co-PI Nadkarni), HALF-PINT Trials: Heart and Lung Failure – Pediatric Insulin Titration Trial; Canadian Institute of Health Research, CIHR 2009-09-15 (PI-Parshuram); The Bedside Pediatric Early Warning System (BPEWS); NIH/NINDS, 5R01HL058669-10 (PI-Pastuszko), Brain Metabolism and Neuroprotection in Cardiopulmonary Bypass; Center of Excellence Grant (PI-Hunt), Laerdal Foundation for Acute Care Medicine (nonprofit); EXPRESS collaborative; Corporate Sponsor Agreement (PI-Nadkarni), Laerdal Medical Corporation, Quantitative Measurement of CPR

INTRODUCTION

More than 12 years have elapsed since the Institute of Medicine published its report, "To Err Is Human," which raised public awareness and called attention to the need for safer health care practice, including improving teamwork and using simulation training.[1] Simulation mirrors or amplifies real clinical situations with guided participatory experiences.[2,3] Simulation training can improve patient safety through a variety of mechanisms, including but not limited to (1) routine training for emergencies, (2) training for teamwork, (3) establishing an environment for discussing error without punishment, (4) testing new procedures for safety, (5) evaluating competence, (6) testing device usability, (7) investigating human performance, and (8) providing skills training outside of the production environment.[4] In 2007, we reviewed existing literature and found evidence to support the premise that simulation-based training improved provider confidence, knowledge, team performance, and process of care in a simulated setting (eg, *simulated settings, T_1*).[5] Simulation-based training encourages errors that occur during the early learning phase of both procedural and nontechnical skills to be resolved in the laboratory rather than on real patients. Simulation-based training provides learners a psychologically safe learning environment without the fear of harming real patients. However, in 2007, there was little proof that simulation interventions actually improved real patient or population safety outcomes (eg, *real patient T_2, or population*

during In-Hospital Pediatric Cardiac Arrest; Center of Excellence Grant (PI-Nadkarni), Laerdal Foundation for Acute Care Medicine (nonprofit), Science of Simulation Education, Implementation, and Dissemination; AHA Innovation Grant (PI-Vetter); American Heart Association ECC Innovation Grant; Student Program for Olympic Resuscitation Training in schools (SPORTS).

Author Contributions: Dr Griswold-Theodorson had access to and takes responsibility for the integrity of the data and the accuracy of the data analysis. Dr Griswold-Theodorson contributed to study conception and design, data collection, analysis and interpretation of the data, drafting of the manuscript, and critical revision of the article for important intellectual content. Dr Ponnuru contributed to study design, data collection, data analysis and interpretation, reviewing and editing of the manuscript, and critical revision of the article for important intellectual content. Dr Davenport contributed to study design, data collection and analysis, and review and editing of the manuscript. Dr Szyld contributed to study design, data collection, data analysis and interpretation, reviewing, editing, and section writing of the manuscript. Dr Deutsch contributed to review and editing of the manuscript and critical revision of the article for important intellectual content. Dr Nishisaki contributed to study design, data collection and data interpretation, reviewing, editing, and section writing of the manuscript. Dr Nadkarni contributed to study design, data collection, interpretation of the data, and reviewing and editing of the manuscript and critical revision of the article for important intellectual content.

[a] Department of Emergency Medicine, Simulation Center, Drexel University College of Medicine, 245 North 15th Street, Philadelphia, PA 19102, USA; [b] Department of Anesthesia and Critical Care Medicine, The Center for Simulation, Advanced Education and Innovation, The Children's Hospital of Philadelphia, 3400 Civic Center Boulevard, Philadelphia, PA 19104, USA; [c] Division of Pediatric Critical Care, Department of Anesthesiology, Critical Care, and Pediatrics, The Children's Hospital of Philadelphia, University of Pennsylvania Perelman School of Medicine, 3400 Civic Center Boulevard, Philadelphia, PA 19104, USA; [d] Department of Emergency Medicine, New York Simulation Center for the Health Sciences, New York University School of Medicine, Floor 3, Room cd375, Bellevue C&D Building, New York, NY 10016, USA; [e] Department of Emergency Medicine, Allegheny General Hospital, 320 East North Avenue, Pittsburgh, PA 15212, USA

* Corresponding author. Pediatric Critical Care Medicine, Department of Anesthesia, Critical Care and Pediatrics, The Children's Hospital of Philadelphia, University of Pennsylvania Perelman School of Medicine, 3400 Civic Center Boulevard, Philadelphia, PA 19104.
E-mail address: Nadkarni@email.chop.edu

outcomes T_3).[5] Since 2007, there has been rapid escalation of research that substantiates the concept that simulation-based deliberate practice and debriefing does improve provider knowledge, skill acquisition and retention, and patient safety in the clinical domain.[6–16] Several studies in the pediatric and maternal–fetal medicine literature demonstrate beneficial clinical outcomes for clinical interventions (technical skills) or nontechnical skills such as teamwork. This article highlights recent pediatric literature that establishes the selected circumstances in which simulation-based efforts have been demonstrated to translate into improved patient outcomes and patient safety in the clinical environment.

TRANSLATING DELIBERATE PRACTICE AND DEBRIEFING TO SAVE LIVES

Park[17] and McGaghie[18] proposed a nomenclature for describing the translational impact of simulation studies as they progress from the simulation laboratory to patient and population outcomes (**Table 1**). At the T_1 research level, studies are conducted to evaluate educational outcomes assessed solely in the *simulation laboratory*. The goal of T_2 simulation research is to evaluate the transfer of a skill from the laboratory to *clinical performance* outcomes. T_3 studies demonstrate that practice via simulation can indeed improve clinical outcomes and *patient safety*. The results of T_3 simulation research can be used to show an improvement in the overall health of a *population or system* and ultimately influence how safe health care is delivered. T_{value} simulation research demonstrates the association of simulation interventions to achieve safer and more efficient care that benefits patients, providers, and systems (eg, *return on investment, T_{value}*). **Table 2** summarizes several key pediatric simulation-based medical education studies that demonstrate the translation of simulation to achieve T_2, T_3, and T_{value} outcomes.

A series of studies conducted by Draycott and colleagues[19–21] demonstrate the translation of simulation-based educational interventions from laboratory (T_1) to patient process of care (T_2), system/population outcome improvements, and decreased liability (T_3, T_{value}). The initial T_1 study demonstrated improvement in obstetric providers' management of simulated shoulder dystocia cases and retention of these skills in simulated scenarios at 6 and 12 months. Next, their T_2 study showed that providers trained using these simulation scenarios were more likely to successfully deliver the baby's posterior arm, perform an internal rotation maneuver, or provide appropriate suprapubic pressure in real patients at risk for shoulder dystocia.[22]

Table 1 Classification of simulation-based education outcomes		
Simulation Education Impact on T_1, T_2, T_3, T_{value} Safety Outcomes		
Simulation-based Education — T_1	T_2	T_3
Increased or improved	Confidence, knowledge, skill, attitudes, and professionalism	Safe patient care practices (process of care)	Patient safety outcomes
Target	Individuals and teams	Individuals, teams, systems	Individuals, systems, and public health
Setting	Simulation laboratory	Real patients and providers	Systems and populations

Data from McGaghie WC, Draycott TJ, Dunn WF, et al. Evaluating the impact of simulation on translational patient outcomes. Simul Healthc 2011;6(Suppl 7):S42–7.

Table 2
Studies demonstrating that simulation training translates to improved patient safety and outcomes

Title, Authors	Setting and Operator	Intervention	Outcome Measures	Results	Conclusions
Maternal and neonatal health					
Does training in obstetric emergencies improve neonatal outcome? Draycott et al,[23] 2006	UK tertiary teaching hospital Obstetric medical staff and midwives	Simulation-based training for obstetric emergencies	5-min Apgar score HIE rates	Statistically significant reduction in 5-min Apgar score less than 6 and HIE	Simulation-based training improves neonatal outcomes
Improving neonatal outcome through practical shoulder dystocia training Draycott et al,[22] 2008	UK tertiary teaching hospital Obstetric medical staff and midwives	Simulation-based training for shoulder dystocia	Retrospective, observational study pre and postintervention 1. Use of techniques to manage shoulder dystocia 2. Neonatal injury rates	A significant reduction in neonatal injury at birth after shoulder dystocia	Simulation-based training improves neonatal outcomes
Didactic and simulation nontechnical skills team training to improve perinatal patient outcomes in a community hospital Riley et al,[24] 2011	3 US community hospitals Labor and delivery staff	Compared curriculum of 3 hospitals: control, TeamSTEPPS alone, and TeamSTEPPS with simulation training	WAOS score: summary metric of adverse event score per delivery	Better WAOS score in a hospital with TeamSTEPPS with simulation training, no difference between the hospitals with TeamSTEPPS alone and control	Both didactic and simulation team training are necessary to improve perinatal patient outcomes in a community hospital
Resuscitation					
Simulation-based mock codes significantly correlate with improved pediatric patient cardiopulmonary arrest survival rates Andreatta et al,[27] 2011	US tertiary teaching hospital Mock code teams led by senior residents	Integration of simulation-based mock codes	Before and after integration 1. CPA survival rates 2. Senior resident self-perception ratings	1. Survival rate increased to ~50% within 1 y correlating with the increased number of mock codes 2. No change in resident self-perception	Integration of simulation-based mock code improves in-hospital CPA survival rates

Study	Setting	Intervention	Outcomes measured	Results	Comments
Regular in situ simulation training of pediatric medical emergency team improves hospital response to deteriorating patients Theilen et al,[37] 2012	UK tertiary stand-alone children's hospital	Implementation of pediatric medical emergency team (rapid response team) with weekly in situ simulation team training including registrars and senior nurses from the wards	Predesign and postdesign 1. Time between warning signs and first response 2. Increased frequency of nursing observations 3. Consultant review 4. Time between first response and PICU admission 5. Hospital mortality	1. Earlier first response time (median 4–1 h), Earlier PICU admission (median 11–7 h). 2. Consultant review obtained more 3. Hospital mortality improved (2.9/1000–1.3/1000 admissions)	Concurrent implementation of pediatric medical emergency team with simulation-based team training decreased response time and improved in-hospital survival rate
Invasive procedures: CVC and colonoscopy					
Acquisition of competence in pediatric ileocolonoscopy with virtual endoscopy training Thomson et al,[39] 2006	UK tertiary care teaching hospital Pediatric gastroenterology trainees from 1997 to 2004	Virtual endoscopy training	Ileocolonoscopy performance in virtual-trained vs standard-trained groups 1. Proportion of attempts of terminal ileum and cecum attainment 2. Lesion recognition rates	1. 36% higher success rate in virtual-trained group over standard-trained group 2. Significantly higher rate of lesion recognition in virtual-trained group	Virtual endoscopy training is superior to standard training to improve pediatric ileocolonoscopy
Simulation-based mastery learning improves patient outcomes in laparoscopic inguinal hernia Zendejas et al,[30] 2011	US tertiary academic medical center	Simulation-based mastery learning curriculum for totally extraperitoneal inguinal hernia repair vs standard practice (no curriculum)	1. Operative time percentage resident participation in procedure 2. Operative performance measured by a global rating scale 3. Intraoperative and postoperative complications	1. Simulation-based mastery learning group was 6.5 min shorter at first postrandomization procedure 2. Resident participation rate was higher in simulation group Both intraoperative (5% vs 35%) and postoperative (3% vs 30%) complication lower in simulation group	Simulation-based mastery learning curriculum decreased operative time, improved trainee performance, and decreased intraoperative and postoperative complications

(continued on next page)

Table 2
(continued)

Title, Authors	Setting and Operator	Intervention	Outcome Measures	Results	Conclusions
Simulation-based mastery learning reduces complications during central venous catheter insertion in a medical intensive care unit. (ADULT) Barsuk et al,[28] 2009	US tertiary care academic hospital PGY-2 and PGY-3 internal and emergency medicine residents rotating through the medical ICU	CVC insertion in traditional vs simulation-based mastery learning program	1. Written and procedure checklist scores 2. Number of skin punctures 3. Presence of arterial puncture 4. CVC adjustment 5. CVC success 6. Pneumothorax 7. Self-confidence	1. Significantly fewer skin punctures, arterial punctures, CVC adjustments, and higher CVC success rate 2. No difference in pneumothorax rate 3. No difference in self-confidence	Simulation-based CVC insertion training with mastery learning (deliberate practice) is associated with better clinical performance
Use of simulation-based education to reduce catheter-related bloodstream infections (ADULT) Barsuk et al,[29] 2009	US tertiary care teaching hospital PGY-2 and PGY-3 internal medicine and emergency medicine residents on medical ICU rotation	CVC insertion in traditional vs simulation-based mastery learning program (historical control and concurrent control using other ICUs within the institution)	1. CRBSI rates in medical ICU 2. CRBSI rates in comparison ICU	1. 84.5% reduction in CRBSI after program implementation 2. CRBSI rate lower than national rate after program implementation	Simulation-based CVC insertion mastery learning program decreases CRBSI
T value					
Management of shoulder dystocia skill retention 6 and 12 mo after training Crofts et al,[19] 2007	UK hospitals Junior and senior doctors and midwives	Before and delayed posttesting after simulation-based training in delivery skills in shoulder dystocia cases (3 wk, 6 and 12 mo)	1. Success or failure of delivery 2. Head-to-body delivery time 3. Performance of appropriate actions 4. Force applied 5. Communication	1. Of those who achieved delivery posttraining, 84% and 85% were able to deliver at 6 and 12 mo. 2. Simulation training resulted in sustained long-term performance	Management of shoulder dystocia skill is retained 6 and 12 mo after initial simulation training

Study	Population/Setting	Intervention	Outcome measure	Results	Conclusion
Cost savings from reduced catheter-related bloodstream infection after simulation-based education for residents in a medical intensive care unit (ADULT) Cohen et al,[40] 2010	US tertiary care teaching hospital PGY-2 and PGY-3 internal medicine and emergency medicine residents on medical ICU rotation	CVC insertion simulation-based mastery learning program	Annual cost for CRBSI before and after simulation-based CVC insertion education	1. 9.95 CRBSI prevented among patients in medical ICU with CVC per y (never event) 2. Net annual savings estimated to be $700,000 3. 7 to 1 return on dollar investment of simulation training	Cost savings from reduced catheter-related bloodstream infection after simulation-based education for residents in a medical ICU
Effect of just-in-time simulation training on tracheal intubation procedure safety in the pediatric intensive care unit Nishisaki et al,[36] 2010	US tertiary care children's hospital PGY-1 through PGY-3 pediatrics residents and PGY-3 and PGY-4 emergency medicine residents rotating through pediatric ICU	Just-in-time simulation-based pediatric intubation training for on-call residents	First attempt and overall success on simulation-trained residents vs traditional trained residents	No difference in tracheal intubation success, but more residents able to perform procedure without added complications	Just-in-time simulation-based pediatric intubation training increased resident attempts in ICU, but no change in success rate
Obstetric safety improvement and its reflection in reserved claims (ADULT) Iverson et al,[41] 2011	US teaching hospital OB/GYN and family medicine attendings	Retrospective review of the number of cases for which money was held in reserve for claims before and after safety improvement measures	Number of reserved claims per policy year	20% decrease per year in reserved claims, which was adjusted for delivery volume, over this time period	Obstetric simulation training was associated with safety improvement and decrease in reserved claims

ADULT: Nonpediatric studies.

Abbreviations: CPA, cardiopulmonary arrest; CRBSI, catheter-related blood stream infection; CVC, central venous catheter; HIE, hypoxic ischemic encephalopathy; ICU, intensive care unit; PGY, postgraduate year; WAOS, Weighted Adverse Outcome Score.

Ultimately, T_3 and T_{value} level of evidence was achieved when they demonstrated that implementation of a mandatory multidisciplinary simulation-based training intervention improved compliance with their clinical practice guidelines and reduced the incidence of neonatal brachial palsy injuries, low 5-minute Apgar scores, and hypoxic ischemic encephalopathy in newborns.[22,23] The training was continued, and the improvement in Apgar scores and the decreased incidence of hypoxic ischemic encephalopathy was sustained over a period of 4 years in their patient population.

Riley and colleagues[24] demonstrated that a simulation-based intervention combined with interdisciplinary team training resulted in a statistically significant 37% improvement in perinatal morbidity scores. They used the Weighted Adverse Outcome Score (WAOS) measure of perinatal morbidity and a culture-of-safety survey (safety attitudes questionnaire) preintervention versus postintervention to compare 3 hospital groups. The first group served as control, and the second hospital received the US Agency for Healthcare Research and Quality (AHRQ)-supported curriculum, the TeamSTEPPS Training didactic training program.[25] The third hospital received both the TeamSTEPPS program and a series of in situ simulation training exercises. They confirmed that didactic instruction alone without simulation was not effective in improving perinatal outcomes. However, comprehensive interdisciplinary team training and in situ simulation deliberate practice improved perinatal safety in these hospital settings.

Similar studies in the adult resuscitation domain support simulation impact on clinical outcomes. Initial pioneering studies demonstrated that deliberate practice to mastery level improved internal medicine residents' retention of advanced cardiac life support skills during simulation evaluations (T_1), improved compliance with evidence-based American Heart Association guidelines by 7-fold compared with traditionally (nonsimulation) trained residents (T_2), and was associated with improved patient survival (T_3).[26] When a similar simulation-based mock code curriculum for pediatric care providers was studied in a US tertiary care teaching hospital, Andreatta and colleagues[27] demonstrated a 50% increase in survival after real pediatric cardiopulmonary arrest. Unannounced simulated cardiac arrest scenarios followed by debriefing for pediatric residents and nurses resulted in sustained improvement in real patient survival after in-hospital cardiac arrest (T_3). Furthermore, a dose–response relationship was demonstrated for frequency of training and associated improvement in clinical outcomes.

Excellent examples of the benefits of simulation-based *procedural skill* training on T_1, T_2, T_3, and T_{value} outcomes can be extrapolated from the adult literature to children. For example, Barsuk and colleagues[28] demonstrated that mastery-based deliberate simulation practice improved central venous catheter (CVC) insertion success and reduced CVC-insertion-related complications in both simulation (T_1) and real patient settings (T_2). The same research group associated this competency-based simulation curriculum with an 85% reduction in CVC-related bloodstream infections when simulation-trained residents rotated through the intensive care unit (ICU) (T_3, T_{value}).[29] Demonstration of T_3 clinically relevant benefits after pediatric procedural simulation-based mastery learning has been accomplished in surgical training and practice. Zendejas and colleagues[30] demonstrated that a simulation-based mastery learning curriculum decreased operative time, improved trainee performance, and decreased intraoperative and postoperative complications and overnight stays after pediatric laparoscopic inguinal hernia repair.

Teamwork training conducted using simulation and debriefing can similarly affect these outcomes. In 2010, Capella and colleagues[31] studied trauma team performance after simulation-based TeamSTEPPS Training. Time to computed tomography, time to tracheal intubation, and appropriateness of time to the operating room were all significantly improved after training (T_2).

GETTING FROM PATIENT SAFETY (T_3) TO RETURN ON INVESTMENT (T_{VALUE})

The return on investment for simulation-based education can include educational benefits, skill retention, efficiency, and/or financial savings. For example, Niles and colleagues[32] showed the effectiveness of rolling refresher pediatric cardiopulmonary resuscitation training with frequent retraining and deliberate practice in a tertiary pediatric ICU to improve resuscitation psychomotor skills (adequate depth, rate, and minimal leaning) on manikins and impact of a multidisciplinary quantitative debriefing program on quality of cardiopulmonary resuscitation during actual code events in our pediatric intensive care unit (PICU).[33] Frequent refresher training and deliberate practice for central line maintenance care showed similar improved competence on manikins (T_1) and patients (T_2) as well as fewer central-line-associated blood stream infections throughout the institution (T_3 and T_{value}).[34,35] A prospective controlled tracheal intubation simulation education program for junior residents immediately before their on-call shift in a PICU allowed less-experienced providers to participate in pediatric tracheal intubations without an increase in tracheal intubation adverse events.[36] Safely increasing learning opportunities can be considered one aspect of T_{value} and may address some challenges created by limited trainee work hours and clinical exposure.

Return on investment may manifest itself as prevention or response to hospital emergencies with good teamwork and communication. A prospective cohort study of all deteriorating inpatients of a tertiary pediatric hospital requiring admission to a PICU the year before, and after, the introduction of a pediatric medical emergency team and concurrent team training suggested improvements in patient outcomes specifically related to the in situ simulation training. Lessons learned by ward staff during regular in situ team training led to significantly improved recognition and management of deteriorating inpatients with evolving critical illness.[37]

LIMITATIONS OF SIMULATION-BASED MEDICAL EDUCATION

Not all recent studies in the literature have demonstrated the transfer of a clinical skill or behavior to an improvement in patient care. For example, Finan and colleagues[38] implemented a simulation-based medical education module on neonatal resuscitation and intubation. First-year pediatric residents completed a 2-hour simulation training session. Clinical intubations were tracked for 8 weeks after the training. The study results showed no association between improved simulation performance and improved clinical performance. However, it may have been unrealistic to expect a short 2-hour session to allow enough practice to affect clinical outcome. Another example is a previously described tracheal intubation education study by Nishisaki and colleagues.[36] In their study, the participating residents did not improve their tracheal intubation success rate. Sound simulation-based training methodology to ensure mastery-level skill acquisition and frequent skill refresher training curriculum to maintain the skills at mastery level are 2 key components for successful simulation-based education translation to safety and improved clinical outcomes.

SUMMARY

The time-honored apprenticeship model may not be the most optimal and effective way to train clinicians. The "see one, do one, teach one" model may give way to "see one, simulate many, do one" model. There is now good evidence that simulation training improves individual and team performance, specifically self-confidence, knowledge, and operational performance on manikins (eg, *simulated settings*, T_1).

Emerging evidence supports that deliberate practice, procedural simulation, and debriefing can improve safe operational performance in clinical settings (eg, *real patient process of care, T_2*) and can result in safer patient and population/system outcomes in selected settings (eg, *real patient and population outcomes, T_3*). Ultimately, a few studies suggest that this can translate into safer and more efficient care for patients, providers, and systems (eg, *return on investment, T_{value}*).

ACKNOWLEDGMENTS

The authors would like to thank Pamela Fried of the Drexel Academic Publishing Service and Ms Alisha Bonaroti for their editorial and administrative participation in this project.

REFERENCES

1. Kohn LT, Corrigan JM, Donaldson MS. To err is human: building a safer health system. Characteristics of state adverse event reporting systems. Washington, DC: The National Academies Press; 2000.
2. Gaba DM. The future vision of simulation in health care. Qual Saf Health Care 2004;13:2–10.
3. Cooper JB, Taqueti VR. A brief history of the development of mannequin simulators for clinical education and training. Qual Saf Health Care 2004;13(Suppl 1): i11–8.
4. Issenberg SB, McGaghie WC, Petrusa ER, et al. Features and uses of high-fidelity medical simulations that lead to effective learning: a BEME systematic review. Med Teach 2005;27:10–28.
5. Nishisaki A, Keren R, Nadkarni V, et al. Does simulation improve patient safety? Self-efficacy, competence, operational performance, and patient safety. Anesthesiol Clin 2007;25(2):225–36.
6. Ericsson KA, Krampe RT, Tesch-Römer C. The role of deliberate practice in the acquisition of expert performance. Psychol Rev 1993;100(3):363–406.
7. Ericsson K. Deliberate practice and acquisition of expert performance: a general overview. Acad Emerg Med 2008;15(11):988–94.
8. Ericsson KA. An expert-performance perspective of research on medical expertise: the study of clinical performance. Med Educ 2007;41(12):1124–30.
9. Cook DA, Hatala R, Brydges R, et al. Technology-enhanced simulation for health professions education: a systematic review and meta-analysis. JAMA 2011; 306(9):978–88.
10. Lynagh M, Burton R, Sanson-Fisher R. A systematic review of medical skills laboratory training: where to from here? Med Educ 2007;41(9):879–87.
11. Yuan HB, Williams BA, Fang JB, et al. A systematic review of selected evidence on improving knowledge and skills through high-fidelity simulation. Nurse Educ Today 2012;32(3):294–8.
12. McGaghie WC, Issenberg SB, Cohen ER, et al. Does simulation-based medical education with deliberate practice yield better results than traditional clinical education? A meta-analytic comparative review of the evidence. Acad Med 2011;86(6):706–11.
13. Sturm LP, Windsor JA, Cosman PH, et al. A systematic review of skills transfer after surgical simulation training. Ann Surg 2008;248(2):166–79.
14. McGaghie WC. Implementation science: addressing complexity in medical education. Med Teach 2011;33(2):97–8.

15. Gurusamy K, Aggarwal R, Palanivelu L, et al. Systematic review of randomized controlled trials on the effectiveness of virtual reality training for laparoscopic surgery. Br J Surg 2008;95(9):1088–97.

16. McGaghie WC, Issenberg SB, Petrusa ER, et al. A critical review of simulation-based medical education research: 2003–2009. Med Educ 2010; 44(1):50–63.

17. Park CS. Simulation and quality improvement in anesthesiology. Anesthesiol Clin 2011;29(1):13–28.

18. McGaghie WC, Draycott TJ, Dunn WF, et al. Evaluating the impact of simulation on translational patient outcomes. Simul Healthc 2011;6(Suppl 7):S42–7.

19. Crofts JF, Bartlett C, Ellis D, et al. Management of shoulder dystocia: skill retention 6 and 12 months after training. Obstet Gynecol 2007;110(5):1069–74.

20. Crofts JF, Fox R, Ellis D, et al. Observations from 450 shoulder dystocia simulations: lessons for skills training. Obstet Gynecol 2008;112(4):906–12.

21. Cass GK, Crofts JF, Draycott TJ. The use of simulation to teach clinical skills in obstetrics. Semin Perinatol 2011;35(2):68–73.

22. Draycott TJ, Crofts JF, Ash JP, et al. Improving neonatal outcome through practical shoulder dystocia training. Obstet Gynecol 2008;112(1):14–20.

23. Draycott T, Sibanda T, Owen L, et al. Does training in obstetric emergencies improve neonatal outcome? BJOG 2006;113(2):177–82.

24. Riley W, Davis S, Miller K, et al. Didactic and simulation nontechnical skills team training to improve perinatal patient outcomes in a community hospital. Jt Comm J Qual Patient Saf 2011;37(8):357–64.

25. Teamstepps. Available at: http://teamstepps.ahrq.gov/. Accessed April 10, 2012.

26. Wayne DB, Didwania A, Feinglass J, et al. Simulation-based education improves quality of care during cardiac arrest team responses at an academic teaching hospital: a case-control study. Chest 2008;133(1):56–61.

27. Andreatta P, Saxton E, Thompson M, et al. Simulation-based mock codes significantly correlate with improved pediatric patient cardiopulmonary arrest survival rates. Pediatr Crit Care Med 2011;12(1):33–8.

28. Barsuk JH, McGaghie WC, Cohen ER, et al. Simulation-based mastery learning reduces complications during central venous catheter insertion in a medical intensive care unit. Crit Care Med 2009;37(10):2697–701.

29. Barsuk JH, Cohen ER, Feinglass J, et al. Use of simulation-based education to reduce catheter-related bloodstream infections. Arch Intern Med 2009;169(15):1420–3.

30. Zendejas B, Cook DA, Bingener J, et al. Simulation-based mastery learning improves patient outcomes in laparoscopic inguinal hernia repair: a randomized controlled trial. Ann Surg 2011;254(3):502–9 [discussion: 509–11].

31. Capella J, Smith S, Philp A, et al. Teamwork training improves the clinical care of trauma patients. J Surg Educ 2010;67(6):439–43.

32. Niles DE, Sutton RM, Donoghue AJ, et al. "Rolling refreshers". A novel approach to maintain CPR psychomotor competence. Resuscitation 2009;80(8):909–12.

33. Zebuhr C, Sutton RM, Morrison W, et al. Evaluation of quantitative debriefing after pediatric cardiac arrest. Resuscitation 2012;83(9):1124–8.

34. Lengetti E, Monachino AM, Scholtz A. A simulation-based "just in time" and "just in place" central venous catheter education program. J Nurses Staff Dev 2011; 27(6):290–3.

35. Scholtz A, Monachino A, Nishisaki A, et al. Central venous catheter dress rehearsal: every line counts. Simul Healthc 2009;4(4):324. Oral Presentation at 10th Annual International Meeting on Simulation in Healthcare (IMSH). Phoenix, January 23–27, 2010.

36. Nishisaki A, Donoghue AJ, Colborn S, et al. Effect of just-in-time simulation training on tracheal intubation procedure safety in the pediatric intensive care unit. Anesthesiology 2010;113(1):214–23.

37. Theilen U, Leonard P, Jones P, et al. Regular in situ simulation training of paediatric medical emergency team improves hospital response to deteriorating patients. Resuscitation 2012. [Epub ahead of print].

38. Finan E, Bismilla Z, Campbell C, et al. Improved procedural performance following a simulation training session may not be transferable to the clinical environment. J Perinatol 2012;32(7):539–44.

39. Thomson M, Heuschkel R, Donaldson N, et al. Acquisition of competence in paediatric ileocolonoscopy with virtual endoscopy training. J Pediatr Gastroenterol Nutr 2006;43(5):699–701.

40. Cohen ER, Feinglass J, Barsuk JH, et al. Cost savings from reduced catheter-related bloodstream infection after simulation-based education for residents in a medical intensive care unit. Simul Healthc 2010;5(2):98–102.

41. Iverson RE, Heffner LJ. Obstetric safety improvement and its reflection in reserved claims. Am J Obstet Gynecol 2011;205(5):398–401.

Patient Safety in Ambulatory Care

Daniel R. Neuspiel, MD, MPH*, Erin H. Stubbs, MD

KEYWORDS

- Patient safety • Medical errors • Medication errors • Ambulatory care • Outpatients

KEY POINTS

- Although often unrecognized, medical errors occur frequently in the pediatric ambulatory setting.
- Medication errors are a common form of outpatient pediatric error, especially in patients receiving multiple prescriptions and with prescriptions written by trainees.
- Risk factors for home medication errors include inadequate communication between parents, providers, and pharmacists; language and cultural barriers; and nonstandard measurement devices.
- A nonpunitive safety culture improves reporting of office-based pediatric errors.
- Electronic health records may both reduce outpatient medication errors and introduce new types of errors.

INTRODUCTION

Because most health care encounters with children occur outside of the hospital, understanding of the types and frequency of errors in this setting is paramount. To date, knowledge about errors in pediatric ambulatory care has been limited, but studies are emerging with information about the types of errors that occur. The most commonly described errors involve medical treatment, communication failures, patient identification, laboratory, and diagnostic errors. Medication errors may be due to errors in prescribing, dispensing, or administration. Patients taking multiple medications are at high risk of an error. One strategy to reduce medication errors is enhanced communication between patients, health care providers, and pharmacists, particularly when a language barrier is present. Electronic prescribing also shows great potential to reduce medication errors and improve patient safety, but may also introduce new sources of error (eg, right drug wrong patient, wrong drug selected, or alert fatigue). Traditional incident reporting systems are not sensitive to the majority of medical errors, are perceived as punitive, and primarily rely on administrative reporting. Office-based voluntary nonpunitive reporting has been effective in detecting errors in the pediatric outpatient setting. Ongoing efforts are needed to introduce a nonpunitive safety culture to promote safe ambulatory pediatric care and prevent harm to children.

Department of Pediatrics, Levine Children's Hospital, PO Box 32861, Charlotte, NC 28232-2861, USA
* Corresponding author.
E-mail address: daniel.neuspiel@carolinashealthcare.org

Pediatr Clin N Am 59 (2012) 1341–1354
http://dx.doi.org/10.1016/j.pcl.2012.08.006
pediatric.theclinics.com

Although children receive the vast majority of their care in the outpatient setting, information on pediatric ambulatory medical errors is just starting to emerge. Research suggests that adverse events and near misses are frequent occurrences in ambulatory pediatrics, but relatively little is known about the types of errors, risk factors, or effective interventions in this setting. Studying medical errors in ambulatory pediatrics is complex, because children receive health care in a variety of locations, including home and school, and by multiple health care providers. This article will review current information on the descriptive epidemiology of pediatric outpatient medical errors, established risk factors for these errors, effective interventions to enhance reporting and improve safety, and future research needs in this area.

DESCRIPTIVE EPIDEMIOLOGY OF AMBULATORY PEDIATRIC ERRORS
Studies of all Types of Errors

Few studies have examined medical errors of all types in outpatient pediatrics. None of these have high sensitivity to detect the majority of these events. The Learning from Errors in Ambulatory Pediatrics study[1] evaluated the scope, range, potential causes, and possible solutions to medical errors in pediatric ambulatory care. Among 14 participating pediatric practices, 147 medical errors were reported. The largest group of errors was related to medical treatment (37%), but errors were also associated with patient identification (22%), preventive care including immunizations (15%), diagnostic testing (13%), patient communication (8%), and other causes. Of the medical treatment errors, 85% were related to medications. Among the medication errors, 55% were related to ordering, 30% to failure to order, 11% to administration, 2% to transcribing, and 2% to dispensing. No denominator data were collected, so the actual error rates could not be determined.

Phillips and colleagues[2] studied medical errors reported by clinicians, staff, and patients in 10 family medicine clinics of the American Academy of Family Physicians National Research Network. Participants were asked to report routinely during 10 weeks and to report every error on 5 specific days. Four hundred one clinicians and staff anonymously reported 935 errors within 717 events, 37% of which came from the 5 intensive reporting days and 61% from routine reports. Staff made 384 (53%) reports, primarily related to patient flow and communication, and clinicians made 342 (47%) reports, mainly medication and laboratory errors. Most (96%) errors reported were related to processes, not to knowledge or skill. Patients reported 18 errors. Among patients affected by errors, there was no breakdown by age, although children were included.

Neuspiel and colleagues[3] reported a voluntary, anonymous, nonpunitive error-reporting project in an outpatient pediatric department in New York City with approximately 36,000 visits per year (2.2 errors reported per 1000 visits per year). In the first year of the project, 80 errors were reported, compared with only 5 errors reported during the prior year via a traditional incident reporting system. Most reports originated from physicians (45%) and nurses (41%). Errors were classified as involving office administration (34%), medications and other treatment (24%), laboratory and diagnostic testing (19%), and communications (18%). The most frequent office administration errors included wrong demographic information or date of visit (9%), misfiled papers in chart (9%), and delays in processing patients due to misplaced registration forms (9%). The most frequent errors attributed to medication and other treatment included errors in vaccine and medication orders (6%), wrong vaccine administered (5%), wrong outside prescription dispensed (4%), incomplete prescription returned by pharmacy (4%), and patient revaccinated too early (4%). Among errors attributed to laboratory and diagnostic testing, the most common were missed specimen pickup (10%) and mislabeled specimens (4%). The most frequent communication errors were patients leaving the practice before ordered vaccines were administered (8%).

In a pediatric outpatient department in Charlotte, North Carolina, with approximately 26,000 visits per year, employing a similar voluntary, anonymous reporting system, Neuspiel and colleagues[4] reported 216 medical errors over 30 months (3.3 errors per 1000 visits per year). Most reports (77%) originated from nurses, physicians, and midlevel providers. The most frequently reported errors were misfiled or erroneously entered patient information (31%), laboratory test delayed or not performed (13%), error in medication prescribing or dispensing (11%), vaccine error (10%), patient not given requested appointment or referral (7%), and delay in office care (7%).

Studies of Malpractice Claims and Diagnostic Errors

One way of looking at the impact of medical errors is via paid malpractice claims. Bishop and colleagues[5] studied data from the National Practitioner Data Bank from 2005 to 2009. Among outpatient claims, 8.4% (95% confidence interval [CI] 7.6–9.2) were for children 0 to 19 years. The most frequent basis for outpatient claims were errors in diagnosis (45.9%, 95% CI 44.4–47.4), followed by errors in treatment or medication (29.5%, 95% CI 28.2–30.9).

Singh and colleagues[6] evaluated diagnostic errors among pediatricians at 3 tertiary care institutions and 109 affiliated clinics via anonymous survey. Among 1362 pediatricians, 726 (53%) responded, and 54% reported making a diagnostic error at least once or twice per month, with higher rates (77%) among trainees. Diagnostic errors causing harm to patients and occurring at least once or twice per year were reported by 45% of respondents. The most frequently reported process source of diagnostic error was failure to gather information through patient history, physical examination, or chart review. The most commonly reported system error was inadequate care coordination and teamwork. Most frequent specific errors were viral illnesses diagnosed as bacterial, misdiagnosis of medication adverse effects, psychiatric disorders, and appendicitis.

Studies of Outpatient Medication Errors

To date, the most widely studied type of error in the pediatric office environment has related to prescribing, dispensing, and home administration of medications. McPhillips and colleagues[7] randomly selected 1933 children receiving a new prescription using automated pharmacy data from 3 health maintenance organizations, 2 using paper prescriptions and 1 using an electronic prescription writer. They determined that 15% of children had potential dosing errors: 8% overdoses and 7% underdoses. In children less than 35 kg, 33% had dosing errors, and more than 1% were prescribed twice the recommended maximum dose. Twenty percent of children under 4 years of age experienced dosing errors, compared with 13% of children aged 4 to 12 years (odds ratio [OR] 1.7, 95% CI 1.1–2.6). Those receiving 5 or more prescriptions were more likely to have dosing errors than children with a single prescription (OR 3.3, 95% CI 1.4–7.7). The most frequent overdosed medications were analgesics (15% overdosed), and the most frequent underdosed medications were antiepileptics (20% underdosed). There were no reductions in error rates in the site using an electronic prescription writer.

A series of publications has emerged from a prospective cohort study at 6 office practices in the Boston area over 2 months.[8–11] Kaushal and colleagues[8] discovered 57 preventable adverse drug events (rate 3%, 95% CI 3%–4%) in the care of 1788 patients. None of the events was determined to be life threatening, but 8 (14%)

were serious. Forty (70%) were related to parental drug administration. The authors determined that improved communication between providers and parents and between pharmacists and parents was the preventive strategy with the most potential benefit to prevent these errors. Children with multiple prescriptions were at increased risk of preventable adverse drug events (OR 1.46, 95% CI 1.01–2.11).[9] Taking more than 1 medication (OR 1.68, 95% CI 1.15–2.46) and age under 5 years (OR 2.35, 95% CI 1.05–5.28) were associated with risk of medication administration errors.[10] Kaushal and colleagues[11] showed that 94% of medication errors with minimal potential for harm and 60% of near misses occurred at the prescribing stage, most frequently due to inappropriate Abbreviations, dosing errors, and illegibility.

Several studies have looked at prehospital antipyretic dosing errors in children seen in pediatric emergency departments. Li and colleagues[12] found that 51% of surveyed caregivers gave inaccurate doses of acetaminophen (62% inaccurate) or ibuprofen (26% inaccurate), especially to infants younger than 1 year of age (relative risk [RR] 1.40, 95% CI 1.06–1.86 compared with older children). Another study determined that 53% of children received an improper antipyretic dose at home.[13] Goldman[14] noted that 47% of parents gave acetaminophen at recommended doses; 12% gave overdoses, and 41% underdosed their children. Among parents with febrile children, 54% would not have come to the emergency department had the fever subsided at home. Parents speaking English as a primary language were more likely to give recommended doses than non-English speaking parents.

Medication errors by pediatric emergency department staff have also been reported. Losek[15] examined errors in the application of standing orders for acetaminophen in a pediatric emergency department (ED). In a 1-week period, there were 122 (78%) correct doses, 15 (10%) underdoses, and 19 (12%) overdoses. The rectal route of administration was associated with significantly greater overdoses (35%, 95% CI 14%–48%) than orally administered acetaminophen (8%).

In the pediatric emergency department of the Hospital for Sick Children in Toronto, Canada, among 1532 children, 10.1% had medication prescribing errors.[16] Error risk was increased when medications were ordered by trainees (OR 1.64, 95% CI 1.06–2.52) and in seriously ill patients (OR 1.55, 95% CI 1.06–2.26). Shaughnessy and Nickel[17] reviewed prescriptions written by 20 family medicine residents. Among 1814 prescriptions, 21% (n = 373) contained at least 1 prescription-writing error, including omissions (6%), unfulfilled legal requirements (1%), incomplete directions (1%), dose or direction errors (3%), unclear quantity to be dispensed (3%), or prescriptions written for nonprescription products (5%). The proportion of pediatric prescriptions was not indicated. Condren and colleagues[18] found errors among 9.7% of prescriptions written by pediatric residents in an outpatient clinic. The most frequent type of error was incomplete information entered (42%), followed by medication dosing errors (34%).

Several investigators have studied ambulatory medication errors in children with specific health conditions. Rinke and colleagues[19] analyzed both inpatient and outpatient error reports involving antidepressants in children under 18 years from the United States Pharmacopeia MEDMARX database from 2003 to 2006. Among 451 error reports, 95% reached the patient; 6.4% required increased monitoring and/or treatment, and 77% involved off-label medication use. The cause of the error was cited as administration in 33% of cases, dispensing in 30% of cases, transcribing in 28% of cases, and prescribing in 7.9% of cases. The most frequent medications cited were sertraline (20%), bupropion (19%), fluoxetine (15%), and trazodone (11%). Outpatient errors involved more dispensing errors and errors due to inaccurate or omitted transcription (both $P<.001$) compared with inpatient errors. No denominator information was available to establish error rates.

Taylor and colleagues[20] studied outpatient oral chemotherapy medication errors in children with acute lymphoblastic leukemia. During a 2-month period at a single center, 1 or more errors occurred in 17 of 172 medications (9.9%). Of the 17 errors, 12 were related to administration and 5 to prescribing; there were no pharmacy dispensing errors. All errors were related to incorrect dosing or failing to administer an indicated medication. Among the 69 study patients, 13 (18.8%) experienced at least 1 medication error.

In a study of medication errors in the homes of children with sickle cell disease and seizure disorders, Walsh and colleagues[21] directly observed medication administration, reviewed medications, and checked prescription doses. In 52 home visits, 280 medications were reviewed, and 61 medication errors were detected (95% CI 46–123), including 31 with potential for injury and 9 with actual injury to the child. Frequent sources of error were when parents failed to fill prescriptions or to change doses due to communication problems. These errors led to further testing or continued pain, inflammation, seizures, vitamin deficiencies, or other injuries. In some cases, communication failures between 2 parents resulted in administration errors and difficulty preparing medications for administration. Among parents using support tools (eg, alarms, reminders) for home medication use, error rates were 44%, compared with 95% among parents not using such tools ($P = .0002$). Patients' physicians were unaware of 80% of the detected errors.

Studies of Immunization Errors

Several investigators have reported studies on immunization errors noting that fragmentation of care leads to unnecessary overimmunization. Feikema and colleagues,[22] using data from the US 1997 National Immunization Survey, found that 21% of children were overimmunized, and 31% were underimmunized for at least 1 vaccine. The largest contributors to overimmunization were having more than 1 immunization provider (OR 2.8, 95% CI 2.4–3.2) and having multiple types of providers (OR 2.0, 95% CI 1.6–2.4). The 1997 costs associated with extra vaccination were estimated conservatively at $26.5 million. Butte and colleagues,[23] in a large urban clinic, determined that 35.5% of pediatric patients had at least 1 invalid vaccine dose. Darden and colleagues,[24] using the 1999 to 2003 National Immunization Survey, determined that among 19- to 35-month-old children, 21.9% were underimmunized, and 9.4% received extra immunizations. Overimmunization was associated with multiple providers (adjusted odds ratio [AOR] 2.3, 95% CI 2.13–2.47) and multiple facility types (AOR 4.67, 95% CI 4.23–5.15).

RISK FACTORS FOR AMBULATORY PEDIATRIC ERRORS

Several risk factors for ambulatory pediatric errors have been pointed out in the studies cited previously:

Young patient age
Weight under 35 kg
Use of multiple medications by child
Communication barriers
Prescriptions by trainees
Lack of teamwork
Incomplete evaluation of patients
Multiple health care providers with fragmented or uncoordinated care
Illegible prescriptions
Improper Abbreviations

Some other specific risk factors for pediatric outpatient medication errors are related to medication measurement devices and barriers due to health literacy, culture, and language.

Measurement Devices and Home Medication Errors

Yin and colleagues[25] studied parental liquid medication administration errors related to dosing instrument type and health literacy. In a single center in New York City, 302 parents were observed for accuracy of a 5 mL dose using several standardized instruments: dosing cup with printed calibration markings, dosing cup with etched markings, dropper, dosing spoon, and oral syringes with and without a bottle adapters. Parents dosed least accurately (within 20% of recommended dose) using the cup with printed (30.5%) and with etched markings (50.2%). Over 85% of parents dosed accurately with the other instruments. After adjustment for confounders, cups were associated with increased odds of making a dosing error compared with oral syringe (printed cup: OR 26.7, 95% CI 16.8–42.4; etched cup: OR 11.0, 95% CI 7.2–16.8). Cups were also more likely than oral syringes to be associated with making large dosing errors (printed cup: OR 7.3, 95% CI 4.1–13.2; etched cup: OR 6.3, 95% CI 3.5–11.2). Dosing errors were also more frequent with limited health literacy (OR 1.7, 95% CI 1.1–2.8). Sobhani and colleagues[26] also found that adults were able to measure liquid acetaminophen more accurately with an oral syringe than a cup, but only two-thirds of participants measured acceptable doses with the syringe.

Yin and colleagues[27] determined the frequency of inconsistent dosing directions and measurement devices among pediatric over-the-counter (OTC) medications at the time (November 2009) the US Food and Drug Administration (FDA) released new recommendations for greater consistency and clarity in dosing directions and measuring devices.[28] They studied 200 top-selling pediatric oral liquid OTC medications during the year preceding the new FDA recommendations for inclusion of a measuring device, consistency between labeled dosing directions and markings on the measuring device, use of nonstandard units and Abbreviations, and presence of Abbreviation definitions. The investigators found that measuring devices were included with 148 of 200 products (74%). There were inconsistencies between medication dosing directions and measurement device markings in 146 of 148 products (98.6%), including missing (N = 36, 24.3%) and superfluous markings (N = 120, 81.1%). Of all products, 11 (5.5%) used atypical measurement units for listed doses. Non-standard Abbreviations for milliliter were used in 97 products. Among products using Abbreviations, 163 did not define at least 1 Abbreviation. The authors conclude that at the time of the new FDA recommendations, top-selling pediatric OTC medications were using highly variable and inconsistent dosing directions and measuring devices.

The readability of retail pharmacy-generated consumer medical information and the features of measuring devices for oral liquids were studied by Wallace and colleagues.[29] Investigators filled similar prescriptions for prednisolone and amoxicillin at 20 different pharmacies in Colorado, Georgia, and Tennessee. Many materials were at ninth-11th grade readability level, too high for many parents, and 3 pharmacies provided no materials at all. One-third of pharmacies provided measuring devices that would require multiple measurements for the prescribed doses.

Health Literacy, Numeracy, Cultural, and Language Barriers

Leyva and colleagues[30] conducted a study to examine the impact of language barriers on medication errors in a Spanish-speaking population in the Bronx, New York. They sought to determine how well Bronx Spanish-speaking Latino parents of children

5 years and younger understand written medication instructions. After being given instructions on administration of ferrous sulfate, only 22% of parents demonstrated correct medication administration (amount and frequency). Subjects reporting comfort speaking English were more likely to demonstrate correct medication amount to be administered (50% vs 21%, OR 3.8; 95% CI, 1.2–12.2) and correct frequency (93% vs 51%, OR 12.4; 95% CI, 1.5–99.1). Both education (OR 1.22, 95% CI, 1.03–1.45) and comfort speaking English (OR 3.81, 95% CI, 1.13–12.86) independently predicted correct medication dosing.

Sharif and Tse[31] surveyed all pharmacies in the Bronx, New York, and visited selected pharmacies to assess computer software used to generate Spanish medication labels. Among 316 pharmacies, 286 (91%) participated. Of these, 209 (73%) provided medicine labels in Spanish. Pharmacies providing Spanish labels mostly frequently (86%) used computer programs to generate them. Lay staff members translated 11% of labels, and 3% used professional interpretation services. Fourteen different computer programs were used to generate Spanish labels, but 3 major programs were used by 70% of pharmacies. The investigators studied 76 medication labels generated by 13 different computer programs, and found that 32 Spanish labels (43%) included incomplete translations (mixture of English and Spanish), and 6 additional labels contained misspellings or grammar errors. The overall error rate was 50%. They concluded that while pharmacies were able to provide Spanish labels, the translation quality was inaccurate and hazardous.

Flores and Ngui[32] also point to racial, ethnic, and language barriers as contributors to increased risk of pediatric errors. Yet in 2004, the majority of pediatricians reported using untrained interpreters to communicate with patients and their families with limited English proficiency.[33]

Adolescents are appropriately given increased responsibility for self-care, with less parental supervision, yet this may increase their risk for home medication errors. Wilson and colleagues[34] evaluated misconceptions and knowledge gaps among teens about OTC medications. They determined that 78% of the adolescents had used OTC medications in the previous month, most commonly ibuprofen and acetaminophen. Although 35% of respondents reported knowing about acetaminophen, 37% did not know it was the same as Tylenol, and many had limited knowledge about adverse effects and contraindications. Hispanic teens reported less use of acetaminophen and had lower knowledge scores than other ethnicities.

Lokker and colleagues[35] note that parents commonly misunderstand labels on OTC pediatric cough and cold preparations. They recruited 182 caregivers from clinics at 3 institutions, and questioned them about the use of 4 common OTC medications. Mean education level of caregivers was 12.5 years, but only 17% had higher than ninth grade numeracy skills. Although all of the medications were labeled with advice to consult a physician for use in children younger than 2 years, over 50% of the time parents would give these products to a 13-month-old child.

Chang and colleagues[36] surveyed parents of febrile children less than 6 years of age hospitalized in Taiwan. After being provided with written medication instructions for antipyretics, one-third of parents had more than 1 misunderstanding for medication timing, time interval of administration, and/or dosage, and almost two-thirds of parents misunderstood acetaminophen adverse effects. Poorer comprehension of instructions was associated with lower academic qualifications.

Costelloe and colleagues[37] found limitations in the ability of parents to measure weights of preschool children at home for calculation of antipyretic dose. Only 40% of parents had home scales, most of which were analog. Research scale weights were heavier than those from home scales, with a mean difference of 0.41 kg (95% CI 0.24 –0.74 kg).

INTERVENTIONS TO ENHANCE REPORTING AND PREVENTION OF ERRORS
Nonpunitive Reporting Systems

In order to improve patient safety in the ambulatory pediatric setting, adequate error reporting is necessary. Traditional incident reporting systems are perceived as punitive, poorly utilized, and missing many clinically significant events. The Institute of Medicine (IOM) recommends a blame-free error reporting system that includes both adverse events and near misses, and a systems-based approach to analyzing errors. Such an approach shifts the blame from individuals to faulty or inadequate systems that contribute to medical errors.[38-40] The American Academy of Pediatrics[41] emphasizes the importance of creating a patient safety culture in which providers and staff understand the importance of patient safety, and constant attention is paid to avoiding errors.

The New York City error reporting project noted previously[3] was partly modeled on a project implemented in an academic adult primary care setting in Charlottesville, Virginia, where clinician-based voluntary reporting was effective in increasing the number of error reports.[42] A similar model was used in an effective nonpunitive error-reporting project in Charlotte, North Carolina.[4] In the Charlottesville, New York City, and Charlotte projects, multidisciplinary teams analyzed reports using root cause analysis and made recommendations for system changes to reduce the likelihood of repeating the same types of errors.

Phillips and colleagues[2] also found that clinic personnel play an important role in error reporting in a family practice setting. While the role of families in recognizing inpatient errors has been noted,[43] caregiver participation in outpatient pediatric error reporting has received little attention.

Strategies to Reduce Medication Errors

Voluntary, nonpunitive error reporting systems are useful for identifying a broad range of errors in the ambulatory setting, and a multidisciplinary team should be engaged to review errors and recommend remedies; however, even with such reporting, many errors will go undetected. Kozer and colleagues[44] suggest that clinicians, pharmacies, and patients must be more proactive in order to reduce medication errors in the outpatient setting. Recommended strategies include the use of computerized provider order entry, use of templates for medication ordering (eg, preprinted forms with specific areas for patient weight, allergies, prescriber's name, and contact information), routine pharmacy auditing, regulations (eg, dose checking required for certain medications), education of trainees in dose calculations, and encouraging teamwork and open communication.

Improving caregiver dosing tools is another important strategy to reduce medication errors in ambulatory pediatrics. Yin and colleagues[45] conducted a randomized trial testing the benefit of a pictographic dosing diagram to improve parents' ability to accurately dose acetaminophen to their infants in an urban hospital clinic in New York City. Including pictographic dosing diagrams with written medication instructions resulted in a 15.2% absolute risk reduction (95% CI 3.8–26.0) in medication administration errors compared to text-only recipients. Benefits of pictogram use were only present among parents with low health literacy. The same group[46] previously demonstrated the efficacy of a pictogram-based health literacy program in decreasing medication dosing errors with liquid medication prescriptions. Hixson and colleagues[47] conducted a randomized trial comparing a sliding card-based dosing tool with product information leaflets alone for measurement and administration of acetaminophen. The median percentage with dosing error was 0% in the dosing card group versus 33.3% in the comparison group (P<.001). The dosing card group had increased numbers of correct dosage intervals and frequencies (74% to 88%, P = .046).

Electronic Health Records and Electronic Prescribing: Solution or New Source of Error?

With widespread adoption and implementation of electronic health records (EHRs), understanding their impact on errors in ambulatory pediatrics is of utmost importance. While EHR may improve patient safety, their rapid timeline implementation in many institutions may have the unintended consequence of increasing errors, and with EHR there are new error types to consider.

Electronic prescribing has the potential to improve patient safety, particularly if the program is incorporated into an EHR, with access to patient medication histories, allergies, and clinical decision support.[48] Kaushal and colleagues[49] reported on a prospective nonrandomized study using pre–post design of 15 electronic prescribing adopters and 15 concurrent controls using paper-based prescriptions. For the adopters, the error rate decreased from 42.5 errors per 100 prescriptions at baseline to 6.6 errors per 100 prescriptions at 1 year (P<.001). For nonadopters, the error rates remained high with 37.4 errors per 100 prescriptions at baseline then 38.4 errors per 100 prescriptions at 1 year. In this study, all illegibility errors were eliminated with electronic prescribing, and most rule violations (failure to follow strict prescribing rules that were unlikely to result in harm) were eliminated.

Jani and colleagues[50] found that electronic prescribing reduced prescription errors in a nephrology outpatient clinic at a pediatric tertiary care hospital. All medication prescriptions were reviewed over a 13-month period during the implementation of an electronic prescribing system. The error rate for handwritten prescriptions was 77.4%, and with electronic prescribing, the error rate was 4.8% (P<.001). The number of error-free visits in this practice increased from 21% to 90% with the use of electronic prescriptions. Electronic prescribing most notably reduced the number of incomplete and illegible prescriptions.

Using a before and after evaluation of an outpatient EHR, Ginzburg and colleagues[51] determined that an integrated, automated weight-based dosing calculator significantly reduced antipyretic prescribing errors for pediatric patients, with the greatest reduction in overdose errors (8.9% before EHR vs 4.0% after EHR, P = .028). Jani and colleagues[52] also looked at medication dosing errors before and after EHR implementation in both outpatients and inpatients at a tertiary care hospital. Prescribing errors occurred in 2.2% of prescriptions prior to the EHR. After implementation, there were 1.2% dosing errors, a 1% absolute reduction (P<.001; 95% CI 1.6–0.5). The investigators also report a decrease in the severity rating of dose errors.

Medication reconciliation tools are another means of reducing medication errors, particularly during transitions of care. Since 2005, medication reconciliation in ambulatory care has been a national patient safety goal of The Joint Commission (TJC), formerly the Joint Commission on Accreditation of Healthcare Organizations.[53] To date, the use of medication reconciliation in pediatrics has primarily focused on the inpatient setting, but its use is equally valuable in ambulatory care. Rappaport and colleagues[54] described a quality improvement intervention to increase use of a medication reconciliation tool in a multispecialty children's integrated health care network. Over a 5-year period, completion of the medication reconciliation tool increased from 0% to 71%, although it remains unclear whether this had a positive impact on patient outcomes.

The use of EHR is recommended to reduce medical errors and improve patient safety, but recent literature suggests there are safety concerns associated with its use. Sittig and Singh[55] aimed to advance the understanding of errors related to health information technology. They defined common errors associated with health information technology:

Computer or network malfunction
Input data truncated
Allowable item cannot be ordered
Incorrect default dose for medication
Patient data entered under wrong name
Incorrect merge of 2 patients' data
Critical abnormal test result alerts are not followed up
Computer discontinues a medication without notifying a person
Billing requirements lead to inaccurate documentation

Singh[56] described additional potentials for errors with EHR use. Increased access to information may reduce diagnostic errors, but it also creates the potential to overlook important data. It remains unclear to what extent clinicians should review the entire computer record. The use of templates in an EHR is potentially problematic, because precompleted notes may contain incorrect information that is easily overlooked. Some templates also import test results that may not have been reviewed, although this is implied once the note is signed. Delayed or lack of follow-up of abnormal laboratory results is another common source of error with EHR use. Additional legal, ethical, and financial challenges have been described with the implementation of EHR.[57]

FUTURE AREAS FOR RESEARCH

More than a decade has passed since the IOM report *To Err Is Human: Building a Safer Healthcare System,*[39] yet safety data in the ambulatory setting remain limited. Tang and Meyer[58] suggest that future efforts should be aimed at developing and validating measures to target known patient safety risks in ambulatory care. These risks include, but are not limited to, potentially long periods between visits, coordination of care among multiple providers, complex medication regimens, stepwise approaches to diagnosis and treatment, and difficulties with access to primary care.

Wynia[59] provided a national agenda with 5 core aims for improving ambulatory patient safety in the next decade:

Study the epidemiology of ambulatory patient safety to better understand how many patients experience health care-related harms in the outpatient setting
Identify an early achievable goal such as timely follow-up of abnormal laboratory and imaging results, a common source of error in ambulatory practice
Engage patients and their families as members of ambulatory safety teams
Link the ambulatory safety agenda to a related high-profile patient safety initiative such as transitions of care, and emphasize the role of the primary physician in patient safety before and after hospitalizations
Develop a network of ambulatory practices capable of conducting research

One area ripe for research is patient engagement and disclosure. Data suggest patients can play a role in improving safety, but engaging patients has remained a challenge. Woodward and colleagues[60] suggest disclosure of errors is the best way to engage patients in safety initiatives. Patients consistently report a desire to be told when an error occurs; however, partial (rather than full) disclosure by the physician most commonly occurs even when the physician supports error disclosure. No studies have investigated the impact of an error disclosure policy. Future research should examine barriers to physician disclosure of errors, impact and outcomes associated with full disclosure, and strategies to engage patients in error reporting and patient safety initiatives.

EHR and electronic prescribing tools show promise in reducing prescription errors, but ongoing efforts are needed. Particular attention should be paid when patients are receiving multiple prescriptions or prescriptions from trainees. Improved education of trainees including medical students and residents is an important area for future work. While prescription errors have garnered substantial attention, errors of dispensing and administering medication are at least as important yet even more difficult to monitor.[61] Uniformity in effective dosing tools for parents may be helpful, and the FDA has already taken important steps in this direction. Improving communication with patients and their parents is another opportunity for future research, particularly when language and cultural barriers are present.

Finally, to improve patient safety, one must continue to encourage error reporting, establish a blame-free safety culture, and increase the recognition of medical errors in all ambulatory pediatric settings. Often, pediatric outpatient practices are unaware that medical errors are common phenomena. A nonpunitive, team-based reporting system may improve reporting, especially among providers and staff. Ongoing efforts should be made to empower patients and their families to reduce the risk for harm in the pediatric office setting.

REFERENCES

1. Mohr JJ, Lannon CM, Thoma KA, et al. Learning from errors in ambulatory pediatrics. In: Henrikson K, Battles JB, Marks ES, et al, editors. Advances in patient safety: from research to implementation. Washington, DC: Agency for Healthcare Research and Quality; 2005. p. 355–68. Available at: http://www.ahrq.gov/downloads/pub/advances/vol1/Mohr.pdf. Accessed June 26, 2012.
2. Phillips RL, Dovey SM, Graham D, et al. Learning from different lenses: reports of medical errors in primary care by clinicians, staff, and patients. J Patient Saf 2006;2:140–6.
3. Neuspiel DR, Guzman M, Harewood C. Improving error reporting in ambulatory pediatrics with team approach. Advances in patient safety: new directions and alternative approaches, vol.1. Washington, DC: Agency for Healthcare Research and Quality; 2008. AHRQ Publication No. 08-0034-1.
4. Neuspiel DR, Stubbs EH, Liggin L. Improving reporting of outpatient pediatric medical errors. Pediatrics 2011;128:e1608. http://dx.doi.org/10.1542/peds.2011-0477.
5. Bishop TF, Ryan AK, Casalino LP. Paid malpractice claims for adverse events in inpatient and outpatient settings. JAMA 2011;305(23):2427–31.
6. Singh H, Thomas EJ, Wilson L, et al. Errors of diagnosis in pediatric practice: a multisite survey. Pediatrics 2010;126:70–9. http://dx.doi.org/10.1542/peds.2009-3218.
7. McPhillips HA, Stille CJ, Smith D, et al. Potential medication dosing errors in outpatient pediatrics. J Pediatr 2005;147:761–7.
8. Kaushal R, Goldmann DA, Keohane CA, et al. Adverse drug events in pediatric outpatients. Ambul Pediatr 2007;7:383–9.
9. Zandieh SO, Goldmann DA, Keohane CA, et al. Risk factors in preventable adverse drug events in pediatric outpatients. J Pediatr 2008;152:225–31.
10. Lemer C, Bates DW, Yoon C, et al. The role of advice in medication administration errors in the pediatric ambulatory setting. J Patient Saf 2009;5:168–75.
11. Kaushal R, Goldmann DA, Keohane CA, et al. Medication errors in paediatric outpatients. Qual Saf Health Care 2010;19:e30. http://dx.doi.org/10.1136/qshc.2008.031179.

12. Li SF, Lacher B, Crain EF. Acetaminophen and ibuprofen dosing by parents. Pediatr Emerg Care 2000;16:394–7.
13. McErlean MA, Bartfield JM, Kennedy DA, et al. Home antipyretic use in children brought to the emergency department. Pediatr Emerg Care 2001;17:249–51.
14. Goldman RD, Scolnik D. Underdosing of acetaminophen by parents and emergency department utilization. Pediatr Emerg Care 2004;20:89–93.
15. Losek JD. Acetaminophen dose accuracy and pediatric emergency care. Pediatr Emerg Care 2004;20:285–8.
16. Kozer E, Scolnik D, Macpherson A, et al. Variables associated with medication errors in pediatric emergency medicine. Pediatrics 2002;110:737–42.
17. Shaughnessy AF, Nickel RO. Prescription-writing patterns and errors in a family medicine residency program. J Fam Pract 1989;29:290–5.
18. Condren M, Studebaker J, John BM. Prescribing errors in a pediatric clinic. Clin Pediatr 2010;49:49–53.
19. Rinke ML, Bundy DG, Shore AD, et al. Pediatric antidepressant medication errors in a national error reporting database. J Dev Behav Pediatr 2010;31: 129–36.
20. Taylor JA, Winter L, Geyer LJ, et al. Oral outpatient chemotherapy medication errors in children with acute lymphoblastic leukemia. Cancer 2006;107:1400–6.
21. Walsh KE, Mazor KM, Stille CJ, et al. Medication errors in the homes of children with chronic conditions. Arch Dis Child 2011;96:581–6. http://dx.doi.org/10.1136/adc.2010.204479.
22. Feikema SM, Klevens M, Washington ML, et al. Extra immunization among US children. JAMA 2000;283:1311–7.
23. Butte AJ, Shaw JS, Bernstein H. Strict interpretation of vaccination guidelines with computerized algorithms and improper timing of administered doses. Pediatr Infect Dis J 2001;20:561–5.
24. Darden P, Gustafson KK, Nietert PJ, et al. Extra-immunization as a clinical indicator for fragmentation of care. Public Health Rep 2011;126(Suppl 2):48–59.
25. Yin HS, Mendelsohn AL, Wolf MS, et al. Parents' medication administration errors. Arch Pediatr Adolesc Med 2010;164(2):181–6.
26. Sobhani P, Christopherson J, Ambrose PJ, et al. Accuracy of oral liquid measuring devices: comparison of dosing cup and oral dosing syringe. Ann Pharmacother 2008;42:46–52.
27. Yin HS, Wolf MS, Dreyer BP, et al. Evaluation of consistency in dosing directions and measuring devices for pediatric nonprescription liquid medications. JAMA 2010;304(23):2595–602.
28. US Department of Health and Human Services, Food and Drug Administration, Center for Drug Evaluation and Research. Guidance for industry: dosage delivery devices for orally ingested OTC liquid drug products. Silver Spring (MD): 2011. Available at: http://www.fda.gov/downloads/Drugs/GuidanceCompliance RegulatoryInformation/Guidances/UCM188992.pdf. Accessed June 26, 2012.
29. Wallace LS, Keenum AJ, DeVoe JE. Evaluation of consumer medical information and oral liquid measuring devices accompanying pediatric prescriptions. Acad Pediatr 2010;10:224–7.
30. Leyva M, Sharif I, Ozuah P. Health literacy among Spanish-speaking Latino parents with limited English proficiency. Ambul Pediatr 2005;5:56–9.
31. Sharif I, Tse J. Accuracy of computer-generated, Spanish-language medicine labels. Pediatrics 2010;125:960–5. http://dx.doi.org/10.1542/peds.2009-2530.
32. Flores G, Ngui E. Racial/ethnic disparities and patient safety. Pediatr Clin North Am 2006;53:1197–215.

33. Kuo DZ, O'Connor KG, Flores G, et al. Pediatricians' use of language services for families with limited English proficiency. Pediatrics 2007;119:e920–7. http://dx.doi.org/10.1542/peds.2006-1508.

34. Wilson KM, Singh P, Blumkin AK, et al. Knowledge gaps and misconceptions about over-the-counter analgesics among adolescents attending a hospital-based clinic. Acad Pediatr 2010;10:228–32.

35. Lokker N, Sanders L, Perrin EM, et al. Parental misinterpretations of over-the-counter pediatric cough and cold medication labels. Pediatrics 2009;123:1464.

36. Chang MC, Chen YC, Chang SC, et al. Knowledge of using acetaminophen syrup and comprehension of written medication instructions among caregivers with febrile children. J Clin Nurs 2012;21:42–51.

37. Costelloe C, Montgomery AA, Redmond NM, et al. Medicine dosing by weight in the home: can parents accurately weight preschool children? A method comparison study. Arch Dis Child 2011;96:1187–90.

38. Committee on Quality of Health Care in America, Institute of Medicine. Crossing the quality chasm: a new health system for the 21st century. Washington, DC: National Academies Press; 2001.

39. Kohn KT, Corrigan JM, Donaldson MS, editors. To err is human: building a safer health system. Committee on Quality of Health Care in America, Institute of Medicine. Washington, DC: National Academies Press; 2000.

40. Aspden P, Wolcott JA, Bootman JL, et al, Committee on Identifying and Preventing Medication Errors, Institute of Medicine. Preventing medication errors. Washington, DC: National Academies Press; 2007.

41. American Academy of Pediatrics Steering Committee on Quality Improvement and Management and Committee on Hospital Care. Policy statement—principles of pediatric patient safety: reducing harm due to medical care. Pediatrics 2011; 127:1199–210.

42. Plews-Ogan ML, Nadkarni MM, Forren S, et al. Patient safety in the ambulatory setting: a clinician-based approach. J Gen Intern Med 2004;19:719–25.

43. Daniels JP, Hunc K, Cochrane DD, et al. Identification by families of pediatric adverse events and near misses overlooked by health care providers. CMAJ 2012;184:29–34. http://dx.doi.org/10.1503/cmaj.110393.

44. Kozer E, Berkovitch M, Koren G. Medication errors in children. Pediatr Clin North Am 2006;53:1155–68.

45. Yin HS, Mendelsohn AL, Fierman A, et al. Use of a pictographic diagram to decrease parent dosing errors with infant acetaminophen: a health literacy perspective. Acad Pediatr 2011;11:50–7.

46. Yin HS, Dreyer BP, van Schaick L, et al. Randomized controlled trial of a pictogram-based intervention to reduce liquid medication dosing errors and improve adherence among caregivers of young children. Arch Pediatr Adolesc Med 2008; 162:814–22.

47. Hixson R, Franke U, Mittal R, et al. Parental calculation of pediatric paracetamol dose: a randomized trial comparing the parental analgesia slide with product information leaflets. Paediatr Anaesth 2010;20:612–9.

48. Abramson EL, Barrón Y, Quaresimo J, et al. Electronic prescribing within an electronic medical record reduces ambulatory prescribing errors. Jt Comm J Qual Patient Saf 2011;37(10):470–8.

49. Kaushal R, Kern LM, Barrón Y, et al. Electronic prescribing improves medication safety in community-based office practices. J Gen Intern Med 2010;25(6):530–6.

50. Jani YH, Ghaleb MA, Marks SD, et al. Electronic prescribing reduced prescribing errors in a pediatric renal outpatient clinic. J Pediatr 2008;152:214–8.

51. Ginzburg R, Barr WB, Harris M, et al. Effect of a weight-based prescribing method within an electronic health record on prescribing errors. Am J Health Syst Pharm 2009;66:2037–41.

52. Jani YH, Barber N, Wong ICK. Republished error management: paediatric dosing errors before and after electronic prescribing. Postgrad Med J 2011;87:565–8.

53. The Joint Commission. National patient safety goals effective January 1, 2012: ambulatory health care accreditation program. Available at: http://www.jointcommission.org/assets/1/6/NPSG_Chapter_Jan2012_AHC.pdf. Accessed June 27, 2012.

54. Rappaport DI, Collins B, Koster A, et al. Implementing medication reconciliation in outpatient pediatrics. Pediatrics 2011;128:e1600. http://dx.doi.org/10.1542/peds.2011-0993 originally published online November 28, 2011.

55. Sittig DF, Singh H. Defining health information technology-related errors. Arch Intern Med 2011;171(14):1281–4.

56. Singh H, Classen DC, Sittig DF. Creating an oversight infrastructure for electronic health record-related patient safety hazards. J Patient Saf 2011;7:169–74.

57. Sittig DF, Singh H. Legal, ethical and financial dilemmas in electronic health record adoption and use. Pediatrics 2011;127:e1042–7. http://dx.doi.org/10.1542/peds.2010-2184.

58. Tang N, Meyer G. Ambulatory patient safety: the time is now. Arch Intern Med 2010;170:1487–9.

59. Wynia MK, Classen DC. Improving ambulatory patient safety: learning from the last decade, moving ahead in the next. JAMA 2011;306:2504–5.

60. Woodward HI, Mytton OT, Lemer C, et al. What have we learned about interventions to reduce medical errors. Annu Rev Public Health 2010;31:479–97.

61. Miller MR, Robinson KA, Lubanski LH, et al. Medication errors in paediatric care: a systematic review of epidemiology and an evaluation of evidence supporting reduction strategy recommendations. Qual Saf Health Care 2007;16:116–26. http://dx.doi.org/10.1136/qshc.2006.019950.

FDA Working to Ensure the Safety of Medical Devices Used in the Pediatric Population

Marilyn Neder Flack, MA, PMP[a],*, Thomas P. Gross, MD, MPH[a],
Joy Samuels Reid, MD[b], Thalia T. Mills, PhD[c],
Jacqueline Francis, MD, MPH[d]

KEYWORDS

- Food and Drug Administration • Center for Devices and Radiological Health
- Medical devices • Surveillance • Total product life cycle • Pediatric device safety

KEY POINTS

- The Food and Drug Administration (FDA) has special provisions in place to protect pediatric patients; this article focuses on medical device safety in this population.
- The FDA ensures device safety throughout the total product life cycle.
- Device registries are promising sources of device safety and effectiveness information.
- New legislation enhances the FDA's ability to protect pediatric patients.
- Recent activities in pediatric radiation safety demonstrate how the FDA approaches device issues.

INTRODUCTION

The Center for Devices and Radiological Health (CDRH) defines the pediatric population as birth through 21 years, and has recognized the need to consider the unique characteristics of different stages of a child's development by identifying the following subpopulations: neonate (birth–28 days), infant (>28 days–2 years), child (>2–12 years), and adolescent (>12–21 years).[1,2] The Federal Food, Drug, and Cosmetic

[a] Office of Surveillance and Biometrics, Center for Devices and Radiological Health, Food and Drug Administration, 10903 New Hampshire Avenue, Silver Spring, MD 20993, USA; [b] Office of Device Evaluation, Center for Devices and Radiological Health, Food and Drug Administration, 10903 New Hampshire Avenue, Silver Spring, MD 20993, USA; [c] Office of In Vitro Diagnostics and Radiological Health (OIR), Center for Devices and Radiological Health, Food and Drug Administration, 10903 New Hampshire Avenue, Silver Spring, MD 20993, USA; [d] Office of the Center Director, Center for Devices and Radiological Health, Food and Drug Administration, 10903 New Hampshire Avenue, Silver Spring, MD 20993, USA
* Corresponding author.
E-mail address: Marilyn.flack@fda.hhs.gov

Pediatr Clin N Am 59 (2012) 1355–1366
http://dx.doi.org/10.1016/j.pcl.2012.08.003
0031-3955/12/$ – see front matter Published by Elsevier Inc.

pediatric.theclinics.com

Act, Sec. 201(h)[321] defines a medical device as an instrument, apparatus, implement, machine, contrivance, implant, in vitro reagent, or similar articles that are not metabolized in the body and not a biologic, drug, or food.[3] Medical devices and their use in pediatric patients was the subject of a 2006 Institute of Medicine study, "Safe medical devices for children," commissioned by Congress.[4]

In regulating devices, the CDRH uses a "total product-life cycle" (TPLC) approach, which seeks to improve device safety and effectiveness by coordinating and integrating premarket evaluation, postmarket surveillance and compliance actions, communication and outreach to consumers and industry, scientific research, standards development, and use of external pediatric expertise. The following sections touch on how the Food and Drug Administration (FDA) addresses pediatric safety issues in each of these areas.

PREMARKET REVIEW OF MEDICAL DEVICES

Medical devices come to market via various regulatory pathways, which are the same for pediatric and adult devices: premarket notification or 510(k), premarket approval, de novo pathway, Humanitarian Device Exemption (HDE), and compassionate use or emergency use.[5] All devices are evaluated using a risk-based regulatory process, with the level of evidence required to ensure a reasonable assurance of safety and effectiveness varying based on the intended use of the product and the technology involved. Some devices require the submission of clinical data, whereas, for others, laboratory testing is adequate to ensure safety and effectiveness. Devices are classified as Class I, II, or III depending on the risk the device poses to the patient and/or the user, with Class III devices posing the greatest risk.

Given the wide range of devices brought to market through various regulatory pathways, the FDA is committed to making sure that if a medical device is to be used in any pediatric patient, a reasonable assurance of safety and effectiveness must be demonstrated in the targeted pediatric subgroup. Some devices have a general indication (eg, syringes or many diagnostic radiographic imaging devices) and can be used in any age group (adults and children), whereas other devices target a specific subpopulation (eg, newborn screening diagnostic tests). Other medical devices may need to be sized for children (eg, heart valves). Manufacturers must recognize the unique host characteristics within each of the subpopulations and, when applicable, address these differences.

To this end, the FDA outlines points to consider for the pediatric population through the *Guidance for Industry and FDA Staff* document, "Premarket assessment of pediatric medical devices."[1] This guidance outlines the general fundamental, scientific, and regulatory principles and types of premarket submission information applicable to establishing a reasonable assurance of safety and effectiveness for all medical devices. In addition, it provides a framework for deciding when special consideration must be given to the pediatric subpopulation for which the device is intended. The FDA identifies common scientific approaches used for assessing safety and effectiveness (eg, biocompatibility, software design, human factors, toxicology, and statistical methods) and clearly advises that the instructions for use should take into consideration special issues for the different pediatric subgroups. By following the guidance, manufacturers are more likely to ensure that appropriate safeguards are in place for a medical device that is intended for the pediatric population.

RECENT STATUTORY ENHANCEMENTS

To spur pediatric device development and bring safe and effective devices to children, Congress passed the *Pediatric Medical Device Safety and Improvement Act of 2007* (Title III of FDA Amendments Act).[6] It provided the FDA with substantial new responsibilities and authorities regarding medical devices that have actual or potential pediatric uses. For example, Title III provides incentives to device manufacturers to create medical devices specifically designed to meet the needs of pediatric patients. It modifies the HDE (regulatory pathway to market for devices for which the intended population is very small) to allow manufacturers of devices specifically designed to meet a pediatric need to make a profit from the sale, which was not previously permitted. Currently, new guidance is being drafted that is designed to help FDA reviewers and manufacturers of medical devices identify and address these issues. In May 2012, Congress passed the FDA *Safety and Innovation Act*.[7] This Act, among many other provisions, enhanced the pediatric safety provisions added in 2007. For example, to further encourage development of devices designed for the pediatric population, in addition to making a profit on devices sold under the HDE,[8] now manufacturers may also request that the product be sold to a larger number of patients than the 4000 limit imposed by the HDE.[7]

PEDIATRIC DEVICE RESEARCH AND STANDARDS DEVELOPMENT

To stimulate pediatric-specific medical device research and surveillance, the FDA has provided funding mechanisms to facilitate gathering and analyzing data regarding safety and effectiveness in this patient population and to create external partnerships. For example, the Critical Path Initiative is an FDA pathway used to provide funding for various research projects, many of which have a pediatric focus. Specific Critical Path initiatives include collaboration with the American College of Cardiology (ACC) on the Improving Pediatric and Adult Congenital Treatment (IMPACT) Registry and an initiative to reduce radiation exposure from pediatric radiographic imaging (see later discussion).

Studies involving human subjects with medical devices are monitored through a designated Bioresearch Monitoring Office. The CDRH monitors ongoing device research through the Early Intervention Program, which focuses on active research of novel medical devices or vulnerable populations, such as the pediatric population, to assure that adequate systems are in place to protect the rights and welfare of human research subjects and to promote high-quality device research.

In addition to research, the development and use of standards is an important tool for evaluating safety and effectiveness for devices used in pediatric populations. Following FDA-recognized standards can reduce the burden to industry by providing a streamlined approach for satisfying many premarket submission requirements.[9] CDRH's Standards Program has committed to investigating the need for standards that address pediatric use issues; input from health care practitioners with pediatric expertise will be an important part of this endeavor.

POSTMARKET SURVEILLANCE OF MEDICAL DEVICES

Once a device is in clinical use, new and unexpected problems may occur with its use, or there could be an unexpected increase in known problems that were not foreseen during the premarket review process. It is imperative that the FDA, device manufacturers, and the clinical community monitor device-related problems. The CDRH uses several surveillance tools to learn about problems with medical devices once they are in the marketplace. Once problems are identified, the CDRH works with device manufacturers to address them using various approaches, which may include (1) recommending recalls or corrective actions, such as updated labeling and improved device designs; (2) communicating information and recommendations to device users; (3) helping manage known risks by providing strategies to facilitate safe use; and (4) mandating and/or conducting observational studies.

Passive Surveillance

Manufacturers and importers are required to submit reports of device-related deaths, serious injuries, and malfunctions to the FDA. User facilities (eg, hospitals, outpatient diagnostic and treatment centers, and nursing homes) are required to submit reports of device-related deaths and serious injuries to the manufacturer and reports of deaths to the FDA.[10] Health care providers and consumers may submit reports voluntarily through the MedWatch program.[11] All reports obtained through this passive surveillance method are housed in the Manufacturer and User Facility Device Experience (MAUDE) database, established in 1996. Most reports in MAUDE (approximately 400,000 per year) are from manufacturers, with a small percentage from user facilities, voluntary sources, and importers. These reports, after redaction to protect the identity of the reporter and the patient, are available on-line for public review.[12]

As is typical of other passive reporting systems, the FDA's system has noticeable weaknesses including (1) data may be incomplete or inaccurate and are typically not independently verified; (2) data may reflect reporting biases driven by event severity, uniqueness, or publicity and litigation; (3) causality cannot be inferred from any individual report; and (4) events are generally underreported. Underreporting, in combination with lack of denominator (exposure) data, precludes determination of event incidence or prevalence.

Despite these limitations, the CDRH safety analysts use techniques to obtain valuable information about emerging device problems from MAUDE. In assessing these reports, in addition to specific patient characteristics, the following factors are considered (1) failure potential resulting from design or manufacturing problems or possible packaging errors; (2) use error potential due to human factors issues, such as inadequate design of the user interface or inadequate labeling (includes instructions for use); (3) use error due to misreading instructions, maintenance error, or incorrect clinical use; and (4) possible adverse environmental factors, including support system failures and adverse device interactions (eg, electromagnetic interference or toxic and/or idiosyncratic reactions).

To assist in detecting new signals, FDA safety analysts use statistical tools, such as Bayesian and other data mining methods, that have been automated to estimate the relative frequency of specific adverse event–device combinations compared with the frequency of the event with all other devices (in the same group) in the database.[13,14] To aid this effort, and reporting and signal detection in general, an extensive hierarchical vocabulary for device failures also has been developed.[15]

Enhanced Surveillance

In 2002, the CDRH launched the Medical Product Safety Network (MedSun) to create collaborations with hospitals to identify, understand, and solve problems with the use of medical devices, and to aid in overcoming underreporting from user facilities.[16,17] Trained reporters, typically risk managers and biomedical engineers, from 290 hospitals across the United States report device-related problems to the FDA using a secure Web site. Not only deaths and serious injuries associated with the use of devices are reported, but also close calls and potential for harm, including human-factor problems with device designs. The MedSun hospitals also participate in CDRH-conducted focus groups, individual interviews, and surveys to learn more about emerging signals and to help the CDRH determine how useful a manufacturer's action has been in improving patient safety.

KidNet, a specialty subnetwork of MedSun, has been implemented in 46 MedSun hospitals beginning in 2000. In an effort to obtain more detailed reports from hospital staff working directly with the equipment, KidNet expanded reporting from the risk manager and biomedical engineer levels deeper into the hospital, to the front-line users (eg, doctors and nurses). Notably, the KidNet sites submitted almost all the reports that MedSun received about problems in the pediatric and neonatal intensive care units. This is one example of a KidNet report that led to a recall of a pediatric product (manufacturer and the reporting hospital are deidentified):

Device: disposable cannula for C02 monitor.

A small piece of the pediatric-neonatal end tidal CO_2 monitor (for intubated children) broke off and got stuck in the infant's tracheostomy tube. Nurse found it before harm was caused.

Location: pediatric ICU.

Outcome: report contributed to a Class I recall (http://www.accessdata.fda.gov/scripts/cdrh/cfdocs/cfRES/res.cfm?id=99419).

To view more examples of reports sent from MedSun hospitals about events occurring in the neonatal intensive care unit, please go to the Search Reports section of the MedSun Web site.[16]

Active Postmarket Surveillance: Sentinel Initiative and Registries

To provide more robust surveillance and complement limited FDA postmarket monitoring systems, the FDA launched the Sentinel Initiative in 2007, which provides a national integrated electronic health care infrastructure for medical product active surveillance in the United States.[18] The surveillance is conducted using nationally distributed data sources (with populations totaling in the tens of millions), transformed to common data models, against which FDA queries (including active surveillance protocols) can be run and aggregate data received. The absence of device-specific identifiers in most Sentinel data sources (eg, those based on claims) limits its current utility for device surveillance. Nonetheless, to prepare for and inform more widespread Sentinel efforts that will be enhanced through implementation of unique device identification (UDI; see later discussion), the FDA is exploring active device surveillance using data from several existing registries and databases, including the Massachusetts statewide coronary intervention registry and the Veterans Health Administration's electronic health records system.[19] In-hospital safety signals (eg, myocardial infarction) for recently introduced interventional cardiovascular devices (eg, drug-eluting coronary stents) have been explored using an automated computerized safety surveillance system, the Data Extraction and Longitudinal Trend Analysis (DELTA) system. DELTA was designed to support flexible prospective safety surveillance applicable to a broad range of medical devices, including those used in pediatric populations.[20]

Another evolving FDA active surveillance effort effectively uses the Consumer Product Safety Commission's (CPSC's) National Electronic Injury Surveillance System (NEISS), which is designed to capture information on injuries in hospital emergency departments (EDs). The FDA collaborated with the CPSC to use NEISS to establish the first national estimates of device-related adverse events resulting in ED visits.[21] More recent efforts have focused on examining reasons for device-related visits to the ED by pediatric patients. These efforts established that contact lenses and hypodermic needles were associated with the greatest percentage of pediatric devices related to ED visits (23% and 8%, respectively), out of nationally projected estimates of 145,000 device-related events over a 2-year period.[22]

National registries, often maintained by professional societies, have become important means to actively monitor postmarket device performance, especially for high-risk devices. Registries have been defined as "an organized system that uses observational study methods to collect uniform data (clinical and other) to evaluate specified outcomes for a population defined by a particular disease, condition, or exposure, and that serves a predetermined scientific, clinical, or policy purpose(s)."[23] The FDA has facilitated the development and/or enhancement of several procedure and/or device registries, including the Interagency Registry for Mechanically-Assisted Circulatory Support (INTERMACS), which attempts to collect high-quality information on procedures and outcomes associated with implanted ventricular-assist devices.[24] Special issues in the pediatric population receiving this therapy are evaluated by the INTERMACS Pediatric Committee, or PediMACS. In another effort funded by the Critical Path Program, the FDA collaborated with the ACC to support the development and implementation of the IMPACT Registry.[25] This registry aims to facilitate pediatric cardiovascular device review, expedite new device approval, facilitate postapproval studies by providing a national framework, and enhance ongoing postmarket surveillance. The FDA has also engaged a pediatric diabetes registry in a collaboration to obtain device information (eg, use of insulin pumps, continuous glucose monitors) related to adverse diabetic incidents.[26]

The FDA use of these registry data sources extends to international collaborations, as exemplified by the FDA-initiated International Consortium of Orthopedic Registries (ICOR), with a goal to understand real world performance of orthopedic devices in both children and adults.[27]

Mandated Postmarket Studies

Another tool that the FDA uses to achieve its surveillance and risk assessment goals is mandated postmarket studies. Depending on the device, these studies may be mandated as part of the approval to place the device on the market, or mandated after the device has already been marketed to further assess important public health issues. Results from these studies may drive revisions to the product's labeling (including patient-related and clinician-related material).

Study approaches vary widely and are designed to capture the most practical, least burdensome approach to produce scientifically sound answers. Examples include: nonclinical testing of the device, enhanced surveillance, observational studies, and, rarely, randomized controlled trials. Current study status, study protocol outlines, and basic study results for the postapproval studies mandated as part of the permission for approval are posted on the FDA's Web site.[28] Of the more than 160 postapproval studies currently underway involving more than three dozen device types, approximately 75% include the pediatric population.

Mandated studies ordered after the device has been marketed are most typically obtained "for cause" (ie, when a significant public health issue has arisen).[29] The FDA has discretionary authority to order a manufacturer of a Class II or Class III device to conduct a postmarket study if the device meets one of a specific set of conditions, one of which is an expected significant use in pediatric populations.

New sponsor-based registries or current national registries can also be used to perform FDA-mandated studies. Over 60 postapproval studies currently underway use registries. For example, the manufacturer of Olympic Cool Cap established a registry to assess the real-world performance of their device to treat neonatal hypoxic ischemic encephalopathy.

Other Data Sources

The FDA has also explored other large data sources to augment existing surveillance capabilities. For example, administrative and claims data captured by health care insurers, such as the Centers for Medicare and Medicaid Services fee-for-service claims, are a potentially valuable source of population exposures and health outcomes of interest. Device use and outcomes can be captured using national and international coding systems, such as Current Procedural Terminology codes and *International classification of diseases, ninth revision, clinical modification (ICD-9-CM)* diagnosis or procedure codes. A pilot study is being conducted, within the 50-state Medicaid and managed care pediatric population, assessing the use and relative hazard of adverse outcomes (retinal detachments, keratopathy, and glaucoma) associated with use of intraocular lenses following cataract surgery.

Administrative and claims data are also being used to explore the prevalence and nature of adverse medical device events, identified by *ICD-9-CM* discharge diagnoses, in a pediatric population that includes significant numbers of children with special health care needs. Underway is a retrospective claims-based cohort study of patients cared for at 42 not-for-profit hospitals in the Pediatric Health Information System, a source that includes data from 70% of the freestanding children's hospitals in the United States, representing 17 of the 20 major metropolitan areas.

Device Identification

The FDA Amendments Act of 2007 directed the FDA to issue regulations establishing a UDI system for medical devices and a proposed rule was issued in July 2012.[30] In conjunction with this initiative, the FDA is leading an effort to develop and implement a strategy for using health-related electronic data from large data sources, such as health insurers and integrated health systems, registries, and other sources, which incorporates UDIs to better understand device safety and effectiveness. Currently, because these data do not contain UDIs, they generally cannot be used to identify specific device exposures in patients.

The incorporation of UDI data into various health-related databases will greatly facilitate many important activities related to public health, including (1) reducing medical errors, (2) reporting and assessing device-related adverse events, (3) tracking of recalls, (4) assessing patient-centered outcomes and the risk-benefit profile of medical devices in large segments of the US population, and (5) providing an easily accessible source of device identification information to patients and health care professionals. UDIs will help expand the scope and impact of important efforts, such as the Sentinel Initiative previously described.

COMPLIANCE ACTIONS: IDENTIFYING RISKS TO THE PEDIATRIC POPULATION

To better incorporate a risk-based approach into compliance actions (eg, recalls) that may result from surveillance data, the CDRH has refined the Health Hazard Evaluation (HHE) process to address the special needs and risks of the pediatric population. An HHE is a risk assessment used to guide the FDA in classifying a recall of medical devices. The HHE helps in determining necessary steps to protect the public health when a device hazard has been identified, as well as what actions are needed by the manufacturer. The HHE assess the nature, scope, and consequence of the hazard; short-term risks (reversible or irreversible); long-term risks (disability, death); and mitigating factors.

INTERNAL COORDINATION AND OVERSIGHT: PEDIATRIC STEERING COMMITTEE AND THE CHIEF PEDIATRIC MEDICAL OFFICER

Internally, the CDRH uses several approaches to address pediatric safety issues. One of these is the Pediatric Steering Committee, a cross-center, multidisciplinary forum that meets monthly to discuss pediatric device-related issues. The Pediatric Steering

Committee provides a forum for discussion of pediatric safety, effectiveness, and ethical issues identified through premarket review, postmarket surveillance, or compliance actions.[31,32] The Committee helps to identify safety issues that may require more intensive evaluation and/or outreach to consumers and industry.

To aid in the work of the Pediatric Steering Committee, to ensure that pediatric medical device issues are assessed throughout the CDRH, and to partner with outside organizations to promote innovation in the development of pediatric devices, in 2010 the CDRH established a new senior-level position, the Chief Pediatric Medical Officer (CPMO), who reports to the Office of the Center Director. The CPMO advocates for pediatric health issues throughout the CDRH, FDA, and nationwide. Within the CDRH, the CPMO works closely with the scientists who review the applications for new devices from medical device manufacturers to ensure, when appropriate, that critical issues that may impact safe use in the pediatric population are considered and addressed. Outside the FDA, the CPMO leads the development of partnerships with the American Academy of Pediatrics and AdvaMed, a professional organization representing device manufacturers, to facilitate communication about ongoing and new device issues to all pediatricians, pediatric health care staff, and pediatric medical device manufacturers.

AN EXAMPLE OF HOW THE CDRH ADDRESSES PEDIATRIC DEVICE ISSUES: THE CASE OF PEDIATRIC RADIOGRAPHIC IMAGING

The FDA's radiological health program[33] has a long history of protecting the public from harms of radiation through regulation, research, and outreach. In February 2010, the FDA bolstered its efforts by launching the Initiative to Reduce Unnecessary Radiation Exposure from Medical Imaging.[34] Although the benefit of a clinically appropriate radiographic imaging examination far outweighs the risk, ionizing radiation exposure to pediatric patients is of particular concern because (1) younger patients are generally more radiosensitive than adults (ie, the cancer risk per unit dose of ionizing radiation is higher), (2) younger patients have a longer expected lifetime for the effects of radiation exposure to manifest as cancer, and (3) use of equipment and exposure settings designed for adults may result in excessive radiation exposure if used on smaller patients. Although studies suggest that pediatric radiologists are succeeding in their efforts to use child-size radiation doses,[35] most pediatric imaging examinations are not performed in children's hospitals[36] and nonpediatric centers may lack the expertise to optimize children's imaging examinations.[37]

So that health care professionals, whether at a community hospital or a pediatric research center, are able to safely image smaller patients more easily, the FDA is encouraging manufacturers to consider radiation safety of pediatric populations in the design of new radiographic imaging devices by including improved hardware features, protocols, and instructions. The FDA included its proposed recommendations to manufacturers of CT, fluoroscopy, and general and dental radiography devices in the draft guidance, "Pediatric Information for X-ray Imaging Device Premarket Notifications"[38] (released May 10, 2012) and announced a July 16, 2012, public workshop[39] to discuss the recommendations, as well as the possible need for including more pediatric use issues in consensus standards for radiographic imaging devices. The draft guidance also proposes that manufacturers who do not adequately demonstrate that their new radiographic imaging devices are safe and effective in pediatric patients should include a label on their device that cautions against use in pediatric populations. In this way, imaging professionals will be able to more easily identify devices designed for pediatric use. Input from the CDRH Pediatric Steering Committee was essential to ensuring that the draft guidance was compatible with the FDA's overall regulatory approach for pediatric medical devices.

The Initiative's goals include not only improved equipment safety features but also improved facility quality assurance and personnel training accomplished through key partnerships with professional organizations, industry, and other governmental agencies. For example, the FDA's Critical Path Program funded projects with the Alliance for Radiation Safety in Pediatric Imaging (ARSPI) to develop the Image Gently—FDA Digital Radiography Safety Checklist[40] and to develop training materials for radiation safety in pediatric fluoroscopy. These educational projects build on the wealth of information already available on the ARSPI Web site[41] and can help health care professionals more safely use radiographic imaging devices already on the market.

To assist facility quality assurance and improvement efforts, the FDA strongly promotes the establishment of registries and databases to track radiation safety metrics (eg, dose data, equipment settings, and adverse events) used for imaging examinations. An example is the American College of Radiology's Quality Improvement Registry for CT scans in children. To support such registries, the FDA is working with imaging device manufacturers to ensure their equipment is capable of automatically recording dose, protocol data, and patient information in standardized formats. Although the long-term goal is to automate the national registries, there is a need for short-term sources of more limited exposure information. To that end, the FDA, the ARSPI, and the Medical Imaging and Technology Alliance are working together on the Image Gently Survey for Digital Radiography to develop technique charts for digital radiographic equipment, categorized by detector type and manufacturer. This project will provide interim data before establishment of American College of Radiology's planned digital radiography dose registry.

To help inform the public about the benefits and risks of pediatric radiographic imaging examinations, the FDA launched a "Pediatric X-ray Imaging" Web site,[42] with targeted information for parents and patients, health professionals, and industry. The FDA encourages parents to act as their child's advocate by asking key questions, such as how the imaging examination will improve their child's health care and whether the imaging facility uses child-sized radiation doses. The Web site also identifies professional responsibilities and resources for referring physicians (pediatricians) and the imaging team (radiologic technologist, medical physicist, and imaging physician or dentist) to ensure that the imaging examination is justified (medically necessary) and optimized (the lowest radiation dose is used that yields an image quality adequate for diagnosis or intervention).

In sum, the FDA has adopted a multifaceted, proactive approach to improving radiation protection for pediatric populations by encouraging improvements for new devices, by providing information to health care practitioners on how to more safely use devices already on the market, by promoting national dose registries, and by educating the public on risks and benefits of pediatric radiographic imaging.

SUMMARY

The FDA protects the safety of the pediatric population in all areas of medical product use, including drugs, biologics, and medical devices. This article provides an overview of how the CDRH uses the TPLC approach to promote and protect the public health with the use of medical devices, especially for the vulnerable pediatric population.

Pediatricians and other pediatric medical experts and health care practitioners nationwide can make important contributions to pediatric device safety by (1) monitoring device use and reporting safety concerns and adverse events through the FDA's voluntary

MedWatch program[11]; (2) participating in safety and quality improvement registries that include pediatric patients; (3) consulting with the hospitals where they have privileges to determine if the hospital participates in MedSun (if so, work with the MedSun hospital lead representative to become the champion for encouraging staff to report problems with devices used on pediatric patients into the hospitals' incident systems so the lead representative may then send them to MedSun); (4) implementing a staff training program that addresses pediatric device safety issues; and (5) contributing special pediatric expertise to the medical device regulatory process by participating in FDA advisory boards, submitting public comment on draft documents (eg, guidance and regulations), and helping develop device consensus standards.

REFERENCES

1. FDA Guidance. Guidance for industry and FDA staff. Premarket assessment of pediatric medical devices. Available at: http://www.fda.gov/MedicalDevices/DeviceRegulationandGuidance/GuidanceDocuments/ucm089740.htm. Accessed October, 2012.
2. FDA Guidance. Guidance for industry and FDA staff. Pediatric expertise for advisory panels. Available at: http://www.fda.gov/MedicalDevices/DeviceRegulationandGuidance/GuidanceDocuments/ucm082185.htm. Accessed October, 2012.
3. Section 201(h), Federal Food, Drug, and Cosmetic Act. Available at: http://www.gpo.gov/fdsys/pkg/USCODE-2010-title21/html/USCODE-2010-title21-chap9-subchapII.htm. Accessed July, 2012.
4. Field MJ, Tilson H. Safe medical devices for children. Institute of Medicine. Washington, DC: The National Academies Press; 2006.
5. FDA web page. Available at: http://www.fda.gov/training/cdrhlearn/ucm162015.htm. Accessed June, 2012.
6. Food and Drug Administration Amendments Act of 2007 (FDAAA) (Public Law 107 250). Available at: http://www.gpo.gov/fdsys/pkg/PLAW-110publ85/pdf/PLAW-110publ85.pdf. Accessed October, 2012.
7. S. 3187: Food and Drug Administration Safety and Innovation Act. Available at: http://www.govtrack.us/congress/bills/112/s3187/text. Accessed June, 2012.
8. FDA web page. Available at: http://www.accessdata.fda.gov/scripts/cdrh/cfdocs/cfcfr/cfrsearch.cfm?cfrpart=814. Accessed June, 2012.
9. FDA Guidance. Guidance for industry and FDA staff. Recognition and use of consensus standards. Available at: http://www.fda.gov/MedicalDevices/DeviceRegulationandGuidance/GuidanceDocuments/ucm077274.htm. Accessed July, 2012.
10. Title 21 Code of Federal Regulations, Part 803. Available at: http://www.accessdata.fda.gov/scripts/cdrh/cfdocs/cfcfr/CFRSearch.cfm?CFRPart=803. Accessed October, 2012.
11. Medwatch Form 3500. Available at: http://www.fda.gov/downloads/Safety/MedWatch/HowToReport/DownloadForms/UCM082728.pdf. Accessed July 2012.
12. Manufacturer and User Facility Device Experience Database (MAUDE). Available at: http://www.fda.gov/MedicalDevices/DeviceRegulationandGuidance/PostmarketRequirements/ReportingAdverseEvents/ucm127891.htm. Accessed June, 2012.
13. DuMouchel W. Bayesian data mining in large frequency tables, with an application to the FDA Spontaneous Reporting System (with discussion). American Statistician 1999;53(3):177–90.
14. DuMouchel W, Pregibon D. Empirical bayes screening for multi-item associations. Proc KDD 2001;2001:67–76. Available at: http://pdf.aminer.org/000/472/638/

empirical_bayes_screening_for_multi_item_associations.pdf. Accessed October, 2012.

15. Event Problem Codes. Available at: http://www.fda.gov/cdrh/problemcode. Accessed June 2012.

16. MedSun: Medical Product Safety Network. Available at: http://fda.gov/medsun. Accessed October, 2012.

17. Bright RA, Flack MN, Gardner SN. The Medical Product Surveillance Network (MedSun). In: Brown SL, Bright RA, Tavris DR, editors. Medical device epidemiology and surveillance. Chichester (United Kingdom): John Wiley & Sons; 2007. p. 63–77.

18. FDA's Sentinel Initiative. Available at: http://www.fda.gov/safety/fdassentinelinitiative/default.htm. Accessed July, 2012.

19. Percutaneous coronary intervention in the Commonwealth of Massachusetts: Fiscal Year 2010 Report. Mass-DAC. Available at: http://www.massdac.org/sites/default/files/reports/PCI%20FY2007.pdf. Accessed June, 2012.

20. Resnic FS, Gross TP, Marinac-Dabic D, et al. Automated safety surveillance to detect low frequency safety signals of approved medical devices: a study from the Massachusetts angioplasty registry. JAMA 2010;304(18):2019–27.

21. Hefflin BJ, Gross TP. National estimates of medical device-associated injuries. Am J Prev Med 2004;27(3):246–53.

22. Wang C, Hefflin B, Cope JU, et al. Emergency department visits for medical device-associated adverse events among children. Pediatrics 2010;126(2):247–59.

23. Gliklich RE, Dreyer NA, editors. Registries for evaluating patient outcomes: a user's guide. Rockville (MD): Agency for Healthcare Research and Quality (AHRQ); 2007 (Prepared by Outcome DEcIDE Center [Outcome Sciences, Inc. dba Outcome] under Contract No. HHSA290200500351 TO1.) AHRQ Publication Number 07-EHC001-1.

24. INTERMACS. Available at: http://www.intermacs.org. Accessed July 2012.

25. IMPACT. Available at: http://www.ncdr.com/impact. Accessed July 2012.

26. T1D registry. Available at: http://t1drxregistry.jaeb.org. Accessed July 2012.

27. Sedrakyan A, Paxton EW, Phillips C, et al. The International Consortium of Orthopaedic Registries: overview and summary. J Bone Joint Surg 2011;93:1–12.

28. FDA Post-approval Studies. Available at: http://www.accessdata.fda.gov/scripts/cdrh/cfdocs/cfPMA/pma_pas.cfm.

29. FDA Section 522 Studies. Available at: http://www.accessdata.fda.gov/scripts/cdrh/cfdocs/cfPMA/pss.cfm.

30. Unique Device Identification. Available at: http://www.fda.gov/udi.

31. Title 21: Food and Drugs. Part 50. Protection of human subjects. Subpart D. Additional safeguards for children in clinical investigations. Availabe at: http://www.accessdata.fda.gov/scripts/cdrh/cfdocs/cfcfr/cfrsearch.cfm?cfrpart=50. Accessed October, 2012.

32. IOM report, Ethical conduct of clinical research involving children, 2004, Available at: http://www.iom.edu/Reports/2004/Ethical-Conduct-of-Clinical-Research-Involving-Children.asp.

33. FDA Webpage, FDA Radiological Health Program. Available at: http://www.fda.gov/Radiation-EmittingProducts/FDARadiologicalHealthProgram/ucm2007197.htm.

34. FDA, Initiative to Reduce Unnecessary Radiation Exposure from Medical Imaging. Available at: http://www.fda.gov/Radiation-EmittingProducts/RadiationSafety/RadiationDoseReduction/default.htm.

35. Arch ME, Frush DP. Pediatric body MDCT: a 5-year follow-up survey of scanning parameters used by pediatric radiologists. Am J Roentgenol 2008;191:611–7.

36. Larson DB, Johnson LW, Schnell BM, et al. Rising use of CT in child visits to the emergency department in the United States, 1995–2008. Radiology 2011;259(3): 793–801.

37. Borders HL, Barnes CL, Parks DC, et al. Use of a dedicated pediatric CT imaging service associated with decreased patient radiation dose. J Am Coll Radiol 2012; 9(5):340–3.

38. FDA Draft Guidance. Pediatric information for x-ray imaging device premarket notifications. Available at: http://www.fda.gov/MedicalDevices/DeviceRegulationand Guidance/GuidanceDocuments/ucm300850.htm.

39. FDA Public Workshop. Device improvements for pediatric x-ray imaging, July 16, 2012. Available at: http://www.fda.gov/MedicalDevices/NewsEvents/Workshops Conferences/ucm301989.htm.

40. Image Gently. FDA digital radiography safety checklist. Available at: http://www. pedrad.org/associations/5364/ig/index.cfm?page=775.

41. The Alliance for Radiation Safety in Pediatric Imaging. Available at: http://www. pedrad.org/associations/5364/ig/.

42. FDA Webpage, Pediatric x-ray imaging. Available at: http://www.fda.gov/Radiation-EmittingProducts/RadiationEmittingProductsandProcedures/MedicalImaging/ucm 298899.htm.

Safe Kids Worldwide

Preventing Unintentional Childhood Injuries across the Globe

Angela Mickalide, PhD, MCHES*, Kate Carr, BA

KEYWORDS

- Unintentional injury prevention • Behavior change • Advocacy • Distraction
- Emerging issues

KEY POINTS

- Safe Kids Worldwide has created, implemented, and evaluated data-driven injury prevention programs to combat leading injury risks to children.
- In addition to the case studies highlighted previously, these multifaceted programs also address other motor vehicle safety issues (eg, hyperthermia prevention); pedestrian safety; fire and burn prevention; drowning prevention; and home safety (eg, poisoning, carbon monoxide, falls, and suffocation prevention).
- Continued attention to encourage behavior change, distribute safety devices, and improve laws and regulations impacting child safety requires a multifaceted, consistent, and direct contribution from all stakeholders.
- Based on the success of the last 25 years and building on the momentum already gained, it is essential that the focus continue to be on reducing childhood injury in the United States and around the world.

INTRODUCTION

Unintentional injury is the number one cause of death to children in the United States[1–3] and the role of health care professionals in promoting patient safety has never been more urgent.[4] The US Centers for Disease Control and Prevention (CDC) recently released its *National Action Plan for Child Injury Prevention*, which describes its vision for reducing childhood injuries and provides a guide for stakeholders in the field.[5] On the global level, the World Health Organization and the United Nations Children's Fund published an overview of childhood injury, including intervention strategies, in the 2008 *World Report on Child Injury Prevention*.[3] Proved injury prevention efforts

Safe Kids Worldwide, 1301 Pennsylvania Avenue, Northwest, Suite 1000, Washington, DC 20004, USA
* Corresponding author.
E-mail address: amickalide@safekids.org

Pediatr Clin N Am 59 (2012) 1367–1380
http://dx.doi.org/10.1016/j.pcl.2012.08.008
0031-3955/12/$ – see front matter © 2012 Elsevier Inc. All rights reserved.

pediatric.theclinics.com

have focused primarily on three strategies: (1) behavior change, (2) correct and consistent use of safety devices, and (3) safety regulations and legislation.[6] Bicycle helmets, smoke alarms, four-sided fencing around pools, and child safety seats are examples of well-established and successful means for reducing child injury.[3]

One organization eager to help health professionals promote patient safety is Safe Kids Worldwide (http://www.safekids.org/worldwide/), a global network of organizations dedicated to providing parents and caregivers with practical and proved resources to protect kids from unintentional injuries. Safe Kids Worldwide works with an extensive network of more than 600 coalitions in 23 countries to reduce traffic injuries, drowning, falls, burns, poisonings, and more. Since 1988, Safe Kids Worldwide has helped reduce the US childhood death rate from unintentional injury by 53%. Yet, there is still much more work to be done to keep kids safe, because approximately 135 million children are born in the world each year.[7]

AGGREGATED INJURY STATISTICS
Worldwide

Globally, 110 children die every hour from an unintentional injury, more than 2600 every day.[2] It is estimated that more than 970,000 children ages 19 and younger died from injuries in 2008, more than 80% of which were unintentional.[2] As children age, injuries make up an increasing proportion of deaths.[3] Beginning at age 10, unintentional injuries are the leading cause of death for children.[3] Road traffic accidents, drowning, fires, falls, and poisoning account for 62% of these deaths.[2] Estimates indicate that more than 95% of injury-related deaths among children occur in low- and middle-income countries.[3] One of the risk areas receiving the greatest attention is motor vehicle–related injury, with experts predicting that these injuries will become the fifth leading cause of death around the world by 2030.[8] Among the emerging risks are increases in cars and lack of child restraint legislation.[8]

Although there are no specific data on the overall global costs of childhood injury, the information that is available is staggering. Motor vehicle–related injuries in developing countries are thought to consume 1% to 2% of gross domestic product, or about $100 billion every year.[3] Although these data speak volumes, they say nothing of the unquantifiable pain and suffering inflicted on individuals, families, and communities.

United States

The United States has made significant progress in reducing unintentional childhood injuries; however, the battle is far from over. Today alone, approximately 25 children will die from a preventable injury.[5] For every child that dies, 25 more are hospitalized.[9] More than 25,000 children are treated in emergency departments each day.[10] The rate of death per 100,000 in the United States is 8.7, compared with Sweden at 2, the United Kingdom at 2.9, Canada at 4.6, and Poland at 6[11]; the lower rates in these countries may be the result of stronger safety-related laws and regulations. The type of injury that children are at greatest risk for evolves as they age. Among infants, the biggest threat is suffocation.[12] By the time a child is between the ages of 1 and 4, drowning becomes the leading injury-related killer.[12] Beginning at age 5 and throughout the remainder of childhood, motor vehicle–related injury is the leading cause of death.[1] As shown in **Fig. 1**, by the time children are between the ages of 15 and 19, unintentional injury comprises the largest portion of all causes of death.[5]

The cost of childhood injury in the United States is high in terms of years of potential life lost and financial costs. It is estimated that in the last decade unintentional injuries

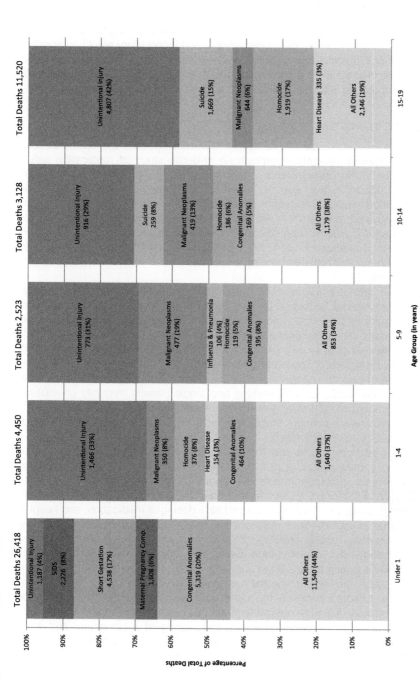

Fig. 1. Five leading causes of death and total number of deaths among children by age group, United States 2009. (*From* Centers for Disease Control and Prevention, National Center for Injury Prevention and Control. National Action Plan for Child Injury Prevention. Atlanta (GA): CDC, NCIPC; 2012.)

accounted for more than 40% of the years of potential life lost among children.[5] This rate is substantially higher than that of other causes of death.[5] When compared with the years of potential life lost for cancer-related deaths, heart disease, and influenza and pneumonia, the rate for injury is 5, 13, and 31 times higher.[5] Exacerbating the toll that injury takes on families and communities, unintentional childhood injury results in approximately $87 billion in medical and societal costs.[5] Taking into account the reduced quality of life among injured children and their families impacted by injury, the costs are estimated to be more than $200 billion each year for the United States alone.[5]

CASE STUDIES IN UNINTENTIONAL INJURY
Medication Safety

Safe Kids Worldwide recently undertook an in-depth study of medication safety among children in the United States. The death rate among children ages 14 and younger from poisoning has been cut in half since the late 1970s.[13] Yet, during the same time period, medication deaths as a percentage of all child poisoning deaths have nearly doubled, as shown in **Fig. 2**.[13] Each day, approximately 165 kids are rushed to emergency rooms for medication-related poisoning treatment.[14] Unsupervised ingestion of medication led to 95% of medication-related poisoning visits to emergency departments, whereas dosing errors made by caregivers were responsible for approximately 5%.[15]

Investigation into the forces behind the medication-related poisoning trends brought to light several factors. A primary factor is the increase in medications in the home, especially prescription pain medications.[16] The aging US population has led to more adults taking prescription medications and often multiple medications.[16] Simultaneously, there has been a rise in multigenerational households in which children may now have greater access to grandparents' medications[17]; one study found that up to 20% of pediatric poisonings involve a grandparent's medication.[18] Complicating medication safety, today's working and single parents may rely on multiple caregivers, making coordination and timing of children's dosages a challenge.[19] Lastly, formulation of medications that taste good and often look like candy may entice toddlers to take them unsupervised.

Through a 3-year partnership with McNeil Consumer Healthcare, Safe Kids Worldwide is taking a multifaceted approach to reducing medication-related poisoning among children, as articulated in a recent report.[20] In partnership with the CDC-led *Up and Away and Out of Sight Campaign*,[14] Safe Kids Worldwide is educating caregivers on the importance of safe storage and safe dosing of medication, and keeping the national poison control center number (1-800-222–1222) easily accessible. A new video illustrates how quickly children can gain access to medication (http://www.safekids.org/safety-basics/safety-guide/medication-safety-guide/). Further, Safe Kids Worldwide is urging the US Food and Drug Administration to allow the pharmaceutical industry to provide dosing instructions on labels for nonprescription acetaminophen for children between the ages of 6 and 23 months to help reduce caregiver confusion. To promote patient safety, health care professionals must educate caregivers about proper storage and dosing of medications and send home safety instructions to reinforce key messages. Easy-to-read medication safety information is available for download at www.safekids.org.

Button Battery Ingestion Prevention

Although several injury-related threats have been endangering children for centuries, others are only just emerging. One such risk is that of button batteries. Button batteries

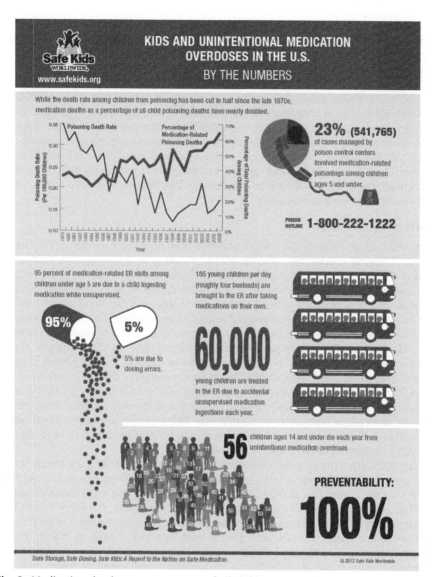

Fig. 2. Medication deaths as a percentage of all child poisoning deaths. (*Courtesy of* Safe Kids Worldwide, Washington, DC.)

are the coin-sized lithium batteries that come in everyday items, such as small remote controls, bathroom scales, reading lights, and greeting cards. These batteries are increasingly common in the home and children are getting a hold of them.[21] Although in many cases the body passes these batteries without issue, the trouble arises when they get lodged, often in the esophagus, and a chemical reaction leads to burns.[14] From 1990 to 2009, the number of children seen in emergency departments for battery-related injury significantly increased, with the greatest increase in exposure during the last 8 years.[21] Approximately 66,000 children ages 17 and younger visited emergency departments for battery ingestion, mouth exposure, or insertion into the ear canal or nasal cavity.[21] This is a troubling trend, especially among children ages 5 and younger, who comprise three-quarters of cases.[21] Increased awareness of the dangers of button batteries, additional laws and regulations to reduce the risk they pose, and continued research into risks are important next steps in this field.

Safe Kids Worldwide has partnered with battery manufacturer Energizer (St. Louis, MO) on a campaign called *The Battery Controlled* to raise awareness and change behavior among adult caregivers about this little-known and emerging risk to small children. Educational materials have been distributed through coalitions and chapters nationwide and a compelling new video illustrates how quickly these ingestions can occur (http://thebatterycontrolled.com/). Health care professionals are encouraged to counsel adult caregivers about keeping common items containing button batteries out of reach of young children and to distribute or refer families to downloadable materials available at www.safekids.org.

Sports Injury Prevention

Each year, approximately 38 million children play organized sports in the United States.[22] Sports injuries are commonplace, resulting in 3.5 million medical visits among children ages 14 and younger annually.[23] Most of these injuries, such as overuse, dehydration, and concussions, are preventable through teamwork among parents, coaches, athletes, schools, safety advocates, athletic trainers, and medical and health professionals. To investigate sports injuries further, Safe Kids Worldwide commissioned a survey of more than 500 children ages 8 to 18 years, 750 parents, and 750 coaches. The resulting report confirmed that children frequently get injured and suggested that behavior change could prevent many of these mishaps.[24] More than one in three children who play team sports reported being injured seriously enough to miss practices or games. Most kids (three in four) said they rely primarily on coaches to keep them safe during practices and games. Unfortunately, young athletes often place themselves in harm's way. For example, approximately 3 out of 10 children believed that even when they are hurt, good players should keep playing their sport unless a coach or adult makes them stop.

Information from the coaches revealed that injuries on their teams are frequent and they want and need more sports safety training. Nine in 10 coaches reported that a child on their team has suffered an injury, emphasizing the importance of safety training. Looking at specific injury risks, such as concussions, the study found that coaches need more education. Half of coaches surveyed believed there is an acceptable amount of head contact (ie, "getting their bell rung," "seeing stars") young athletes can receive without potentially causing a serious brain injury. Making injury prevention even more of a challenge for coaches, nearly half of them reported receiving pressure from parents or the kids themselves to play an injured child during a game.

Parents are taking many steps to reduce injury risk, yet misperceptions and uninformed behaviors about sports are all too common. Important steps, such as taking children for preparticipation physical examinations and making emergency contact information easily accessible, are being taken by parents. However, a better understanding of sports injury is necessary. For example, the survey revealed that 9 in 10 parents underestimated the length of time kids should take off from playing any one sport during the year and 4 in 10 underestimated the amount of fluids a typical young athlete needs per hour of play.

Based on the findings, Safe Kids Worldwide, in partnership with founding sponsor Johnson & Johnson (New Brunswick, NJ), launched a sports safety campaign aimed at keeping young athletes safe. Key messages focus on the importance of preparticipation physical examinations and consistent use of safety gear; preventing dehydration, overuse injuries, and concussion; and having an emergency plan in place if a child sustains an injury. Safe Kids Worldwide developed a tip sheet using the letters in "coaches" as a mnemonic device, as shown in **Fig. 3**. Health care professionals should discuss these messages with young athletes and their caregivers during routine office visits. In addition, any athletes with suspected concussions should be examined and monitored closely before they are allowed to return to play, following the guidelines listed in **Box 1**.[25] Further, US residents should be encouraged to learn more by participating in one of the hundreds of Safe Kids Worldwide coalition-led

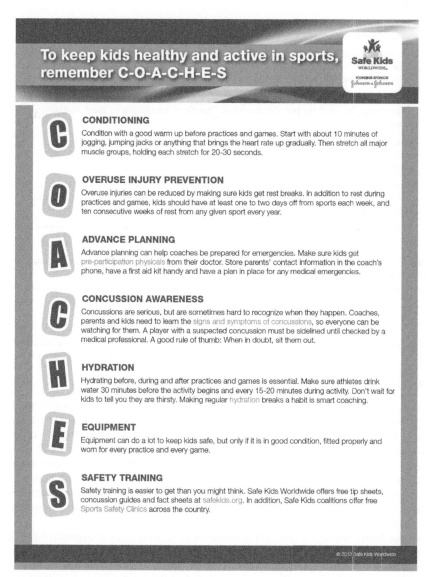

Fig. 3. Safe Kids Worldwide developed a tip sheet. (*Courtesy of* Safe Kids Worldwide, Washington, DC.)

Box 1
Need for rest

1. Encourage athletes to strive to have at least 1 to 2 days off per week from competitive athletics, sport-specific training, and competitive practice (scrimmage) to allow them to recover physically and psychologically.

2. Advise athletes that the weekly training time, number of repetitions, or total distance should not increase more than 10% each week (eg, increase total running mileage by two miles if currently running a total of 20 miles per week).

3. Encourage the athlete to take at least 2 to 3 months away from a specific sport during the year.

4. Emphasize that the focus of sports participation should be on fun, skill acquisition, safety, and sportsmanship.

5. Encourage the athlete to participate in only one team during a season. If the athlete is also a member of a traveling or select team, then that participation time should be incorporated into the aforementioned guidelines.

6. If the athlete complains of nonspecific muscle or joint problems, fatigue, or poor academic performance, be alert for possible burnout. Questions pertaining to sport motivation may be appropriate.

7. Advocate for the development of a medical advisory board for weekend athletic tournaments to educate athletes about heat or cold illness, overparticipation, associated overuse injuries, and burnout.

8. Encourage the development of educational opportunities for athletes, parents, and coaches to provide information about appropriate nutrition and fluids, sports safety, and the avoidance of overtraining to achieve optimal performance and good health.

9. Convey a special caution to parents with younger athletes who participate in multigame tournaments in short periods of time.

Data from Brenner J. Overuse injuries, overtraining, and burnout in child and adolescent athletes. Pediatrics 2007;119:1242.

---

sports safety clinics for coaches, parents, and young athletes being held across the country; a complete list of these events is available at www.safekids.org/sports.

Child Passenger Safety

In 2009, motor vehicle–related incidents were the leading cause of death among children ages 1 to 19 and the second leading cause of unintentional injury–related death among infants (children younger than 1 year of age).[26] According to the National Highway Traffic Safety Administration (NHTSA), in 2009 there were 4077 motor vehicle–related fatalities among children[27]; of these deaths nearly 85% were among children as occupants (Lorenzo Daniels, NHTSA, written communication, June 2012). In addition to the fatalities, according to NHTSA more than 400,000 children were nonfatally injured as occupants (Lorenzo Daniels, NHTSA, written communication, 2012).

Undoubtedly, one of the greatest achievements in child injury prevention has been in child passenger safety. When installed and used correctly, child safety seats have been shown to reduce fatal injury by 71% and 54%, respectively, for infants and toddlers in passenger cars.[28] It is recommended that children sit in a back seat for every ride and are in the appropriate restraint for their age, weight, and height.[28,29] Children should ride in rear-facing child safety seats as long as possible and should remain in a rear-facing child seat until they are at least 2 years of age or reach the highest weight or height allowed by the manufacturer of the child safety seat.[28–31] Once able to graduate to a forward-facing child seat, children should again remain in this type of seat as long as possible, often until they are 65 or 80 pounds.[28–30] After outgrowing a forward-facing seat, children are safest in a booster seat that enables the adult seat belt to fit properly.[29,32] Finally, a child no longer requires a booster seat when the lap belt of an adult seat belt lays snuggly across the upper thighs and the shoulder belt lays across the shoulder and chest.[28,29,31] In 2009, it is estimated that 309 children younger than age 5 were saved because of restraint use.[28]

For the past 15 years, Safe Kids Worldwide has partnered with the General Motors Foundation to promote the correct and consistent use of child restraints through the Safe Kids Buckle Up program. More than 80,000 events have been held, more than 1.5 million car seats have been inspected, 137 mobile car seat checkup vans are in communities nationwide, and 505 permanent inspection stations have been established. In addition, Safe Kids Worldwide is the certifying body for more than 34,000 car seat technicians and 1500 instructors. Yet, according to a recent Safe Kids Worldwide study progress has been mixed.[33] On the positive side, a large percentage of child restraints are being used correctly in some capacity on arrival and placement of car seats in the right direction (eg, forward- or rear-facing) is very high. Areas that require further improvement include correct use of seat belts, harnesses, lower anchors, and top tethers. To promote patient safety, clinicians should encourage all families to read and follow their car seat and vehicle owners' manuals carefully, or seek out a car seat checkup event or fitting station in their community, locations of which can be found at www.safekids.org.

SPECIAL CONSIDERATIONS INFLUENCING INJURY RISK

With the proliferation of mobile devices and the incorporation of them into vehicles, a topic coming to the forefront as a risk factor for childhood injury is distraction. Whether it is a parent taking a call, texting, or surfing the World Wide Web while supervising a child in the water, an adult on a cell phone while driving or a child listening to music with a headset while crossing the street, distraction is increasingly common. Available data address the significance of inattention and the need for in-depth research in a variety of risk areas. For example, in 2010, more than 3000 people died in motor vehicle crashes involving driver distraction and an estimated 400,000 sustained injuries.[34] Further, approximately 42% of all cooking fire deaths and 44% of the cooking fire injuries occurred when cooking equipment was left unattended.[35] In addition, one-quarter of children who died from drowning were under the supervision of a distracted individual.[36] Finally, a survey from Texas found that among children who fell from apartment windows or balconies, the supervising adult was distracted in 85% of cases.[37] Clinicians should counsel caregivers about the need to be fully present when supervising their children at home, at play, and in traffic. Children should be advised to use new technologies, such as cell phones, portable music players, and tablets, at the right place and time to stay out of harm's way.

Health care professionals should also be aware of the role adult literacy may play in increasing injury risk among children. A nationally representative survey found that approximately 93 million adults, more than 40% of the US adult population, read at or below basic literacy levels.[38] Even more concerning, 43% of adults with the lowest literacy levels live in poverty.[39] Poverty, which is another risk factor for injury, combined with low literacy further emphasizes the need for clear, highly illustrated safety-related communication to parents and caregivers.[40] Many easy-to-read downloadable safety materials are on the Safe Kids Worldwide Web site.

Lastly, the changing demographics and home environments of today have introduced another challenge for clinicians as they promote patient safety. Cultural competency has, and will continue to be, an important skill set for health professionals to acquire. In 2011, the US Census Bureau estimated that more than half of children younger than age 1 were of ethnic or racial minority[41] resulting in an even more pressing need for health care providers to be sensitive to a wide range of knowledge, attitudes, and beliefs in the clinical setting. Also, changing home structures, including a rise in single-parent households during the 1990s and an increase in multigenerational households, suggests that several caregivers may be responsible for any given child.[17,19] Thus, the most effective prevention efforts may require counseling with several caregivers and safety education should be tailored to their individual roles.

SUMMARY

The mission of Safe Kids Worldwide is to prevent unintended injuries to children. Cofounded in the United States as the National SAFE KIDS Campaign in 1987 by Dr Martin R. Eichelberger, a surgeon at Children's National Medical Center, and Herta Freely, a public relations professional, the organization is dedicated to preventing unintentional childhood injury across the country. By bringing together health and safety experts, educators, corporations, foundations, governments, and volunteers, Safe Kids Worldwide now works to protect children around the globe. Using rigorous research, local program implementation, and awareness campaigns to drive behavior change, Safe Kids Worldwide works tirelessly to meet one objective: protect children from preventable injuries.

With coalitions in 49 states, the District of Columbia, and Puerto Rico, this organization has provided families with more than 530,000 smoke alarms, distributed more than 2 million bicycle helmets, and donated and installed 530,000 car seats to families who needed them. Volunteers are integral to the network; during the past 24 years, Safe Kids Worldwide volunteers have provided more than 13.5 million hours of service in their communities.

Safe Kids Worldwide is a trusted partner to the CDC, US Consumer Product Safety Commission, Federal Emergency Management Agency, US Fire Administration, NHTSA, and National Transportation Safety Board, and Fortune 500 companies, including Johnson & Johnson, FedEx, and General Motors. Safe Kids Worldwide's partners recognize the core competency in developing and delivering research-based programs that promote safe practices to protect children.

In addition to forging partnerships at the national level, their coalition leaders collaborate with hundreds of other diverse partners to implement programs, expand outreach efforts, and disseminate safety information. Coalitions partner with public health departments and other government agencies; children's hospitals and other health care institutions; fire departments; law enforcement agencies; local chapters of such organizations as the National Volunteer Fire Council, International Association of Fire Fighters, National Safety Council, Parent Teacher Association, and National Head Start Association; and service organizations, such the Kiwanis, Lions, and Rotary clubs.

Safe Kids Worldwide has created, implemented, and evaluated data-driven injury prevention programs to combat leading injury risks to children. In addition to the

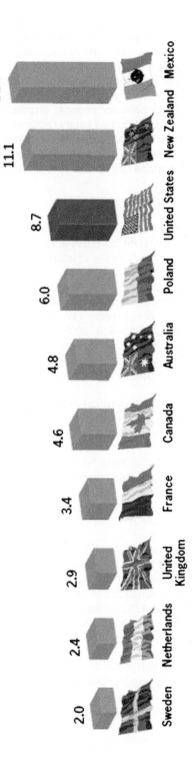

Rate per 100,000 population

Fig. 4. Childhood injury rates worldwide (*Courtesy of CDC vital signs, CDC April 2012*).

case studies highlighted previously, these multifaceted programs also address other motor vehicle safety issues (eg, hyperthermia prevention); pedestrian safety; fire and burn prevention; drowning prevention; and home safety (eg, poisoning, carbon monoxide, falls, and suffocation prevention). Detailed information on program objectives, materials, and metrics can be found at www.safekids.org.

Keeping children safe requires an ongoing effort from all stakeholders involved. Continued attention to encourage behavior change, distribute safety devices, and improve laws and regulations impacting child safety requires a multifaceted, consistent, and direct contribution from all stakeholders. Based on the success of the last 25 years and building on the momentum already gained, it is essential that the focus be on reducing childhood injury in the United States and around the world (**Fig. 4**).

REFERENCES

1. Centers for Disease Control and Prevention, National Center for Injury Prevention and Control. Web-based injury statistics query and reporting system (WISQARS). Available at: http://www.cdc.gov/injury/wisqars/index.html. Accessed June 14, 2012.
2. World Health Organization. 2008 injury estimates for children ages 19 and under. Unpublished raw data. Geneva (Switzerland): World Health Organization; 2012.
3. World Health Organization. World report on child injury prevention. Geneva (Switzerland): World Health Organization; 2008.
4. Centers for Disease Control and Prevention, National Center for Injury Prevention and Control. Web-based injury statistics query and reporting system (WISQARS). Available at: http://www.cdc.gov/injury/wisqars/index.html. Accessed May 17, 2012.
5. Centers for Disease Control and Prevention, National Center for Injury Prevention and Control. National action plan for child injury prevention. Atlanta (GA): Centers for Disease Control and Prevention, National Center for Injury Prevention and Control; 2012.
6. Carlson Gielen A, Sleet DA, DiClemente RJ, editors. Injury and violence prevention: behavioral science theories, methods and applications. San Francisco (CA): John Wiles & Sons, Inc; 2006.
7. United Nations Statistics Division. Annual number of births (births). Available at: http://data.un.org/Data.aspx?d=SOWC&f=inID%3A75. Accessed June 26, 2012.
8. World Health Organization. Global status report on road safety: time for action. Geneva (Switzerland): World Health Organization; 2009.
9. Levi J, Segal LM, Kohn D. The facts hurt: a state-by-state injury prevention policy report. Washington: Trust for America's Health; 2012.
10. Centers for Disease Control and Prevention, National Center for Injury Prevention and Control. Web-based injury statistics query and reporting system (WISQARS). Available at: http://www.cdc.gov/injury/wisqars/index.html. Accessed June 5, 2012.
11. Centers for Disease Control and Prevention. CDC vital signs: child injury. Available at: http://www.cdc.gov/vitalsigns/ChildInjury/index.html. Accessed July 16, 2012.
12. Centers for Disease Control and Prevention, National Center for Injury Prevention and Control. Web-based injury statistics query and reporting system (WISQARS). Available at: http://www.cdc.gov/injury/wisqars/index.html. Accessed June 6, 2012.

13. Centers for Disease Control and Prevention. CDC WONDER compressed mortality file, underlying cause-of-death. Available at: http://wonder.cdc.gov/mortSQL.html. Accessed February 15, 2012.

14. Centers for Disease Control and Prevention. Put your medicines up and away and out of sight. Available at: http://www.cdc.gov/features/medicationstorage/. Accessed February 9, 2012.

15. Budnitz DS, Salis S. Preventing medication overdoses in young children: an opportunity for harm elimination. Pediatrics 2011;127(6):e1597–9.

16. Bond GR, Woodward RW, Ho M. The growing impact of pediatric pharmaceutical poisoning. J Pediatr 2011;160(2):265–70.

17. AARP Public Policy Institute. Multigenerational households are increasing. Available at: http://assets.aarp.org/rgcenter/ppi/econ-sec/fs221-housing.pdf. Accessed February 9, 2012.

18. McFee RB, Caraccio TR. Hang up your pocketbook: an easy intervention for the granny syndrome: grandparents as a risk factor in unintentional pediatric exposures to pharmaceuticals. J Am Osteopath Assoc 2006;106(7):405–11.

19. Population Reference Bureau. The rise and fall of single-parent families. Available at: http://www.prb.org/Articles/2001/TheRiseandFallofSingleParentFamilies.aspx. Accessed February 16, 2012.

20. Baker JM, Mickalide AD. Safe kids, safe dosing, safe kids: a report to the nation on safe medication. Washington: Safe Kids Worldwide; 2012.

21. Sharpe SJ, Rochette LM, Smith GA. Pediatric battery-related emergency department visits in the United States, 1990-2009. Pediatrics 2012;129(6): 1111–7.

22. National Institute of Arthritis and Musculoskeletal and Skin Diseases. Childhood sports injuries and their prevention: a guide for parents with ideas for kids. NIH Pub. 06–4821. 2006.

23. American Academy of Orthopaedic Surgeons. A guide to safety for young athletes. Available at: http://orthoinfo.aaos.org/topic.cfm?topic=A00307. Accessed October 24, 2011.

24. Mickalide AD, Hansen LM. Coaching our kids to fewer injuries: a report on youth sports safety. Washington: Safe Kids Worldwide; 2012.

25. Brenner J. Overuse injuries, overtraining and burnout in child and adolescent athletes. Pediatrics 2007;119:1242.

26. Centers for Disease Control and Prevention, National Center for Injury Prevention and Control. Web-based injury statistics query and reporting system (WISQARS). Available at: http://www.cdc.gov/injury/wisqars/index.html. Accessed June 8, 2012.

27. National Highway Traffic Safety Administration. Fatality analysis reporting system (FARS) encyclopedia. Available at: http://www.nhtsa.gov/FARS. Accessed June 19, 2012.

28. National Highway Traffic Safety Administration. Traffic safety facts, 2009 data: occupant protection. Washington: National Highway Traffic Safety Administration, National Center for Statistics and Analysis.

29. Committee on Injury, Violence, and Poison Prevention. Child passenger safety. Pediatrics 2011;127:788–93.

30. Medline Plus. Child safety seats. US National Library of Medicine, National Institutes of Health. Available at: http://www.nlm.nih.gov/medlineplus/ency/article/001990.htm. Accessed October 26, 2011.

31. National Highway Traffic Safety Administration. Traffic safety facts, research note: child restraint use in 2006: use of correct restraint types. Washington: National

Highway Traffic Safety Administration, National Center for Statistics and Analysis; 2007.

32. National Highway Traffic Safety Administration. Car seat recommendations for children. Washington: National Highway Traffic Safety Administration, National Center for Statistics and Analysis; 2011.

33. Decina L, Lococo K, Joyce J, et al. A look inside American family vehicles: national study of 79,000 car seats, 2009-2010. Washington: Safe Kids Worldwide; 2011.

34. National Highway Traffic Safety Administration. Available at: http://www.distraction.gov/content/get-the-facts/facts-and-statistics.html. Accessed June 18, 2012.

35. National Fire Protection Association. Archived news release: 2007, NFPA releases mitigation of cooking fires report. November 2007. Available at: http://www.nfpa.org/newsReleaseDetails.asp?categoryid=1545&itemId=36866&cookie_test=1. Accessed June 18, 2012.

36. Covington T. What child death review teams can tell us about drowning. Paper presented at the National Drowning Prevention Symposium. San Diego, March 8, 2012.

37. Istre GR, McCoy MA, Stowe M, et al. Childhood injuries due to falls from apartment balconies and windows. Inj Prev 2003;9:349–52.

38. National Assessment of Adult Literacy, US Department of Education, 2003. Available at: http://nces.ed.gov/naal/kf_demographics.asp#1. Accessed February 11, 2012.

39. ProLiteracy. The impact of literacy. Available at: http://www.proliteracy.org/page.aspx?pid=345. Accessed June 18, 2012.

40. Singh GK, Kogan MD. Widening socioeconomic disparities in US childhood mortality, 1969-2000. Am J Public Health 2007;97(9):1658–65.

41. US Census Bureau. Most children younger than age 1 are minorities, Census Bureau reports. May 17, 2012. Available at: http://www.census.gov/newsroom/releases/archives/population/cb12-90.html. Accessed May 21, 2012.

Index

Note: Page numbers of article titles are in **boldface** type.

Pediatr Clin N Am 59 (2012) 1381–1387
http://dx.doi.org/10.1016/S0031-3955(12)00183-6
0031-3955/12/$ – see front matter © 2012 Elsevier Inc. All rights reserved.

pediatric.theclinics.com

Moving?

Make sure your subscription moves with you!

To notify us of your new address, find your **Clinics Account Number** (located on your mailing label above your name), and contact customer service at:

Email: journalscustomerservice-usa@elsevier.com

800-654-2452 (subscribers in the U.S. & Canada)
314-447-8871 (subscribers outside of the U.S. & Canada)

Fax number: 314-447-8029

Elsevier Health Sciences Division
Subscription Customer Service
3251 Riverport Lane
Maryland Heights, MO 63043

Printed and bound by CPI Group (UK) Ltd, Croydon, CR0 4YY

08/05/2025

01864754-0002